Library of Congress Catalog Number 86-062931
ISBN 0-9617722-0-4
Printed in the United States of America

A Biography of
M. Leonarda Lentrup
S.Sp.S.

by Ann Gier

This Fire Ever Burning

Dedicated to All Missionaries
at Home and Abroad

Acknowledgements

To the many Sisters, relatives, and friends of Mother Leonarda who wrote their remembrances of her after her death, my sincere thanks. It was from these personal accounts as well as from House Chronicles, letters from and to Mother Leonarda, from her Chapter Conferences, and from her personal Diary that I gathered the facts and information to write this biography.

To the Sisters who helped with the translation of Mother Leonarda's letters, thank you.

A very sincere word of thanks to my aunt, Mrs. Bernice Kruse Stanislawski, for her translation of Mother Leonarda's diary. The diary was written in small notebooks in very small German script, the ink already faded in many places, and it was indeed, a difficult task, not only in trying to decipher it but in trying to see it.

To all who helped with the typing, my sincere thanks.

But most of all, I thank Sister Kathleen Kane, the present Provincial Superior in Techny for asking me to take up once again and complete the biography I had started thirty years ago and was forced to stop. To Sister Kathleen and her Council, thank you!

August 6, 1985
Feast of the Transfiguration

Prologue

A quiet Sunday morning was interrupted by a car winding its way along the narrow road. In the car sat a nun, petite and frail looking, somewhat worn, showing the signs of more than thirty years of everyday exposure to the tropical sun in her lined face. She sat intent upon her mission and for today, at least, totally oblivious to the hot African sun which brightened the greenness of the plush tropical vegetation. She loved this second country of hers and its people. This was a land where morning and evening came upon one with the suddenness of a burst of applause, and where the stars seemed closer to earth than anywhere else in the world. Suddenly the shrill call of a large black crow pierced the heavy, musty stillness. The nun scanned the road ahead and realized she had just about reached her destination: the leper colony outside the city of Accra, Ghana, West Africa.

The ride was nothing unusual, a simple repetition of what she had been doing for over twenty-five years. The lepers of Ghana were the extra special people in her life—equal in importance to the girls she taught in Forms five and six in St. Mary's Secondary School, Accra. Her monthly or twice monthly visits to the lepers were a give and take situation.

They were a joy to her; a blessing to the maimed and suffering lepers, who looked forward to her visits with extraordinary anticipation. They waited for her smile, her words of consolation. She was the one comfort in their life, which was ravaged by a hideous, crippling disease. Somehow as the petite nun went about giving out pieces of clothing, small pictures from old greeting cards, soothing lotions, and speaking to them of hope and a hereafter of happiness, these lepers momentarily forgot or pushed in the background the agony of missing limbs, or faces partially destroyed by the disease. They came from the whole leper colony—some on crutches; some shuffling along on stumps of what were once legs; the half blind leading the blind; some simply moving forward as best they could until they all came into one large open room—an open space with wooden beams and thatched roof—and here they waited to hear her words of encouragement and love and hope.

Once someone said to a nun who worked among the lepers of China, "I wouldn't do that for a million dollars!" And she quietly replied, "Neither would I." If someone told Sister Jane in Africa the same thing, her reply would probably be the same. These people were not statistics with a dollar value to her. They did not mean a salary at the end of the month. To her they were members of the human race just like herself. Right now they needed someone who cared, and she was there. For courage to go out to them with open heart and arms, she tapped the deep wellsprings of her womanliness and her missionary spirituality and gave them of her woman's gift of consolation, dedication and love and her missionary strength and endurance.

The dust lay thick upon her desk. Another China dust storm! Nothing to do but clear away a space large enough for her to work on and start correcting papers and then get back to studying her Chinese.

In the background, as she looked out the window, stood Fu Jen University, impressive, large, beautiful in Oriental design, administered by the missionary priests and brothers of the Society of the Divine Word, and already carving its niche of fame in anthropological research and in all its faculties. Fu Jen Middle School stood close by. Sister Ellen let her eyes roam over the panorama. Fu Jen was already a monument in Peking. Who could foresee that one day in the not too distant future its halls would be stilled, and then in the 60's it would rise again like a Phoenix, even more impressive and beautiful, in Hsinchang, on the outskirts of Taipei, Taiwan.

This moment, however, Sister Ellen saw only the present before her, and it all seemed like a dream. Here she was, teaching a people steeped in the richness of their ancient culture. An amazing people! What could she do for them? She gave them of her dimensions of knowledge and faith, devoted love and enduring hope; and in return received from them the courtesy, respect, and quiet wisdom that is so vital a part of Chinese culture.

* * * * *

The young women marching in their caps and gowns had just completed four years at Holy Ghost College in Manila, Philippines. With their degrees in their hands they stood before life. Sister Ann surveyed the line of young women. She had some of them in her classes. They were an artistic people, happy and loving. In her classes she had tried to instill in these young women qualities of leadership; she had shown them the relationship between the infinite and the finite so that going out as they were now to face life, they would recognize their duties toward human society, the Church, and the State.

In another part of Manila, at Lourdes Hospital, other young women were getting their caps. These were the caps of the registered nurse, for the Sisters were also engaged in this activity—hospital work, and a school of nursing.

* * * * *

The dispensary was crowded, as it usually was, on this hot day with temperatures soaring above the 100-degree mark. There seemed to be no end to the illnesses and disease of these poverty stricken people of Indore. Yet in spite of their pains, they waited quietly and patiently, for this was India, a land of beauty and extremes, home to millions of bronzed people with their exquisitely sculptured facial features and their dogged stamina to bear up under suffering of all kinds.

From the window of the small convent close by Sister Perfecta looked at her people. She had come to India years before, and although her activity was in education, she was not unfamiliar with the dispensary work carried on by some of her co-workers. Moments like this came rarely, for there was always an over abundance of work. Thus she savored every second of this passing reflection as she mentally put in proper perspective: God, life, mission. The piercing cry of an infant getting some necessary medical treatment brought her back to the reality of eight A.M. She smiled, went to the small table, gathered some books, and proceeded to leave the room to meet her students in the classroom.

* * * * *

In this kaleidoscope of pictures there is a common prism. The women in the pictures were all Holy Spirit Missionary Sisters; they were all Americans; they all came from the American Province of the Order founded in Techny, Illinois, a little area just a few miles north of Chicago, at the beginning of the twentieth century. What's more, they all were probably *what* they were and *where* they were because of the fortitude and magnanimity of one woman. This is the story of that woman.

It is always a challenge to give life to pen and ink and to bring before the reader a flesh and blood life and vibrant spirit. To bring before the reader in this last quarter of the twentieth century, a period greatly engrossed in the "ego"; a period in which pleasure seems to supersede all else, even overruling the right to life; a period in which logical reasoning and wisdom have, in many instances, been replaced by the voice of the mob and individual convenience; a period of great scientific strides and at the same time self-destructive forces; a period in which luxuries somehow have become necessities; a complex, complicated, searching, confused period of history; a period in which the Church began "opening windows" and began taking a long, hard look at itself; a period in which religious Orders in the Church began a revitalization process, keeping the pristine spirit and motive of the Founder or Foundress and fitting it into the needs of this period of time;—to relate to this world the story of a woman whose life was the very antithesis of all that is considered "biographical fascination" today—a woman who built a network of works of charity and yet possessed a baffling simplicity and humility; to tell the story of a woman who reached out in kindness and understanding to others, yet believed that for herself corporal penance was a means of purifying and deepening the soul; a woman whose entire life was wrapped in the love of God and her fellow human beings—such a life can only be told in the simple way in which it was lived.

During the years she lived on earth she touched the lives of many people in many ways. It is time now that others should be touched by this gracious woman.

* * * * *

Elizabeth Lentrup, now Mother Leonarda Lentrup

Chapter One

. . . Truly you have formed my inmost being
You knit me in my mother's womb.
I give you thanks that I am
fearfully, wonderfully made;
Wonderful are your works.
My soul also you knew full well;
Nor was my frame unknown to you . . . .
—Psalm 138/139

Melody suffused the land. Its source seemed but a fleck of dust against an opalescent sky. High, very high in the sky a lark was singing, and the strains of its song rained downward drenching fields and meadows with melody.

Autumn had prodigally spilled its russet colors all over the countryside of Ahlen, a small town situated just southeast of the district of Muenster in the province of the great "west plains"—Westphalia. The farmland surrounding the town yielded grains of all kinds, but now that the harvest had been stored away, the land rested in the warm rays of a setting sun.

How much history lay tucked away in those silent fields and stately linden trees! What tales could they tell of old Westphalia—how Caesar invaded the area with his army and was met head on by the brave and warlike inhabitants of Westphalia at the time, the Sicambrians; how Drusus and Tiberius, sons of Augustus, came with their armies and made their conquests; how Charlemagne conquered with sword and "iron tongue" and so on down through the period of frequent uprisings following the Protestant Revolution until finally the great "west plains" were wrapped in the laws and the pride of the most recent innovator, Otto Von Bismarck.[1]

But there was peace now. Some workers were trudging home from the fields after another day of harvesting. Here and there quaint little farmhouses with their low-hanging roofs were snuggled in the folds of the sloping plains. Over in the distance, in the town of Ahlen, a coal-mining town, the white stucco houses with their black trimmings looked like huge checkerboards set up on display.

All this was "home" to Elizabeth Lentrup, who, in the youthful joy of her fifteen autumns, thought nothing could be so beautiful and peaceful as sunset over her beloved Ahlen. She was returning home after her day's lesson in sewing and embroidery with the widow Frau Niehaus.[2] Every Westphalian girl of the late 1800's took pride in becoming efficient in these arts which would equip her to be a practical housewife some day. Today on her return home, Elizabeth was caught by the song of the lark and stood just for a moment scanning the skies for a glimpse of the sweet songster.

She was alert and eager, full of joyous vitality which seemed anxious to pour itself out. Her face was pleasant and attractive and reflected an inner spirit of warmth and kindliness. Even in her youthfulness there was a certain determination about her, visible in the way she searched for that bird. Her brown eyes were warm and seemed endlessly deep as if they penetrated things far beyond this world. Finally she saw the tiny speck of a bird, and her mouth puckered into a smile of delight. "O Ho! There you are, you happy little bird. You thought no one could find you. You are mistaken. No one with such a beautiful song can hide."

Music always cast a spell over her and touched a sympathetic chord in her heart. Even now she was competing with the skylark:

Goldne Abendsonne
Wie bist du so schoen . . . .

Her voice was already deep and resonant as she sang of the golden evening sun, which was balancing itself on the crest of the horizon. Hardly a stanza was completed when the reverie was pierced by a child's call.

"Elise, Elise, come home quickly." Her little brother Anton waved frantically as he ran toward her.

"What is the matter, Tony? Has something happened at home?" asked Elizabeth while scrutinizing the little six-year-old for some traces of mischief.

"No—o—o! Mama said I should go outside to see if you were coming. Then I ran through the field and saw you here at the creek. Say, Elise, what were you looking at? I can't see anything."

"Oh, I was looking at a lark. I like to hear the

skylark sing."

"Is that all?" came the disappointed reply. But in the next moment, little Anton was all filled with childish enthusiasm again. "Do you know what, Elise? Grandpa Lentrup promised to take me fishing early in the morning some day, even before Mama is awake. But we won't fish in this little creek; we'll go to the big river Lippe. I'm going to get a whole pan of worms, too."

"That's nice, Tony, but won't you be too sleepy early in the morning? And you'll be hungry, too. If Mama isn't awake, who'll make your breakfast and lunch?"

"Well, Elise, you can make some marzipan for us, and we'll take that along."

Elizabeth smiled at the little one's plans, but she was anxious to find out why her mother sent Anton to look for her. That was unusual, indeed.

"But, Tony," she began, "you didn't tell me why Mama sent you to look for me."

"I don't know why," answered the perplexed youngster. "She said something that Uncle Bernard was coming. Do you know Uncle Bernard, Elise? I don't."

Elizabeth gasped. "Uncle Bernard—home from America! Oh, how wonderful! No, you probably don't know Uncle Bernard, Tony; but come, let's run home. We don't want to miss any of his stories about America." And before the lad knew what was happening, his sister had grabbed his hand and was running the short distance home. She didn't want to miss one single thing her uncle was telling about the United States.[3]

As the Lentrup family sat grouped around Uncle

Bernard, they made a happy picture. Frau Lentrup sat in the old armchair holding her usual basket of knitting on her lap. She was a native Westphalian and came from the Schulze-Allendorf family, one of the old families of Ahlen. Her face was kindly but determined, and the children knew her to be a strict mother, but just. Each child was given his appointed task to perform upon his return from school, and Frau Lentrup saw to it that the work was done promptly and well. No carelessness or idleness was tolerated by this energetic woman, who educated her children by example as well as by word. Each morning her footstep was the first one heard when she arose early to begin her day's work; it was the last one heard at night as she passed from room to room to see if her children were comfortably sleeping. It was she who encouraged the older children to begin their day by assisting at Mass even though it meant a forty-five minute walk to the Church. Although she had just turned forty, her life already had been a full one—filled with blessings, toil, and charity.[4]

Almost eighteen years had passed since she first met Heinrich Lentrup, a middle-class farmer of Ahlen, and consented to become his wife. Josephine Allendorf, as Frau Lentrup, proved a faithful wife and mother. Nine times God had blessed their wedded life and let them share in His creative power. Josephine gave birth to nine children, four boys and five girls. Theodore came first; and then on March 8, 1874, Elizabeth was born. She was followed by Maria, then Anna, Heinrich Junior, Antonia, Theresia, Anton, and Karl, each one adding more joy to the Lentrup family. Little August, the tenth and last child, came the following year, 1890. These were busy years for the young mother, but she had an honest, hard-working husband to ease and help carry the increasing burdens.

Heinrich toiled energetically on his one hundred fifty acres of farmland. His grain was good, and his pigs provided some of the best "Westphalian hams." The linens that his children wore were the products of his own flax fields. Herr Lentrup was the opposite of his somewhat strict wife. His rather placid and even disposition made him easily accessible to his growing children who found in him their refuge and confidant in all their little troubles and problems. The neighbors and the pastor of St. Mary's Church admired the christian charity and zeal of this devout man who worked so quietly and prayed so fervently.[5]

This evening, Herr Lentrup was silently enjoying his brood of youngsters as they pelted poor Uncle Bernard with their curious questions. The big maplewood clock was solemnly ticking the hours away, but still the questioning and story telling continued. Elizabeth was the leader of the group.

"Did you see every part of the United States, Uncle?" she asked.

"Every part! Dear Elise, it would take me more than five years to see every part. It is a large country and beautiful."

"Do they have many farms there, Uncle Bernard?" questioned young Theodore, whose ambition was to be a farmer like his father.

Uncle Bernard chuckled. "Yes, Theo, they have farms and plenty of farmers; but let me tell you this. You could build a city on some of their farms."

"Uncle Bernard, a city?" came the astonished

chorus. "What do you mean?"

"I mean that their farms are big, 'gross,—sehr gross,' " he demonstrated, flinging out his arms. "You see there is much land in the West, and nobody lives on it. They have very big cattle farms, ranches, they are called. Why, I think some of their ranches are as big as Ahlen."

"Really, Uncle Bernard?" a doubting Theodore asked; "as big as Ahlen? But Ahlen is a big town. We have almost five thousand people living in Ahlen, and we have three churches: two Catholic and one Protestant."

"Yes, and one hospital," interrupted Maria, "and . . ."

"And four breweries," teased Uncle Bernard. "You might as well add that if you want to have a complete picture of Ahlen."

"Oh, Uncle Bernard, I would love to see America," sighed Elizabeth. "When you go to America again, will you please take me along?"

"Well, Elise, it takes some money to go there. Will you be able to pay your passage over the ocean?" he asked in mock seriousness.

"Oh, yes, Uncle, I shall work."

The old clock in the corner chimed ten, and Frau Lentrup thought that was late enough for her children to be listening to stories. They all knelt to say evening prayers, which the father led in his deep, sonorous voice, a bit louder than usual, because little heads were drooping on either side of him.

That night Elizabeth lay in bed a long time thinking of the United States. She wondered how she could get there and where she would live. Would it be in a big city like New York or maybe Chicago? No, she thought, not Chicago; that seemed too far away. Perhaps she would settle in some small town, a small one like Ahlen. Yes, just a small town.

But while she mused, she felt down in the depths of her mind another urge tugging at her, a feeling she couldn't quite understand. What was it? She felt as if she had a duty to perform but was not totally certain of what that duty was. Was she, after all, supposed to be a Hausfrau of Ahlen just like her mother and grandmother? Would she ever get to America, or was it possible she would travel to another part of the world? Her thoughts were too unclear. She couldn't sift them out. Sleep overtook her searching into the future and she dreamed of Uncle Bernard's America.

Elizabeth's dreams, however, were not to be realized for some time. There were other immediate obligations to fulfill as big as this one that confronted her now at the close of the year 1889.

Almost twelve months had passed since Elizabeth left the little school house in the district of Halener, some two miles distant from her home. Many memories were wound up in those eight years of schooling under the capable instruction and guidance of Herr Abeler.

The little Halener school house had been built in 1878, and it stood on a historic spot. Several hundred years ago, just a little to the south, had been the ancient fortifications of the town of Ahlen, which at that time enjoyed its hard-won juridical powers. The highest point of the present Ahlen-Warendorf highway still retained its old name "Galgenberg" dating back to those early times when the execution of criminals took place on this very spot.[6]

When Elizabeth began going to school on April 1,

1880, the little country school housed only twenty-five pupils ranging between the ages of six and fourteen. Each day the children hiked the two miles to school, and in the late afternoon walked back home.

Elizabeth's many talents manifested themselves in the early years of her education, and Herr Abeler was kept in constant suspense to see which of his two star pupils would lead the class. Elizabeth and Lieschen Beese, a close companion of hers, were continually vying with one another for the first place in scholastic achievement. The knowledge and accomplishments of these two girls gave the teacher many an opportunity to be justly proud of them. On one occasion, when the district supervisor came on his regular inspection tour and witnessed the fine work of the two girls, he kept repeating, "I have never seen the likes of such industry and studiousness. They are to be admired."

It was on a late afternoon in March 1888, that Herr Abeler called on the Lentrups. The sun was slowly dropping itself into the pocket of land and sky and was leaving in its place streaks of gold, azure, and crimson. Birds sat on the branches of surrounding trees and chirped loudly like merchants selling their wares in an outdoor market. Herr Abeler stopped momentarily to light his pipe. He viewed the surrounding countryside with a pleased and satisfied grin as if he had been an artist critically examining one of his works and liked what he saw. This was a familiar walk, for it took him to the Lentrup family; and he was a frequent visitor at that home. For several weeks he had been discussing Elizabeth's future with her parents. Today he brought along the girl's report card for March 27, 1888, as if to prove his point. It read: "Religion, Arithmetic, Geography, Drawing—Very good. No mark below Good. Conduct and Diligence—Excellent."[8]

"Elizabeth is a fine young woman," the teacher told Heinrich and Josephine Lentrup. "She has not only remarkable talents of the mind but is also gifted with a charming and disarming personality. She should continue her education and receive training in becoming a teacher."

The Lentrups agreed. Yes, Elise was special in a way. She managed the children beautifully and had a way of getting them to listen to her. Josephine thought of the marzipan Elizabeth made today as a reward for something the children had done. Yes, she'd do well as a teacher.

Elizabeth, however, was not so easily convinced. "I don't have the essential qualities to be a teacher," she told her parents and teacher. "I just cannot see myself as a teacher. I don't think I should continue studying."

The matter was tossed about during several more discussions, but Elizabeth remained adamant. Finally the plan of her being a teacher was dropped, but her parents would not concede to her stubbornness all the way. She would have to continue her education. Heinrich simply told his daughter, "If you don't want to be a teacher, then you must learn to be a good housewife and 'Bauernfrau.' Your mother agrees with me that you should go to the Franciscan Sisters in Freckenhorst to learn home economics."

Elizabeth was hardly satisfied with this turn of events. She had absolutely no desire to go to the Franciscan Sisters or any Sisters for that matter.

"Anna," she confided to her younger sister, "I don't want to go to the boarding school in Freckenhorst. I haven't ever been with nuns or in a Sisters' school. I'm sure, Anna, I could learn much more about home economics if I worked in a hotel or had the actual experience."

Anna was delighted. "Elise, I'm so happy, so happy you don't want to go. I would miss you so much!"

"All right then, Anna. You must help me persuade Mama and Papa not to send me. If we both beg them, maybe they'll change their minds; and I won't have to go."[9]

Thus she tried every stratagem to change her parents' decision, but it was to no avail. This time her parents were definite and determined. However, two years passed after her leaving the Halener school before Elizabeth started the second part of her schooling. One day shortly after Easter in 1890, Herr Lentrup and his young son, Theodore, drove the already homesick Elise to the convent school.[10]

Freckenhorst was just about twenty-four miles northwest of Ahlen, but traveling by means of horse and wagon made the journey seem long.

Two weeks after her arrival, Elizabeth sat at her little wooden desk and began her first letter to her loved ones in Ahlen. She didn't know just what to write, for the pangs of homesickness were still gnawing away at her young heart; but she did have to tell them something. Two big tears ran down her cheeks as she began:

Dear Parents, Brothers, and Sisters:

You will be anxiously awaiting my first letter to you from Freckenhorst. I still feel no better. I hope that you are all very well. I am.

Did Father and Theodore arrive safely? How are Grandfather and Grandmother? When is Grandfather's feastday?

I cannot tell you much news for I am here only two weeks. Let me say just a few words about the order of the day. We rise at 5:15 A.M., dress, tidy up our room, go to the chapel at 6 o'clock, recite our morning prayers, assist at Holy Mass, and then take our breakfast. After breakfast, we first take a short walk through the garden with one of the Sisters. Then everyone goes to her assigned work. The first week, I was in the Sisters' kitchen, and now I am in the new laundry. At 12 o'clock, we take our dinner. This is followed by a lesson in needlework till 3:30. After a small afternoon snack, we have religion class, mathematics, and business correspondence. From five to six, we write recipes in our cook books. At 6 o'clock we go to chapel for devotion. Supper is at 7 o'clock, followed by recreation. At 8:30 we say our evening prayers and go to bed.

There are about seventy girls here, and there is plenty of life. What gives me the greatest joy is that Wilhelmina Wissling is together with me in the same class. Now I will close, dear parents, brothers, and sisters, and with heartiest greetings from Reverend Mother and the Sisters I remain your loving daughter,

Elise[11]

Her eyes were still shining with brimming tears as she sealed the envelope, but she felt better now that the letter was written. Her parents would be happy.

It didn't take long though before Elizabeth did a complete turn around. Now she felt so completely at home among the kindly Franciscan Sisters, that she gladly would have prolonged the year. Her companions and the Sisters in the school were now the recipients of her love and kindness. As in Ahlen, so here, too, she grew in the esteem of others because of her magnanimous nature. There was nothing feigned about her. Her simplicity and sincerity were refreshing. She was developing into a beautiful young woman, healthy and lovely, with the fair features of her mother. A smile lingered continuously on her lips and brightened her brown eyes. She was as happy as any girl her age could be and was always ready for fun or festivities.

It was during this year, too, that another change, deeper than anything physical, affected her. One could notice a certain serenity and determination behind her fun-loving ways. Elizabeth had resolved upon something, but it was a locked secret to all.[12]

Did she find the answer to that tugging at her heart, that strong inner urge she felt when she dreamed of going to America?

Toward the end of the year 1890, the sacrament of confirmation was administered to the girls at Freckenhorst by the Archbishop of Muenster, and Elizabeth was one of the happy recipients. The reception of this sacrament was a significant moment in her life. Her whole future pivoted on a deep devotion to the Holy Spirit. Was it at this time that the spark was kindled in her—that spark which would become the fire ever burning in her heart—the burning desire to give herself completely to God in the service of others? Later in life, her untiring zeal to promote a greater knowledge and veneration of this Divine Spirit among others was to prove one of her most lovable characteristics. She hardly ever talked to anyone without in one way or another mentioning the Holy Spirit. But as a young girl of sixteen, how much did she realize what her future held?[13]

On the first day of the new year, 1891, she thought it appropriate to write a few lines to Herr Abeler, her former teacher. The circumstances at this time of letter writing were different, and she wrote with the lightness of a happy year. In her neat penmanship she began: "Esteemed Teacher . . ." Then her thoughts raced back to the carefree years spent under this solicitous man. Yes, she had much for which to be grateful to him and thus her pen wrote on:

A holy duty admonishes me to send you today, on the first day of the New Year, my sincere good wishes. I hope that you will receive many blessings, but, above all, that you will remain the teacher in our parish for many years and may see many capable students graduate from your school. It is only now that I realize how much I owe to you, and today I shall double my prayers for you so that our dear Lord may richly repay all that you have done for me and for my brothers and sisters. In order that my prayers may become more efficacious, I shall unite them with the Holy Sacrifice of the Mass, which is said here daily.

There was no homesickness in her now, and she freely went on describing the joys of her boarding school days:

There is only about a quarter of a year left for me to stay in this convent home. I like it very much, for it has become a second home for me. When I return, I hope to be a good support to my Grandmother. We have many little joys, celebrations, and festivities here. On De-

cember sixth, good St. Nicholas visited us and brought many gifts.

The feast of Christmas was most beautiful. At midnight, we had our first solemn high Mass of the day. At 6:30 in the morning there was a low Mass followed by the second solemn high Mass during which we sang a three-voiced Mass. In the afternoon at 5 o'clock, we opened our gifts and thus closed the celebration of a wonderful day.

Repeating my best wishes for a blessed New Year, I remain

Your grateful,
Elise Lentrup [14]

In April, her year of training in home economics was completed. Again she brought home a favorable report with a special note commending her for her practical and economical mind in performing her duties at Holy Cross Boarding School in Freckenhorst.[15]

Elizabeth went to her widowed Grandmother Allendorf's large farm to take over the duties as manager of the household and farm. Her practical mind and solid training made her well suited for the great responsibility. What she had thus far acquired in theory, she now enriched with experience.[16]

Whenever an opportunity presented itself, she traveled the short distance to visit her parents. The younger members of the family were always happy when they saw big sister Elise coming home.

They would run to her with shouts of "Elise, make some marzipan for us."

Another would pull her arm and beg, "And some 'Plaetzchen,' Elise. Make some 'Plaetzchen' for us."

Smilingly Elizabeth would wrinkle her brow in a

serious way and ask, "How shall I make the marzipan? Who will tell me how to make it?"

Immediately, there would be a running to and fro with, "I'll get the sugar. I'll crush the almonds."

Then Elizabeth would set to work and make the sweet sticks of marzipan and the little nut-filled cookies. These were happy times for the children. They loved Elizabeth, who was a second mother to them. All sought her advice, even Theodore, her older brother.[17]

As a lovely woman of nineteen, Elizabeth found satisfaction and joy in many things: her household chores, in music, and in helping others. The young folk of the parish found her a social asset to their gatherings and parties. As she grew into young womanhood, her external beauty was enhanced by an inner beauty and strength which gave her whole demeanor an air of tranquillity. She was indeed looked upon as one of the most desirable young women of her parish.[18]

1. "Westphalia," *Catholic Encyclopedia,* Vol. XV, p. 602. "Ahlen," *Encyclopedia Brittanica,* Vol. I, p. 152.

2. Letter of Elizabeth Lentrup to Reverend Arnold Janssen, S.V.D., August 12, 1894 (in the archives of Sacred Heart Convent, Steyl, Holland).

3. Document 1, reminiscenses of Sr. Alfonsa, S.Sp.S. de A.P., sister of Elizabeth Lentrup (in the archives of Holy Spirit Convent, Techny, Illinois).

4. Document 1.

5. Document 1.
Document 2, reminiscenses of Sr. Luperia, O.S.F., sister of Elizabeth Lentrup (in the archives of Holy Spirit Convent, Techny, Illinois).

6. Document 7, reminiscenses of Herr Julius Abeler, the grade school teacher of Elizabeth Lentrup and intimate friend of the family (in the archives of Holy Spirit Convent, Techny, Illinois).

7. Document 7.

8. Report card of Elizabeth Lentrup from the Halener School (in the archives of Sacred Heart Convent, Steyl, Holland).

9. Document 1.

10. Document 1.

11. Translation of a letter of Elizabeth Lentrup to her family, April 30, 1890 (in the archives of Convent of the Holy Spirit, Techny, Illinois).

12. Document 4, reminiscenses of one of her school girl friends (in the archives of Convent of the Holy Spirit, Techny, Illinois).

13. Document 13, pre-entrance papers of Elizabeth Lentrup sent to Reverend Arnold Janssen, S.V.D. (in the archives of Sacred Heart Convent, Steyl).

14. Translation of a letter of Elizabeth Lentrup to Herr Abeler, January 1, 1890 (in the archives of Convent of the Holy Spirit, Techny, Illinois).

15. Report card of Elizabeth Lentrup written by Mother Feliciana, O.S.F., August 28, 1890, Freckenhorst (in the archives of Sacred Heart Convent, Steyl).

16. Document 12.

17. Document 3, reminiscences of Elizabeth Lentrup's sister, Antonia (in the archives of Convent of the Holy Spirit, Techny, Illinois).

18. Document 12.

Chapter Two

. . .O God, that all times you may find me as you desire me and where you would have me be, that you may lay hold on me fully, both by the Within and the Without of myself, grant that I may never break this double thread of my life.

—Teilhard de Chardin

The world in the last quarter of the nineteenth century was simmering with quests for expansion and dominion. Nations were competing with one another to become world powers and to flaunt their flags proudly over conquered lands on all continents. "Colonies" became the watchword of growth in power, and an insatiable appetite for colonization and authority was gnawing at the vitals of most European nations, even the smallest. The world had gone out on a tour of conquest.

Germany, too, played its part in acquiring new possessions in Africa and Oceania. She had expanded her empire to almost a million additional square miles; but, what is more, she had taken under her protection millions of new subjects. Politicians, merchants, and settlers were interested in the new lands as additional sources of money and revenue, but there was only one group really concerned about the millions of new subjects. These were the missionaries, who saw in the newly acquired land not only power and wealth but a great responsibility.[1]

For the most part, the zeal of the nation's imperialism did not deeply affect the quiet lives of the Westphalian farmers. They lived on the land that probably had been cultivated by their ancestors and had been handed down from generation to generation as a family heirloom. There was little need for them to bother about the jungles of Africa or the primitive lands of Oceania.

To Elizabeth, working on her grandmother's large farm, the thought of Africa and other far away lands had but one significance: there were people living in those countries who were also searching for truth and happiness. More and more Elizabeth became possessed with the desire of giving herself completely to God and humanity. Already in her boarding school days at Freckenhorst, she had been fired with the zeal of working for God's people as a missionary. Now as she quietly went about her work in the fields or in the farmhouse, she realized that her life was not meant to be spent among her own Westphalians, but elsewhere. It came to her more and more clearly in the silent depths of her soul that she was not meant to be that "Bauernfrau" her father spoke of. She understood and respected the dignity and greatness of marriage and physical motherhood. Yet, she herself felt called to be both a mother and virgin. She was being powerfully drawn toward a missionary life, in which vocation she could use all of a mother's power to love and give life, and all of a virgin's enriched and dedicated love.[2] Where she would carry out her missionary apostolate was not yet clear to her. China and Africa always seemed to be the two places to which her thoughts usually turned.

While Germany and the world in general were going on their venturesome trips of conquest, inside Germany a different kind of battle was being waged. In fact, it was actually known as a battle, the "Kulturkampf," the battle of cultures, and was ushered into Germany's pages of history by Otto Von Bismarck, a man bent on his own personal political conquests. Like so many political personages both before and after him, Bismarck had to find an excuse for his own inadequacies, a scapegoat to be driven out with the faults of the nation on its back thus giving the leader free reign in a supposedly "free" country. Hundreds of years before him, Nero used a similar ploy when he blamed the early christians for Rome's problems. Now Bismarck selected as his scapegoat the Catholic Church and more precisely, the religious orders in the Catholic Church. In June 1872, just two years before Elizabeth Lentrup was born, Bismarck passed a law expelling the Jesuits and all other religious orders from the territory of the German empire. In 1873, he passed the "May laws" which limited the power of the Church over its members.[3]

Thus it was that Elizabeth's life would be influenced by the laws of Bismarck.

During the very days when Elizabeth, as a little girl, made her daily trips along the Ahlen-Warendorf road to the little schoolhouse of Herr Abeler, the future of her life was being uniquely patterned out for her by two remarkable women. None of the three women, Helen Stollenwerk, Hendrina Stenmans, or young Elizabeth knew each other. In 1882, when Elizabeth was busy learning how to read and write, in another part of Westphalia Helen Stollenwerk was saying her farewells at Aachen to answer the great desire of her heart: to be a missionary. However, it was not as easy as it may sound. There had been a long story preceding that farewell and a longer one which followed.

For almost thirteen years Helen had been waiting to find the answer to her ardent desire of becoming a missionary Sister. Time and again she met with disappointments of one kind or another, for there were as yet no mission congregations of women in Germany. She had knocked at the doors of several convents, but none of them had missions in China, the land to which she desired to dedicate her life and energies. Finally, there seemed to be a faint echo of an answer to her wish. Father Craemer of Aachen told her of a certain priest, Arnold Janssen, who had just recently founded a mission society for priests and Brothers. He had established the seminary for his Society of the Divine Word, as it was called, in Steyl, Holland, since the "Kulturkampf" forbade religious Orders in Germany. Rumor had it, that he contemplated founding a mission congregation for women also. Helen immediately wrote to Father Janssen telling him of her desires and of her willingness to work for the people in mission lands. The reply was not exactly encouraging, but Helen thought it held hope for the future. Anrold Janssen told Helen that he had no immediate plans for a missionary sisterhood, but that she was welcome to come and work as a maid in the seminary kitchen. There were some misgivings about this arrangement among the members of her family, but Helen accepted; and on December 30, 1882, she came to Steyl to begin her duties as a maid. She was thirty-one years old. It took someone with an unshakeable and solidy grounded faith, an enduring hope, and a generous love to accept such an invitation as the prelude to the founding of a mission congregation of women. Helen had what it took.

Two years later, Hendrina Stenmans, another young woman, desirous of becoming a missionary Sister, joined Helen in the kitchen of the seminary in Steyl.

Although the two women were not professed religious in the proper sense of the word, that is, women who had taken the three vows of Poverty, Chastity, and Obedience, they, nevertheless, led a life of regular routine with designated times for prayer, work, and recreation. The Sisters of Providence who were in charge of the seminary kitchen at the time admired the heroic zeal and fortitude of these young women. From day to day, Helen and Hendrina lived with the hope that soon the Founder would inform them that the decision had been made, and that he would establish his mission congregation of women. But Arnold Janssen was a man not prone to haste in the works of God. He was the precise mathematician who had to have exact answers, even in prayer. He deliberated over the matter, prayed, and sounded the depths of these two women in various ways to see if they had the proper spirit and stability upon which he could build his missionary sisterhood.

Seven long years of maid service passed before Helen had the joy of hearing that a decision had been made. December 8, 1889, was the birthday of this new congregation. They were officially known as the Missionary Sisters Servants of the Holy Spirit whose aim, after that of self-sanctification, was to work for the propagation of the faith in mission lands. Thus, after almost twenty years of patient waiting, the two women realized their vocation. Later Helen and Hendrina were known as Mother Maria and Mother Josepha and were considered co-foundresses of the congregation. Other young women had joined them already during their time of service in the seminary kitchen.[4]

To say that this new Congregation of women in the Church was blessed in its co-foundresses is an understatement. The congregation sprang from such fertile seed—these two women—that its roots have a depth many misfortunes cannot shake.

The new congregation developed rapidly. In 1895, just six years after its founding, the first Missionary Sisters Servants of the Holy Spirit were sent to an overseas territory. They established a mission in South America: Valle Maria, Entre Rios, Argentina. This was just the beginning. There followed in quick succession over the next decades the opening of missions in all parts of the world: Togo, Africa, 1896 (until 1918); New Guinea, 1899; U.S.A., 1901; Brazil, 1902; China, 1905; Japan, 1908; Holland, 1910; Germany, Austria, and the Philippines, 1912; Mozambique, Africa, 1912 (until 1918); Indonesia, 1917; Paraquay, 1920; Poland, 1921; Czechoslovakia, 1931; India and England, 1933; Chile, 1934; Italy, 1937; Australia, 1940; Switzerland, 1942; Hungary, 1943 (until 1945); Ghana, Africa, 1945; Spain, 1951; Taiwan, 1953.[5]

Indeed, the motto of the new congregation: "May the Holy Triune God live in our hearts and in the hearts of all people" was being realized in all parts of the world because of the intrepid zeal and indomitable courage of these missionary women.

It was to this very new Order in the Church that Elizabeth was attracted. It was a mission congregation which placed equal emphasis on the active apostolate in the missions and a deep spiritual life with a loving devotion to the Holy Spirit. In her own life, Elizabeth had already, in a way, led this two-fold idea.

The month of August was always a busy one for every Westphalian housewife. It was a busy one for Elizabeth, too, and the long rows of shining jars of preserves bore witness to her day's work. She worked energetically and intently, but her mind was far from the steaming pots of preserves and the cleanly washed jars. That urge within her, that impelling force which urged her to give her all to God for humanity; that great desire for an unselfish life of personal sanctification—all had become like a burning fire within her soul, and she wanted to feed that flame and scatter its warmth over the whole world. At last the desire could be pent up no longer; it crystallized into a definite decision. She would write for admission into the Congregation of Missionary Sisters Servants of the Holy Spirit.

Quietly, Elizabeth slipped away one evening to

her room. There was a silent prayer, and then she dated a sheet of stationery: August 12, 1894. She pondered a moment over the opening sentence, then decided to give just a brief biographical sketch of herself to Reverend Arnold Janssen to whom she was writing.

Having completed the short introductory paragraph, she plunged immediately into the real purpose of her writing and continued:

The thought of going to the poor people in mission lands first came to me when I was fifteen years old through the reading of the Yearbook of the Holy Childhood Association. But, since I was still too young, I did not give the matter any further thought. However, after three years, the same thought came to me again; and from then on I have been thinking that the Divine Savior, in His infinite goodness and kindness, would give me the great grace to offer my life for the poor in mission lands. This inmost compassion which I have for the poor unfortunate ones, and this ardent wish to work for their salvation and to win souls for heaven, urges me in my resolve to offer my life for them. Therefore, in order to attain my goal and the fulfillment of my desire, I come to you and beg you for admission into the Convent of the Missionary Sisters. I have written nowhere else for admission.

I shall try with all my strength to obey the Rule of the Congregation conscientiously and faithfully, and I shall strive to imitate the virtues of the Divine Heart of Jesus. I must acknowledge that I am not worthy of so great a grace as to be admitted. The realization of my unworthiness weighs heavily upon me, and yet, the Call is so beautiful that I can only confide in the Divine Heart of Jesus and trust that, in his goodness and love, He will compensate for that which I, of myself, cannot do.

She had expressed the inmost sentiments of her soul and wanted to sign her name, but first she added a few more lines of information regarding her health and financial status.

I am very healthy. When I was seventeen, I had a mild case of anemia, and in early childhood I suffered an attack of jaundice for about three weeks; but nothing more.

My property amounts to 4,000 Marks which sum I inherited from my grandparents.[6]

The letter was finished, and Elizabeth now waited anxiously for the answer to her application.

She had not spoken to anyone of her intentions except to her confessor, Father Theodore Grabe, who encouraged her and promised to do all he could to help her. In fact, it was Father Grabe who told Elizabeth of the missionary Sisters in Steyl and of their activities; for she, not knowing of any Order of missionary sisters in Germany, had been considering entering an Order in Argentina.[7]

Father Grabe had many opportunities in the next few months of holding true to his promise to help her; for once Elizabeth's intentions were made known, opposition was not slow in coming. This time it was her parents who objected to her plans. She knew that she would have to put up a bold fight to carry out her plans, but she had not counted on the main opponent who called at the Lentrup home one brisk fall evening.

Reverend Father Jenne, the old pastor of St. Mary's Church in Ahlen, was not a little provoked at the decision Elizabeth had made.[8]

"Who put this idea in your head, Elizabeth?" he questioned as he stood rubbing his cold hands over the burning logs in the fireplace. "It's just a passing fancy, something that comes and goes in the life of most young women. I know how it is," he continued all the while riveting his gaze upon the quiet Elizabeth, "first they want to shut themselves up in a convent and leave everything; then a young man comes along, and soon they are married." Finishing his little speech, the old pastor walked over to Elizabeth to see if the effects of his words were already visible. But he was disappointed. There was no change in Elizabeth. Even her lingering smile was still there.

"My vocation is not a passing fancy, Herr Pastor," she quietly answered.

"We have already talked to Elizabeth, Father," added Frau Lentrup.

Elizabeth's vocation was a severe blow to her mother. For several days she had been trying to reason with her daughter, explaining how necessary Elizabeth was at home, how the younger children relied upon her, and how she would miss her help around the house.

"You see, Elise, how sad your mother is. It would be better to stay home a little longer and help her," the pastor began again. "What do you say, Herr Lentrup?"

Heinrich Lentrup was a little noncommittal on this delicate subject. His answer was a soft monosyllabic, "Ach, I don't know. Elise should know what she wants." And he went on smoking his pipe. The huge puffs of smoke he blew out in rapid succession showed that he was not quite in favor of this conversation. Father Jenne thought highly of Mr. Lentrup, one of his faithful trustees of the parish. He liked his deep, quiet piety which mingled so harmoniously with his life of toil and labor; but he could not agree with him today.

"What is to become of the parish," demanded the priest, "if all the best girls go to the convents? The best girls should be for us, for the parish. They are just what we need to build up good Catholic families. They are the ones who will make good, good housewives and mothers."

Elizabeth laughed. "Father Jenne, never fear that all the good girls will go to the convent. There are many, many good girls in Ahlen to marry and raise fine children; and, besides, I shall always pray for the parish and for you, my Pastor. Now let me get you a warm drink."

Elizabeth went to prepare a cup of hot coffee for her pastor. She knew that he had only the welfare of the parish at heart; but she knew, too, that God's call was something too intense to be disregarded, and she had resolved to follow it, cost what it may. The remainder of the evening's visit was spent in discussing other topics, and Elizabeth was left in peace.

Days sped by, and still her mother found it hard to consent. Obstacles seemed to be placed in her way on all sides. Whenever there was an opportunity, Elizabeth would slip away to St. Mary's Church, there to bury herself in the silence of her God, away from the din of opposition and pray that God's will be done. She knew that it was her choice of a missionary Order which caused her mother the greatest grief.[9]

"But why must you enter a missionary sisterhood, Elise?" she had asked when Elizabeth told her about her vocation. "Why must you go so far away? Why do you wish to go to Africa or China where we shall never hear from you again? Enter some Order that does work in Germany."

How could Elizabeth tell her mother of the firm desire burning in her heart? How could she explain this missionary vocation—this powerful urge? St. Paul had explained it in one sentence: "With us, Christ's love is a compelling motive. . . ."[10] Yet, would these words console her mother?

How does one explain to her family this deeper self dedication she desires? Every person has a duty to live a God-centered life and to see that this life is diffused into the whole world. Yet, there are those few who go the "extra mile"—the professed religious who by their total renunciation of all earthly possessions and by complete dedication to God live in the world as living examples that the Kingdom of God is truly not of this world. Would such an explanation satisfy a mother, heartbroken at the thought of losing a daughter? How does one explain the joy and at the same time the pain of this call to be a religious? What words does one use to describe adequately the longing of the soul to help all mankind as a missionary? Elizabeth was experiencing now an aloneness, a mysterious frustration in life, something she would meet with many times in her future,—a time of intense inner vision where the answers are all within but find no outward clarification in human language.

The scenes of conflict she was experiencing with her family passed before her as she knelt in the quiet church, but then they all seemed to fade away into insignificance. The call of God was much stronger when compared to all the objections waged against her answering that call. There was only one thing to do: say, yes, to God. She asked the Holy Spirit for his gift of Fortitude, so that she would have the courage to make the step God asked of her. She prayed for her family that the separation might not grieve them too deeply.

The reply to the letter she had written in August came very soon. The Reverend Arnold Janssen had fixed her entrance day for the latter part of September. Elizabeth could hardly hope to be free to go so soon especially with the way her mother felt when she had told her of her plans. Troubled and uncertain about the whole matter, Elizabeth sought advice from Father Grabe, who promised to write to Father Janssen and explain the situation. In the course of the months, Father Grabe did write several times explaining various matters to the Superior General Janssen. One letter of September 20, 1894, gives a clear insight into some of the troubles Elizabeth was having. Father Grabe writes:

From your letter, it is evident that you have already definitely fixed the entrance day for September 29. However, I fear that the Mother will object very strongly to this early date since I could hardly obtain her consent when Elizabeth first expressed her wish to enter a religious congregation. I am sure she will not let her daughter go so soon.

Mr. Lentrup, who in all other matters, is the master of the house, lets his wife have complete charge of the daughter in this case. I am sure he wishes to spare the Mother. . . .I know that if I would exert my authority to the full, I could force a consent from Mrs. Lentrup; but I am unwilling to proceed in such a way unless circumstances should make it imperative.

Mrs. Lentrup had intended to compel Elizabeth to marry; but after my energetic remonstrance, she abandoned the plan and did not take up the idea again. Other than this trouble, there is nothing to fear concerning Elizabeth herself.

May I then, Reverend Father, urgently petition you to postpone Elizabeth's entrance day until after Easter . . . .[11]

Four days later Father Janssen wrote to Father Grabe:

The entrance day of Elizabeth Lentrup is postponed . . . .Please convey to her my friendliest greetings and admonish her in the Lord to make use of this delay to perfect herself more in all virtues and prepare herself better to be a servant of God in the religious life.[12]

Finally, on March 9, 1895, a letter came from Father Janssen reading:

The entrance day of Elizabeth is permanently fixed for March 30, 1895. May God the Holy Spirit bless and bestow graces upon Elizabeth that she may be a worthy religious . . . .[13]

The weeks preceding her departure for Steyl were spent at home where Elizabeth tried to do all she could to show her love and gratitude to her family and friends. Mother and daughter worked side by side. They were so much alike in their ways, their industry and courage. Together they sewed the petticoats and nightgowns and towels, which were requirements on Elizabeth's wardrobe list from Steyl. The trunk in the corner of the bedroom was slowly being filled with the white and black of a nun's trousseau.

There was still another matter to be taken care of. Elizabeth went to see Dr. Bernemann, the family physician in Ahlen, for a physical exam. The doctor's report stated that Elizabeth was strong and healthy,[14] a fact which made her extremely happy since her mother had also pleaded that she was pale and sickly and was anxious about her daughter's health. Because of this over-anxiety on the part of the mother, Elizabeth had to undergo two physical examinations. Father Grabe in explaining the two reports to the bewildered Father Janssen summed up the whole matter rather succintly in two sentences:

> *Because of the express wish of the parents, Dr. Bernemann once again examined her, and the result is very good. Elizabeth has a pale complexion, but that is of no importance.*[15]

There were frequent interruptions by visitors, too, at the Lentrup home these days. Friends from the neighborhood of Ahlen wanted to see their favorite Elise before she left and brought with them their little farewell gifts—products of their own lands and labors.

The day of separation and good-byes came. Elizabeth climbed into the wagon with her father. Some of the neighbors had come to bid her "Auf Wiedersehen." Elizabeth smiled at them all and even had to laugh when she overheard some solicitous neighbors console her mother with the words: "Ach, Frau Lentrup, she is too pretty and too active to stay in the convent long. Cheer up! She'll soon be back, and then you'll have your Elise again."[16] How little did they know the mettle of the soul which animated that attractive face and external beauty!

The freshness of spring suffused itself over the

whole countryside. A few birds had come back already from winter quarters and perched on branches heavily laden with fat buds impatient to burst into bright green leaves. Elizabeth was enjoying her ride. How different this ride from her first one to Freckenhorst. Then she was filled with sadness and homesickness. Now she experienced only a deep joy and peace. She leaned toward her father and said softly, "Go slowly, Papa. It's all so beautiful, so beautiful."

Herr Lentrup looked at his daughter and smiled affectionately, "Ja, Liebchen, are you homesick already?"

"Oh, no, Papa, but spring is so beautiful here in Ahlen. I love to see how all the trees and bushes come to life again. It makes me want to sing just as David did in the Psalms, 'How wonderful, O Lord are all your works.' I feel like a carefree child again in the newness of spring. Do you think it is just as lovely in Steyl, Papa?"

"Ja, spring is spring, Elise, and Steyl is just over the border of Holland, so spring cannot be much different. Now, here we are at the rectory, Elise. Do you want to ask Father Jenne for his blessing?"

Herr Lentrup busied himself with the horses while Elizabeth went up the stairs of the parish rectory. Father Jenne was happy that she had come. His evening's visit some months ago was lost in the past, and he could only wish Elizabeth God's blessing.

"Well, Elise," he said, his eyes twinkling, "if you cannot stay home to be a good 'Hausfrau,' then go where God calls you and be a good nun." With that he placed his hands on the girl's head and blessed her.

Elizabeth said "Good-bye" to her confessor, Father Grabe, who had been her one stand-by during the months of trial. In the future he would always be ready to help her.

During the remainder of the trip to the Netherlands' border, Elizabeth was silent most of the time. Her thoughts were filled with varied emotions. Slowly, she was leaving this land of her birth, never to return. True Westphalian that she was, her land was dear to her and so were its people. They were serious-minded people, for the most part, hard workers, staunchly religious, but a little wary of quick friendships. The Rhinelanders used to say that "one had to eat a sack of salt with a Westphalian before a friendship could be struck"—exaggeration, yes, but descriptive of the Westphalian's cautious and prudent nature. Yet, once a friendship was made, one could be sure of their loyalty and fidelity. They had a fine sense of humor. Elizabeth was taking some of these qualities with her, qualities that would be indispensable in the work that lay ahead.

Once over the border into Holland, it was not far to the little village which sheltered the new foundation of missionary Sisters. Steyl was a small, friendly town, skirted on one side by the slowly moving Maas River, which had one time been an important asset in the town's industrial life. Now, however, the river only added to the scenic beauty of Steyl, but the town itself was taking on new importance as a training center for missionary priests, Brothers, and Sisters. Unable to find a suitable spot in Germany for his Orders because of the "Kulturkampf," Arnold Janssen had been directed to Steyl; and after finding a favorable location, he built St. Michael's Mission House, the first seminary of the Society of the Divine Word. Just recently he had purchased the old Notre Dame Convent for his congregation of Sisters.[17]

Actually, this was the third home for the young community. On July 13, 1888, the four young women who worked in the seminary kitchen moved into a small one-story house which had been purchased by Father Janssen. Three shady linden trees grew in front of the house, and so the students of the seminary dubbed it the "Convent of the Three Linden." The four candidates called it their little "Nazareth" because of the extreme poverty.

In the following year, the Capuchins exiled from France and living in a near-by monastery leased their home to Father Janssen, since they could return once more to their own country. The Superior General designated the monastery as the new home for the candidates, his future Sisters. The twilight procession of the women led by Father Janssen from the Convent of the Three Linden to the Capuchin Monastery was of singular importance. It took place on December 7, 1889, and the following day, December 8, the Feast of the Immaculate Conception of the Blessed Virgin Mary, became the birthday of the new congregation. The candidates loved their new home because it had a greater semblance to a convent and made them feel closer to their goal. However, in just a year's time, they were again told to move.

A short distance from the seminary was the Notre Dame Convent in which some Augustinian Nuns, exiled from Germany during Bismarck's time, lived. Now that things were more peaceful in Germany, the nuns wished to return to Essen and therefore offered to sell the convent to Father Janssen. He readily accepted it as the third home for his Sisters. This was the house the missionary Sisters had until 1904, when their own convent, Sacred Heart Motherhouse, was built.[18]

It was the old Augustinian Convent that Elizabeth entered on March 30, 1895. The two Foundresses, Mother Maria, the Superior, and Mother Josepha, her Assistant, greeted her upon her arrival. She was joyfully welcomed into the group of smiling Sisters! Happiness emanated from all of them and even seemed to be reflected in their cheerful dresses. Arnold Janssen, the Founder himself, selected for his Sisters a singularly lovely habit: a light sky blue dress and scapular with a white veil and cincture. Over the scapular and around the neck hung a red ribbon upon which was suspended a cross and a symbol of the Holy Spirit, the Dove.

Though many of the Sisters were no longer youthful in physical age, yet in the religious life they were all young members of a new congregation. Just one year ago, on the Feast of a great Doctor of the Church, St. Gregory the Great, March 12, the two Foundresses and the ten oldest novices made their first vows. This had been the first religious profession ceremony in the new congregation, and it is beautifully described in Mother Maria's own words:

At last our long cherished desire was fulfilled. Through the holy vows we had united ourselves intimately with our dear Savior. Now we could give full vent to the emotions we felt. With the most joyous affections of our hearts we could praise and bless the good God, who in His loving providence had guided and directed all in such a wondrous fashion, and thank Him for all graces and blessings, especially for our vocation to the religious life. We could place before Him all the undertakings of our community, the holy Church, and our dear relatives. Oh, there was so much to say and to offer! The time was all too short.

Elizabeth recognized in the two Mothers, who had already taken her into their heart and home, the ideal Holy Spirit Missionary Sister. Their obedience, simplicity, and deep love of God manifested itself even in their words and actions. With such good and noble Mothers to turn to, Elizabeth did not find it too difficult to say "Good-bye" to her father when the time came for his return trip to Ahlen.

But it was not easy for Herr Lentrup to leave behind his oldest daughter; and when he returned home without her, his children saw their father in tears. The separation had meant so much to him! Nevertheless, he told his wife and children that Steyl had made a great impression on him, and he asserted: "Father Arnold is a holy man."[20]

For Elizabeth, the pain of separation was somewhat mollified by her meeting with the Sisters and the excitement of the occasion. Entrance into the postulancy did not call for much ceremony. Elizabeth merely donned a plain black dress and a little black bonnet and became thereby the seventy-seventh postulant to enter the six-year old congregation. It was the custom at that time, in the congregation, to address the postulants by their family name. Thus, Elizabeth was called Sister Lentrup.

The simple ceremony completed, other formalities had to be attended to. First and foremost among these was the visit to the Reverend Founder. Mother

Josepha, the postulant Directress at the time, accordingly introduced the newcomer to Father Janssen. Elizabeth knew him only through correspondence. Now she had the opportunity of seeing him face to face, and she was impressed, as most people were, by his penetrating gaze. At first, he seemed all sternness; but Elizabeth noticed that in his right eye there was a merry twinkle, and the right corner of his mouth was turned upwards into an incipient smile. The interview was brief; nevertheless in those few minutes Elizabeth learned that not only had she been given two solicitous Mothers and a delightful group of Sisters, but that she was now under the spiritual guidance of a saintly priest. If Elizabeth was inspired by the holiness of the Reverend Founder, he was equally impressed by the virtuous serenity and determination of the young postulant. In fact, it was not long before he showed what great confidence he placed in her.

Now that Elizabeth had met all the Superiors and had been initiated into the preliminaries of her convent life, she was ready to begin in earnest her life of dedication.

1. Carlton Hayes, *A Political and Social History of Modern Europe* (New York: Macmillan Company, 1924), pp. 547-560.

2. P. Grendel, S.V.D., Golden Jubilee Message, 1939.

3. *The History of Nations: Germany,* Vol. XVIII, pp. 440-441.

4. Sister Assumpta, S.Sp.S., *The Life of Mother Maria Stollenwerk and Mother Josepha Stenmanns,* trans. Servant of the Holy Spirit (Techny, Illinois, 1931), pp. 7-27.

5. Diamond Jubilee Book of the S.Sp.S.

6. Translation of the letter of Elizabeth Lentrup to Reverend Arnold Janssen, August 12, 1894 (in the archives of Sacred Heart Convent, Steyl).

7. Document 2.

8. Document 7.

9. Document 2

10. II Cor. 5:14.

11. Translation of the letter of Father T. Grabe to Father A. Janssen, September 20, 1894 (in the archives of Sacred Heart Convent, Steyl).

12. Translation of the lettr of Father Janssen to Father Grabe, September 24, 1894 (in the archives of Sacred Heart Convent, Steyl).

13. Translation of the letter of Father Janssen to Father Grabe, March 3, 1895 (in the archives of Sacred Heart Convent, Steyl).

14. Physical examination report of Dr. Bernemann, Ahlen, August 18, 1894 (in the archives of Sacred Heart Convent, Steyl).

15. Translation of the letter of Fr. Grabe to Fr. Janssen, September 5, 1894 (in the archives of Sacred Heart Convent, Steyl).

16. Document 1.

17. Herman Fischer, S.V.D., *Life of Arnold Janssen,* trans. F.M. Lynk, S.V.D. (Techny, Illinois: Mission Press, 1925), pp. 132-135

18. Sister Assumpta, pp. 40-45

19. Sister Assumpta, p. 52.

20. Document 1.

Chapter Three

. . .It was he who "gave gifts to everyone"; he appointed some to be apostles, others to be prophets, others to be evangelists, others to be pastors and teachers. He did this to prepare all God's people for the work of Christian service, to build up the body of Christ . . . .

—Ephesians 4:11-13

When Elizabeth's father told his family that Father Arnold Janssen was a holy man, he had appraised Father Janssen correctly. Arnold Janssen was an intensely spiritual man, a man of prayer, a mystic. He had a very special devotion to the Mother of God, the Angels, and the Saints. Yet, in naming the mission orders he founded he went to the very core of religion and spirituality. His mission society for priests and Brothers he named the Society of the Divine Word, taking St. John's sublime title for Christ as expressed in the opening verses of his Gospel. To his congregation of missionary Sisters he gave the title,

Missionary Sisters Servants of the Holy Spirit, dedicating his Sisters to the Third Person of the Blessed Trinity. In this Father Arnold was ahead of his time. In the latter part of the 19th century, the Holy Spirit was still very much the "Forgotten Guest." It would be decades later that writers would begin calling the second half of the twentieth century the age of the Holy Spirit, a most appropriate title for an age scientifically referred to as the atomic age or energy age.

Thus in their very titles the priests, Brothers, and Sisters were constantly reminded of the profundity of their calling and their sacred obligation to spread the Good News of the Word for which task they needed the wisdom, fortitude, and love of the Holy Spirit.

From its very inception, the Congregation of Holy Spirit Missionary Sisters was characterized by a profound spiritual depth shown in its liturgy, adoration hours before the Blessed Sacrament, intervals of prayer during the day.

The women entering the postulancy were taught that the missionary's life must be a prayer-work combination. Although the two co-Foundresses never realized their desire of going to some far-off mission, still both were very much aware of the needs and training of the aspirants to the religious-missionary life. Both knew that the missionary's spirituality must be the reservoir and source of strength and power for the apostolic zeal and fervor needed for work in mission lands.

With this objective in mind Mother Josepha, who was the postulant directress at the time of Elizabeth's entrance, trained and motivated the young women in her care. In little ways Mother Josepha brought before her postulants opportunities for sacifice.

There were many sacrifices that the young postulants could practice during those early years of the congregation. If they had the privilege of being trained by the very Founders of the congregation, they also had the burden of its initial poverty and hardships. Yet, Mother Josepha knew how to spur the zeal of her charges.

One of the works of Catholic Action that the Founder encouraged the Sisters to foster as early as 1893, when the congregation numbered only twenty-five novices and eight postulants, was that of opening their doors to lay retreats. It was on just such an occasion when thirty women came to the little Notre Dame Convent to take part in one of the lay retreats that Mother Josepha went to her postulants with a question. There were not enough beds for these retreatants. So Mother Josepha approached her postulants with her characteristic smile which previewed a special request.

"I am going to the hayloft to sleep tonight, so that I can give my bed to a retreatant," she began. "Are there any volunteers to go with me?"

Every hand shot up.

A half hour later, Elizabeth and her companions were carrying their most necessary bedding up the ladder to the hay loft where with suppressed giggles they improvised sleeping quarters for the night.

For the postulants this was a novelty, but there would be other times in Elizabeth's future and in the future of some of her companions when novelty would give way to stark reality as they viewed the impoverished conditions in which they were expected to live.

In September, 1895, a great event took place in the little convent. On the eleventh of that month, the first mission departure celebration was held, and four Sisters received their mission crosses from Father Janssen. In the afternoon, after singing a special hymn to Mary, "Hail Star of the Sea," the Sisters left for Argentina.[1]

Two months later on November 1, 1895, Elizabeth Lentrup received her blue and white habit and was formally accepted into the novitiate. At the altar she also received a new name, not to replace her baptismal name—no, that was hers forever—but rather to add another dimension to her life with a new name signifying a special relationship with God and her mission in the world. When the priest addressed her with the words, "Elizabeth Lentrup, from henceforth you will be called Sister Leonarda" her fervent answer, "Thanks be to God" summed up the real joy that flooded her soul.

The novitiate meant an intense training in the spiritual life, in the study of the Constitutions, the Rule Book, and in character development. It meant an intensive study of the religious life, a growth in virtue, and a thorough preparation for the great day of taking her vows, the climax of her months of preparation, and the beginning of her life of complete dedication.

Elizabeth had the co-Foundress, Mother Josepha, a truly valiant woman, as her directress in the postulancy. Now in the novitiate she had as her novice mistress another woman of solid spirituality and outstanding kindness. Indeed, God surely smiled at this new congregation in the Church by giving it outstanding women as its first leaders and teachers.

Sister Theresia was the novice mistress. Her novices said of her that her corrections and admonitions were always mingled with great sincerity and gentleness so that no one would leave her saddened or depressed. Once she had to admonish one of her novices, but later she thought she had been unnecessarily harsh with the novice. Not wanting to minimize the seriousness of the matter for which the novice was admonished, but at the same time wanting to take away some of the sting of the correction, Sister Theresia asked her assistant, Sister Raphaele, to make it a point to meet the novice before evening prayer and say some kind words to her. Sister Theresia concluded, "Else I fear she will not sleep well."

From this woman already so mellowed and so rich with the Fruits of the Holy Spirit, the novices could imbibe a true realization of their vocation to the missionary apostolate.

Later in life, Sister Theresia was favored with special graces in prayer and could communicate most intimately with Christ.[2]

Elizabeth and her companion novices spent some time in the kitchen preparing the huge tubs of vegetables for the priests, Brothers, and students at the seminary. Potatoes were especially in abundance. One novice was assigned to clean and refill all the lamps in the house; another took care of the bread and butter; another helped in the sewing room. Elizabeth's training and experience at home in the household duties enabled her to perform these tasks and other work assigned to her in the kitchen with efficiency and thoroughness. These were the happy and quiet days of the novitiate.

For Sister Leonarda, the novitiate also meant a

deep interior growth. More and more she realized the sublimity of her call to be a missionary Sister, and above all, to have the privilege of bearing the title, Servant of the Holy Spirit. Love and devotion to the Holy Spirit took solid root within her during these months of spiritual training. She was especially fond of the Quarter-Hour Prayer, a custom introduced by the Founder in both his societies. Every quarter hour at the stroke of the clock, the Sisters recited aloud short acts of faith, hope and charity, an act of spiritual communion, and a petition for the Seven Gifts of the Holy Spirit. Thus, every fifteen minutes the Sisters were reminded again of the Divine Presence within them.

Sister Leonarda's companions in the novitiate were an interesting group. There was even one of the German nobility among them. Princess Amelia Von Croy, daughter of Lieutenant-General Prince Von Croy and Princess Johanna, entered Steyl in 1894, at the advanced age of sixty. Only Father Janssen, Mother Maria and Mother Josepha knew of her noble birth for she desired it to be secret so that she might not be considered any different from the rest. Her age did not hinder her from following the regular order and even of joining the other younger novices in their burst of enthusiasm to be sent to the missions.[3]

During Sister Leonarda's second year in the novitiate, another big event took place—another departure, but this time not to the foreign missions. It was the departure of some missionary Sisters to another wing of the house to begin a new Congregation of Servants of the Holy Spirit of Perpetual Adoration.[4]

For some time Father Janssen had been considering the founding of a third congregation, a community of cloistered Sisters who would devote their lives to prayer for the missions and missionaries, especially those of his two societies. Consequently, on December 8, 1896, the new congregation was established, and its first members were volunteers taken from among the missionary Sisters. One of those to leave the ranks of the missionary Sisters was Sister Michaele, especially chosen by the Reverend Founder to be a pioneer in the new division. She possessed a stable and firm character, a practical mind, a cheerful disposition, keen intelligence, and a great understanding of people.[5] She had held the office of Director of Studies in the congregation of the missionary Sisters, and her departure was a real loss to them. Nevertheless, the missionary Sisters knew that this newly formed army of perpetual adorers of the Blessed Sacrament would henceforth be a powerful aid to their work in the apostolate, and they were happy that the nucleus was chosen from their number.

Sister Leonarda's sincere desire for foreign mission work kept her from volunteering for the cloistered branch. Two years later, however, her sister, Anna, entered this congregation. Then there were two of the Lentrup family consecrated to the special service of the Holy Spirit: Elizabeth as a Missionary Sister Servant of the Holy Spirit, and Anna as a Servant of the Holy Spirit of Perpetual Adoration. The cloistered Sisters wore a rose-colored habit and white veil. As they knelt in adoration before Christ in the Blessed Sacrament, they loosely draped a white tulle veil over their heads, and the soft material fell gently to the floor. The habit was singularly beautiful, and because of the rose color, the Sisters came to be called the Pink Sisters.

Back in Ahlen, Frau Lentrup, who had so opposed giving her eldest daughter to a mission congregation, found that God was asking more of her than just one child. After Anna left for Steyl to become an Adoration Sister, Maria, the second oldest girl, also followed the call to become a Franciscan Sister of St. Mauritz in Muenster. The three oldest Lentrup girls were now all peacefully settled in their convents, and poor Father Jenne had lost some of his best "Bauernfrauen" of the parish. It was God's gain. Sister Luperia, the Franciscan, and Sister M. Alfonsa, the Adoration Sister, would serve God faithfully and lovingly for over a half century of prayer, work, and the practice of virtue.

On June 13, 1897, Sister Leonarda pronounced her first temporary vows of poverty, chastity, and obedience. Now she was, indeed, what she had so long desired to be, a Missionary Sister, and her hopes for an early appointment for the foreign missions were high. But her Superiors informed her that for the time being she was to help with the teaching at the Motherhouse. So it was that the girl who once argued with her parents and teacher that she did not have the needed qualifications to be a teacher would now spend the next three years teaching.

*****

The new century dawned upon the world with blessings and disasters. It was the year of Jubilee solemnly opened by Pope Leo XIII, who invited

Catholics the world over to make the pilgrimage to Rome for the Holy Year Indulgences and to receive the accompanying spiritual graces.

But in other parts of the world, the smoldering embers of unrest, discontent, and hate were being fanned and kept alive. England was using all her military strength in the Boer War in Africa. The United States had just emerged from her war with Spain and was beginning to enter upon the world's stage as one of its great powers.

The average citizen of the world at this time, however, was perfectly at peace and contented. He considered this era one of progress and development. Little did he see the hidden fires rumbling in that gigantic volcano which one day would erupt into World War I.

In the far East, Chinese reactionaries instigated by the Dowager Empress Tzu-hsi formed a society known as the "Boxers" whose goal was to rid China of foreigners. After the murder of some missionaries and diplomatic officials, the rebellion was crushed by Japanese, American, and European troops.[6]

Although the world situation did not affect the lives of the Sisters in Steyl, the Boxer rebellion catastrophe was deeply felt by the missionary Sisters. The Chinese crisis had been the cause of poignant anxiety for the Reverend Founder, whose priests were working in China, and the Sisters prayed incessantly for God's protection upon the Divine Word Missionaries. Their prayers were heard, and not one priest of the Society lost his life at that time.[7]

Already in the second month of the new year, 1900, the Sisters felt the sting of grief when their beloved co-Foundress, Mother Maria, was taken with a severe illness which resulted in her death. Her death was doubly felt by the missionary Sisters since, at the wish of the Reverend Founder, she had resigned her office as Mother General of the Missionary Sisters in December 1898, to enter the cloistered division and once more became a simple novice, again beginning the religious life. She, the co-Foundress of one congregation, was now employed in the very simple chores of a novice and was subject to the very Sisters whom she herself had admitted and trained. On her death bed, she pronounced her vows as a Servant of the Holy Spirit of Perpetual Adoration. It was very sad for the missionary Sisters not to have their revered Foundress with them in her last hours![8] All this was also not as the Founder had planned it. His reason for asking this humbling sacrifice of Mother Maria was that he found in her soul the precious link that he wanted to use to show the spiritual bond between the two congregations. He saw in Mother Maria sterling qualifications for both the active and the comtemplative life. God also saw that she was ready, and He called.

*****

Thus the year unfolded month after month with mixed feelings of peace, joy, and sadness in the world at large as well as in the convents in Steyl. Even Sister Leonarda was to have her little shock before the year was over.

It happened on the Feast of the Immaculate Conception, December 8. Some of the Sisters were just concluding their annual retreat; and, as it was always necessary during the time of retreat, the other Sisters were employed in various duties around the house performing the tasks of the retreatant Sisters. Sister Leonarda was usually appointed to be the cook because of her handiness in kitchen work. While she was bending over one of the big kettles and stirring its contents vigorously, she was interrupted by a Sister who breathlessly blurted out: "Sister Leonarda, come quickly to the chapel. Father General wants all the Sisters present while he reads the appointments of the new officials."

Sister Leonarda hurriedly removed her apron, adjusted a few things in the kitchen in order to avoid a burned dinner, and rushed to the chapel. She came in just at the moment when the Reverend Founder read from his paper: "Sister Theresia is appointed Assistant Superior and Sister Leonarda, novice mistress."[9]

The new novice mistress gasped and ran out of the chapel. All her hopes of carrying the mission cross to far-away lands vanished, and in her utter disappointment she gave vent to tears. Because everything had happened so quickly, the baffled Sister thought that perhaps she had not heard correctly. After all, she had been rather distracted by her work in the kitchen; and she may not have heard the correct name. Inquiry only assured her that what she had heard was only too correct.

In her new position, she was succeeding her own novice mistress, Sister Theresia, who became the Assistant to Mother Josepha. Just three years ago, Sister Leonarda herself had been a novice, and now she was considered capable enough by the Reverend

Founder to take over the training of the novices, one of the most important duties in the congregation.

The novices knew Sister Leonarda, for she had been their teacher in several classes and sometimes acted as substitute choir directress for Sister Gabriela; but although they esteemed Sister Leonarda as a teacher, they were sorry to lose Sister Theresia. Consequently, when Mother Josepha came to introduce the new mistress, she found the situation a difficult one for there were tear-stained faces on both sides. The novices lamented the loss of Sister Theresia, and Sister Leonarda lamented the loss of her opportunity for the missions. But, when they looked at who they were and where they were, the scene appeared somewhat ridiculous, The gloomy spell was broken by Sister Isidora, one of the novices, who approached Sister Leonarda and consoled her with the words: "Don't feel bad, Sister Leonarda; we are good novices."[10] This naive statement uttered with the simplicity that only little Sister Isidora could muster was just the thing needed to bring smiles to everyone.

Sister Leonarda's term as novice mistress was short-lived. Yet, in less than five months, she left an indelible impression upon her charges. One evening the novices were gathered together for their usual hour of recreation. Their young mistress was delayed in coming, and the novices took the opportunity to discuss their new mistress. One by one they were picking out this good quality and that.

"She is certainly a kind mother to us," put in Sister Isidora.

"And look how considerate she was to me in my recent illness," added Sister Johanna.

Another novice remarked, "I don't know just

why it is, but ever since Sister Leonarda is with us, I have such a joyful feeling and a real incentive to pray and sacrifice."

"Well, you know where she gets all her own joy and that deep spirit of sacrifice," Sister Johanna wisely explained. "She gets it from the Tabernacle. Every Sunday after evening prayers, she remains in chapel a long time kneeling at the altar. I know. I've seen her."

The novices' lively panegyric was abruptly interrupted by the entrance of Sister Leonarda herself. Everything was hushed, and the novices fell to a silent preoccupation with their needlework. The air breathed suspicion, and Sister Leonarda detected it.

"What were you talking about, Sisters?" she questioned.

Everyone was silent.

"Come now," she urged, "you were having a lively conversation."

Everyone was silent, but the needles kept going in and out rhythmically.

"Then, my Sisters, if you cannot tell me what the recreation topic was," Sister Leonarda continued in a quiet manner, "I cannot draw favorable conclusions. So, you will each say Psalm 50 tonight before going to bed and pray that you may choose a more suitable topic for recreation. And if you have spoken of anyone, say another prayer for her."[11]

Every novice breathed a sigh of relief. Each one wanted to laugh at her own indiscretion and inability to answer Sister Leonarda's question, but laughing would have made the matter worse. It was better to say the Psalm and let it go at that.

Sister Leonarda could be just that abrupt in her

ways, a natural result, no doubt, of her character and temperament, which under the divine guidance of the Holy Spirit would, in time, be polished of its rough edges. In general, she showed a remarkable capability in dealing with souls. Although she was considerably young when given her first office, and that a very important one in the congregation, her direction of the novices did not reflect a youthful zeal of office which immediately seeks to "reform," cost what it may, rather than to direct and encourage. From the very beginning, Sister Leonarda manifested a special delicacy in working with those in her care. She was firm but gentle, a characteristic quality of one tenderly devoted to the Holy Spirit and faithful to His inspirations; for the Divine Spirit in his work as Sanctifier, continually cleanses the soul even with painful fire, but always works gently for the good of the soul and its progress in divine love.

Sister Leonarda's own deep interior life provided her with the requisites needed to train the novices in virtue. Time and again, she would tell the novices to say a prayer to St. Joseph each day asking him to be their guide in the spiritual life. Then, too, her own simplicity made it possible for her to rejoice with the little joys of the young souls entrusted to her. When they received their promotion to make their vows, she was so filled with joy over their great privilege that her face became all aglow with happiness.[12] Above all, she was distinguished for her magnanimity and understanding. It is most necessary to see her growth in Christlikeness first because from this steady and firm growth proceeded the ability to use her talents to the utmost. The Reverend Founder, a priest skilled in the guidance of souls, never would have uttered this singular praise of her: "She is one of our most capable Sisters. . . ."[13] if he had meant "capable" only as far as external activities are concerned. He meant "capable" because she had already learned to "put on Christ."

Work with souls is a slow, gradual process, just as the changes of nature come about quietly and gradually; and spring always came to Steyl slowly but beautifully. Every day the grass was a little greener, the air, a little warmer, and nature, more expectant; just as everyday the novices realized more and more what it meant to become a Servant of the Holy Spirit as Sister Leonarda unfolded to them the hidden treasures of their vocation and taught them to live their lives in great intimacy with the Divine Spirit.

Now that spring was here again, the novices were happy to go out to the garden once more with hoes and spades. Everything went on as usual, and it was entirely unexpected when Sister Theresia assembled the novices one day and told them that Sister Leonarda had received her appointment to go to the United States. Sister Theresia added: "It would be nice if you prepared a little farewell program for Sister Leonarda. She will probably leave in a few weeks."

Too bewildered to say more, the novices muttered a halfhearted, "God bless you" and were silent.

They prepared a farewell program for their mistress, but on the day it was given, no one could complete one stanza of the song; and they repeated the lines over and over again until someone finally added the last two lines. The poor novices really felt miserable over their second loss of a good spiritual mother; but the next day they were admonished by Mother Josepha who wondered what kind of Missionary Sisters they would be, anyway.[14]

Sister Theresia, however, consoled them with a happy glimpse into the future. "Sister Leonarda is going to prepare a home for you," she said, "and new activities in the United States."

Yet, it was true! As the Foundress and first superior of the new foundation in the United States, Sister Leonarda fulfilled these words to the letter.

The day of departure was set for April 26, the Feast of our Lady of Good Counsel. Sister Leonarda took four Sisters with her, among whom were Sister Foureria and Sister Martina, staunch co-workers and faithful subjects of the young Superior, who had just had her twenty-seventh birthday a month ago. She was still in temporary vows, having been professed but three and one-half years. Age did not matter, though; the Reverend Founder looked deeper than that, and he found the soul he needed to establish the Congregation of Missionary Sisters Servants of the Holy Spirit in the United States.

1. Sister Assumpta, S.Sp.S., *The Life of Mother Maria Stollenwerk and Mother Joseph Stenmans,* trans. Servant of the Holy Spirit (Techny, Illinois, 1931), p. 58

2. Sister Sixta, S.Sp.S., *Gottes Kraft in Schwachen Haenden* (Steyl: Mission Press, 1951).

3. Sister Assumpta, p. 67.

4. Sister Assumpta. p. 128.

5. Hermann Fischer, S.V.D., *Mutter Maria Michaele, Mitgruenderin und erste Generaloberin der Steyler Anbetungchwestern* (Steyl: Mission Press, 1938).

6. M. J. Kerney, *Compendium of History* (Baltimore: John Murphy Co., 1909), p. 697.

7. Herman Fischer, S.V.D., *Life of Arnold Janssen,* p. 356.

8. Sister Assumpta, p. 141.

9. Document 14, reminiscenses of Sister Johanna, S.Sp.S. (in the archives of Convent of the Holy Spirit, Techny, Illinois).

10. Document 15, reminiscenses of Sister Isidora (in the archives of Convent of the Holy Spirit, Techny, Illinois).

11. Document 14.

12. Document 14.

13. Document 4.

14. Document 14.

Chapter Four

Jesus drew near and said to them: "I have been given all authority in heaven and on earth. Go, then, to all peoples everywhere and make them my disciples: baptize them in the name of the Father and of the Son and of the Holy Spirit, and teach them to obey everything I have commanded you. And remember! I will be with you always, to the end of the age."

—Matthew 28:18-20

The waters of the Atlantic were a misty grayish blue. Sister Leonarda stood at the ship's railing, enjoying the fresh air and feeling the coolness of the salty sprays as the waves hit against the ship. It had been a rather uneventful trip, except, of course, for the apples. She chuckled quietly. The Sisters had decided things were too dull, so they thought they would have a little fun with the apples which Sister Leonarda had taken with her from Holland and which she had planned to keep for their first meal in the new country. However, the Sisters had an appetite for apples on the ship and kept asking Sister Leonarda for the apples, saying it would help their sea-sickness. They were bound to wear out their leader's determination. Finally, Sister Alexia took out her violin and began playing some plaintive melody and then went into a serenade walking like some troubadour around Sister Leonarda until the latter was laughing tears. She got out the apples and gave them to the Sisters—but not all. She still had some left to enjoy in their new home.[1]

Sister Leonarda mused. What a mystery the religious life was! How full of paradoxes, so it seemed. Spiritually it had a depth that rested in the fathomless profundity of the Divine; and yet the religious could find a refreshing lighthearted joy in something so trivial as a playful teasing to get an apple. The three vows gave the religious woman a freedom to love and laugh and enjoy the simple things of life in a way few people could understand.

As Sister Leonarda stood there reflecting on the religious life, the Nordam kept its steady course through the waters on its way to the United States. Her reflections on the religious life turned to thoughts about the country which was her destination. There were many questions in her mind. What kind of country was the United States? What would she meet with when she got there? What kind of people were the Americans of the U.S.? In the course of the last few weeks Sister Leonarda had asked herself these questions many times. Her memory flipped pictures of Uncle Bernard's U.S. She had so wanted, at that time, to go back to the United States with Uncle Bernard, and now twelve years later she was going to that country but in an entirely different capacity and with a challenging responsibility. When she had entered the Convent in Steyl, she had wanted to be a missionary in Africa or China, but instead she was now going to a country that opened its doors to Europeans, Asians, Africans, and peoples of all lands. In the vast expanse of land known as the United States one could find immigrants from just about every corner of the earth.

In 1901, the United States was a young, sprawling country; and like a gangling youngster not quite familiar with its growing limbs and adolescent body, and perhaps developing too rapidly, this country at the beginning of the 20th century was also feeling the pains and frustrations of its rapid growth.

The country emerged from the fire and bloodshed of a war for freedom—freedom from social and political tyranny; from religious and ethnic persecution. The nation came into existence bearing scars of burned out towns and villages, and the wounds of its citizens. From its beginning as a nation the watchword for all who would enter its shores was freedom, liberty, human rights. Down through the rushing time of two centuries, much would go down in its history under the banner, or the guise, of freedom and human rights.

It was a country with a unique personality. The coins of the country epitomized it; "E Pluribus Unum"—From many, one—many people from all places of the world making up one distinct nation.

It was at once the idealist and the shrewd practical business mind; the traditionalist and preserver of the past, and at the same time, the refuge for the avant-garde. It opened its arms, raised its torch, and lit the way for the poor, the despised, the downtrodden, the disillusioned, the ambitious, the scholar, the merchant, the craftsman, the farmer, scientist, and artist, the adventurer and dreamer. All people who wanted a chance to live with the basic freedoms necessary for a peaceful life; all people who wanted an opportunity to use their aptitudes and talents and make something of themselves—all these were welcomed to this country. But, "E Pluribus Unum" included the well-meaning as well as the charlatan and drifter, the honest as well as the unscrupulous. It meant cooperation as well as dissension because freedom has as many interpretations and causes as people fighting for it.

Thus the country came to be the "melting pot of nations" and ideas.

By 1901, the young country had already been through the bloody revolution for its freedom from tyranny and unjust taxation; the War of 1812, which gave birth to the classic "do not trespass" document: the Monroe Doctrine; the pathetically tragic Civil War to abolish slavery and preserve the Union; the Spanish American War to limit or crush Spain's interests in the Americas. The country had felt the repercussions from slavery and the post Civil War Carpetbaggers who surely set back Reconstruction; the Know-Nothing Party with its anti-Catholic and anti-immigrant policy; the Ku Klux Klan and its lawlessness and violence; the sad and often violent subduing and final subjugation of the Indian tribes, the aborigines of this beautiful land.

Unlike the European or Asian countries with their centuries of history and tradition, this country was anti-monarchical, anti-aristocratic, anti-feudal, and anti-privilege.[2]

European writers and philosophers scoffed at it for it was a country that had "no monarchy, no hereditary aristocracy, no tradition of culture, no landed gentry . . .no established Church, no secret police, no royal council of state, no house of peers, no 'society,' no feudal tenure . . . ."[3] And yet, what philosophers scoffed at were the very reasons which called many to these shores.

To understand the American one must see this person in the light of the country's brief but extremely rich and colorful history—history that is tragic yet hopeful, violent but also compassionate, turbulent, yet peaceful, simple and complicated; stressing equal rights yet giving rise to an "aristocracy" and privileged class of its own: the millionaire and multi-millionaire, the railroad and oil tycoons, the steel magnates, and other people of wealth.

People overseas erroneously equated "American" with the latter privileged class, but the very wealthy, even though they contributed to the country, made up a small percentage. Beyond this group was the backbone of the country: the city factory worker putting in twelve or more hours a day in horrendous work conditions at the time; the coal miner earning a livelihood in the dark and often treacherous recess of the earth; the farmer often battling soil conditions, insects, drought, storms; all the everyday faceless and nameless people—only statistics—yet the ones who really built the country, kept it going and gave it a new spirit and a fresh vitality. And what is more, in this country, it was possible for people such as these to rise above their poverty to become statesmen, professors, bank executives, or even president of the country.

The American character and personality evolved from all of this. Actually, one might say the American character was the melding of traits inherited from the forefathers of many lands with the distinct characteristics of this new land. The two blended into a new personality. The stability and perseverance traits of the "old country" mixed with the new spirit of daring and adventure, with the recklessness and restlessness of youth and its flair for show and ostentation, for candor and trust, its constant movement, never standing still, always hurrying here and there—and all these traits mixed with the character of the land: immensity and plenty, vastness and prodigality—resulting in a personality that was generous, self-reliant, hard-working, and willing to sacrifice, boisterous, boastful, indulgent, understanding and forgiving in some ways, prejudiced in other ways, but always open to the new and always championing the cause of freedom and human rights.

In 1901, the country was still loosely bound by a lot of "little old world" sections in cities; immigrants tended to flock to their own people. it would be only following the First World War that the American personality would begin to take on meaning as a distinct nationality.

To this country, then, breath-takingly beautiful in the grandeur of its natural wonders, and to these people with such a variegated personality, Sister Leonarda and her companions were quietly wending their way across the Atlantic. To understand the people of another nation and to accept them as they are demands a keen insight and a fine perception of the human person. There is something so deeply unique about each nationality that it escapes the understanding of an "outsider." The missionary is always aware of this. She knows she cannot fit the personality of another country into the mold of her own country's personality. Accepting each person as a unique individual in the uniqueness of his own country was one of Sister Leonarda's most beautiful traits. For this she would be deeply loved.

The late afternoon sun was casting its final rays on Wednesday, May 8, 1901. In Hoboken, New Jersey, the passengers were debarking from the Nordam, and there were laughter, shouts of welcome and a confusion of happiness surrounding travelers, relatives and friends. The five Sisters from Steyl, Holland, were a bit unsteady as they tried to stand on stable ground with somewhat shaky "sea legs." Somewhere in the hubbub of shouts and laughter and a strange language, they heard someone calling out, "Grüss Gott, Schwestern! Herzlich Wilkommen!" They looked about them. Yes, someone was welcoming them. They were the only Sisters they could see. The sound of their own language thrilled them. They were in a strange country, being welcomed by strange people, but in a language they understood. The friendly cordiality and kindness warmed them. Nothing goes so directly to the heart of a person as one's language, especially when heard in unfamiliar surroundings.

They saw a man and woman waving to them and moving through the crowd. Mr. and Mrs. Frank Heinemann and their daughter Pauline were soon standing before the Sisters, and introductions were made. The Heinemanns took care of the Sisters' immediate needs and then took them to the Leo House, a stopping place for German Catholic immigrants. The Sisters spent the night here.[4]

At two o'clock the following day, Sister Leonarda and her companions boarded a train for Chicago. Near Buffalo, the Sisters experienced some consternation when they found themselves in the middle of an excited group of passengers all talking at once and every word unintelligible to the bewildered newcomers. The Sisters finally concluded that some accident had occurred. And so it had—or almost had! The rails of the track spread so much that there was danger of their coach de-railing. Not knowing what to do, the Sisters stood perplexed as the other passengers hurried back and forth. A kind gentleman saw the Sisters' predicament, came up to them, and offered to take them to the pullman car because he said that it was not right for the Sisters to be in that crowd at midnight. The gentleman meant well, his offer was kind, but Sister Leonarda's mind was filled with the last admonitions given her by the Reverend Founder and Mother Josepha. Their words kept ringing in her ears: "Remember you will be in a new country. Do not readily listen to any stranger that may approach you." Realizing her responsibility as senior of the group, Sister Leonarda graciously declined the man's offer. He smiled, for he must have sensed the situation of the poor Sisters; but he would not be dismissed so easily. He saw to it that their luggage was taken care of and that they themselves were comfortably seated in a different coach. Later, when Sister Leonarda became acquainted with the American people and their customs, she laughed many times over this incident and expressed her sincere gratitude for the kind man's solicitude.[5]

The train arrived in Chicago on Friday at seven o'clock in the evening. The Sisters were warmly welcomed by Father John Peil, Superior of the Divine Word Fathers, Father Richards, and Brother Wendelin, and a few Chicago friends.

The priests and Brothers of the Society of the Divine Word had gone to the United States as early as 1895. At the time of the Sisters' arrival, the Society had just opened St. Joseph's Technical School for boys in the little village of Shermerville, some ten miles north of Chicago.[6]

Shermerville was just one of the many villages springing up around growing cities throughout the country. The Galloways from Pennsylvania had settled this area around 1836. Most of the first settlers were English, but from about 1840 on, German immigrants began buying up the land. At one time, it was possible to purchase an acre of this farmland for about $1.25. In its youthful years, Shermerville had a most unflattering nickname. It was known as the saloon town. However, in 1901, when the Sisters came to begin their foundation in Shermerville, the village was already gradually developing into a respectable rural area. There was a population of about three hundred and approximately sixty houses. Business buildings included one meat market, one general store, one coal and feed store, one harness store, one stone cutter, and the railroad station for the Chicago, Milwaukee, and St. Paul Railroad. And, yes, there were still some remnants of the early days in the presence of five saloons. In 1923, at the suggestion of E. W. Landwehr, the name was changed to Northbrook in an attempt to bury the old reputation.[7]

The location, rich in farm land and open spaces, offered room for expansion for the Divine Word Fathers and the Holy Spirit Missionary Sisters. From the little village of Shermerville, in the years to come, scores of priests, Brothers, and Sisters would journey out to carry the mission cross to mission lands. But this was the joy of the future! Now, there were only the hardships of a new foundation which was as yet hardly begun.

An hour before midnight, the tired travelers found themselves in the chapel of St. Joseph's Home where a solemn hymn of thanksgiving, Mary's hymn: "My soul magnifies the Lord" was sung for their safe journey. The Sisters then walked a short distance to the small frame house which was their new convent. There, Mrs. Barbara Happ, Mrs. Mathias Happ, Mrs. Julia Donovan, Miss Gaesfeld, and Miss Lucy Bracktendorf awaited them with cups of hot coffee and a little refreshment. Sister Leonarda was surprised at this thoughtfulness on the part of these busy women, who waited for the Sisters even at this late hour. She would never forget their kindness on this first night in a strange land and a strange convent. Down through the years, none of the Holy Spirit Missionary Sisters would forget these women, who so generously befriended their Foundress and her companions.

The early morning hours were already ticking away before the Sisters lay down for a few hours' rest.[8]

When the Sisters had gone to bed, Sister Leonarda opened her suitcase and took from it a small notebook. She sat down, took a pen and opened the book to the first page and wrote:

"God Holy Spirit, all for love of Thee!"

Then she turned the page and jotted down in diary form: "Each person while on earth gives but a very small part of her life, just a dot; each lifetime on earth is but an infinitesimal point in time. Every human being lives on earth to prepare for a greater life to come. A person lives here temporarily, but one day will be eternally happy. So it is that in each one's life there may be a task, a calling, a special mission—yet all are but moments lost in eternity.

"We also find such important moments in our holy Church, in society at large, and in religious societies. Thus this is now such an important moment in the life of us five Sisters and in the life of our Congregation, namely, the establishment of a branch of our Order in a new land.

"There are now two hundred Sisters in the Congregation, six branch houses, and forty Sisters in these houses. The youngest branch is our foundation in the United States. We five Sisters: Sister Alexia, Sister Clara, Sister Foureria, Sister Martina, and I, Sister Leonarda, left Steyl, Holland, on April 26, 1901. Arrived in New York, Wednesday, May 8, and in Chicago, May 11. We have been sent to establish the Congregation of Missionary Sisters, Servants of the Holy Spirit in the United States."[9]

In such concise words, Sister Leonarda began her great work on earth.

The little house was poor, very poor, indeed! It looked quite forsaken and unstable from the outside, but the inside was even more miserably wretched and ill-furnished. Sister Leonarda needed but to glance about her to read what her role and that of her Sisters would be, at least in the beginning.

Not the least perturbed by their small dwelling, the Sisters excitedly examined every nook and corner of their new home. They found that it would not be necessary to waste any steps in walking from one place to another. By entering the front door, they came into a little hall, which was also the sacristy. On one side of the small corridor were a reception room, the chapel, and a very small room, the office, for Sister Leonarda. On the opposite side were the kitchen and dining room. A few steps to the right or to the left, and the Sisters would be either in the chapel or the dining room. On the second floor were two very small bedrooms and a storeroom. That was the convent.[10]

The inspection tour being complete, the Sisters set about unpacking the few necessities they had brought with them. They could bring along only whatever their trunks would hold, and so they had but the bare necessities for cooking and the like.

One of the first rooms the Sisters wanted to clean and arrange was the chapel. Father Peil had promised to bring the Blessed Sacrament on the twelfth of May, their first Sunday in the United States; and the Sisters wanted to make their chapel as beautiful as circumstances allowed.

Evening shadows were slowly resting upon the cottage and the surrounding wilderness when Sister Leonarda cheerfully called her Sisters together. The unpacking was finished, the house had been given a few decorative touches, and now Sister Leonarda opened her purse and poured out its contents on the table. They all counted. Forty-seven cents![11] On this sum of money the Sisters were beginning a new foundation. Sister Leonarda put the coins into the purse again and laughed.

"You see, Sisters," she said, "this is just our one percent—not even that, and besides it is only material aid. God will add his ninety-nine percent of blessings. We need only trust in Him." She was so cheerful about it all that none of her Sisters could feel depressed or saddened in spite of their rather grave, as some people might call it, financial situation. Instead, they fell right in line with their leader and determined to forge ahead.

Each Sister took upon herself some part of the work in making their little convent a livable place and in setting about providing their necessities. Sister Clara took care of the kitchen; Sister Alexia had a garden laid out during the first week—and that to her credit and ingeniousness—for she lacked all necessary implements. Sister Foureria took care of the home and helped with the laundry. Sister Martina took care of all the "finishing touches" and did the extra work. The convent was so small and their community so small also that their tasks were not impossible, except that they were in need of many necessities.

On Sunday, May 12th, true to his promise, Father Peil brought the Blessed Sacrament to the Sisters' chapel, and the tiny room used as a chapel suddenly took on the proportions of a magnificent basilica, for the One who gave the chapel meaning was as truly in their poor room, a makeshift chapel in a tottering frame house, as He was in some splendid, stately cathedral.

The Sisters needed His Sacramental Presence in their midst, for their work was just about to begin, and He would be their Strength and Courage, their

Refuge and Consolation when the going would be arduous and uncertain.

It was the following day when Sister Martina happened to glance out the window as the Sisters returned from Mass, that she gave a cry of alarm which brought Sister Leonarda into the room. They both looked and saw a single file procession of Brothers advancing toward the convent with baskets of clothes. What could it mean?

Puzzled, the Sisters opened the door for the smiling Brothers and were greeted with: "Welcome! Look what we have saved for you!"[12]

The Brothers were being facetious, but their words were sadly significant. In a way, they marred the beginnings of the Holy Spirit Missionary Sisters in this country and shackled the Sisters with a label that would carry on even into the 1960's and 1970's—the label that the Holy Spirit Missionary Sisters from Steyl were simply in existence to work for the needs of the priests and Brothers of the Society of the Divine Word—to staff their kitchens and do their laundry. Somehow among the members of the Society of the Divine Word the idea carried through for decades that the Sisters were uneducated women and could do only housework in the Society's kitchens and laundries. Even in the 1960's, when by that time, scores of Sisters had already received degrees in various fields in universities across the United States; when many Sisters were in charge of schools as Principals and Headmistresses, as Heads of College Departments, as Administrators of Hospitals; when others were engaged in intensive research and Doctorate studies; and still others had degrees in home economics, dietetics, household management; when the Sisters were known over the country for the superb talent of some of their members shown in works of art and exquisite embroidery and other fancy needlework; when scores of other Sisters in the Congregation had received their R.N.'s and degrees in science—even then, more than fifty years after the Sisters came to the United States, there were still some members of the Society of the Divine Word here in the U.S. who had the same mental attitude toward the Sisters that those first priests and Brothers had in 1901 when the Brothers brought over their heaping baskets of clothes and said, "Look what we have saved for you."

The sharp pain of a poignant sorrow went through the soul of Sister Leonarda. It was as if in this one moment the faces of young women who came to this Order flashed before the Foundress. Her sensitive soul saw many of them laying aside their burning desire to work as missionaries at home and abroad because of this other work that had to be done. In this one moment she had a premonition of the disheartening decisions she would be forced to make in the future and that other Superiors after her would have to make. For just a second there was silent communing with God in her soul.

The smiling Brothers were still standing before her, and Sister Leonarda, knowing that the Congregation of Missionary Sisters was still connected to the Society of the Divine Word and hence subordinate in many ways to the priests, could do little else than accept. Her vow of obedience was dear to her, and she recognized in this situation the need for a resigned obedience.

There was no need to inspect the baskets which the Brothers just set down, for the Sisters knew very well what they contained; and, after the first shock, they laughed heartily at those heaps of clothes. When they had all enjoyed a good laugh, Sister Leonarda said, "Now, Sisters, let us begin at once." In no time at all, everyone was darning socks or sewing on buttons or patching shirts for the priests, Brothers, and small boys of St. Joseph's Technical School. The school numbered forty pupils, and the amount of torn clothing had been left to accumulate when word came that the Sisters were coming; but the Sisters worked with a will, determined to empty the baskets before another washday rolled around.[13]

Months of toil and sacrifice followed for the little group of five, for they now did the kitchen work for the priests, Brothers, and students, and the laundry work, and the sewing. If they grew weary and despondent, because this was a far cry from the missionary work they had anticipated doing, they had only to look at their leader, a brave woman of faith and indefatigable strength of will. She plodded on ahead, and the others followed.

One summer evening as the Sisters sat busily sewing outdoors on the veranda during their recreation period, they were surprised by the visit of an elderly woman who introduced herself as Mrs. Janssen. Sister Leonarda, wholly unaware of the good woman's motive in coming, remarked pleasantly, "It is certainly very thoughtful of you to visit us, Mrs. Janssen. We are still quite new in this country, and we are always eager to make more friends."

The woman looked at Sister Leonarda and dryly

answered: "I want you to do something for me."

At this, Sister Leonarda, only too eager to be of assistance anywhere, asked: "Well, now, Mrs. Janssen, what can we do for you? What do you wish?"

"I want to stay here," came the immediate reply.[14]

Sister Leonarda was taken aback by this unexpected answer. She tried to explain to the good woman that the small convent was hardly large enough for the Sisters. Where could they put her? They could offer her very little comfort, indeed, no comfort at all. Thus Sister Leonarda reasoned with the woman, but Mrs. Janssen held to her request and would not leave.

All that Sister Leonarda had said by way of refusal was only too true, yet there was another reason for refusing Mrs. Janssen's request, a reason which lay deeply sheltered in the heart of each Sister. They knew that, sooner or later, they would have to undertake a work of charity to establish themselves more firmly in the country, and their unanimous wish was that they might establish an orphanage. Now as Mrs. Janssen spoke to them, each Sister mentally clung to that fond desire, for fear that this incident would be its failure.

At length, Sister Leonarda could no longer resist the pleas of the old Mrs. Janssen and consented to have her stay with the Sisters.

The consent was but an exterior acquiescence. Deep within Sister Leonarda held on to the hope that she would be able to establish an orphanage as the first charitable undertaking in the United States and that Mrs. Janssen's stay was but a temporary arrangement. She knew that at that moment all the

Sisters were also clinging to that hope.

However, Mrs. Janssen was overcome with joy when Sister Leonarda said she could stay. Each day she was happier, and, of course, such happiness had to spill out. Thus, in no time at all, Mrs. Janssen's joy and good fortune became food for gossip around the neighborhood, and in a very short time the Sisters saw their last hopes for an orphanage vanish in a puff of unfulfilled desires as they welcomed two more elderly women to live with them.

It was impossible to shelter all in the little cottage. Another place had to be provided as sleeping quarters for the women. This was accomplished by renovating a near-by barn into sleeping rooms. Three single rooms were arranged on the first floor, and a dormitory was prepared on the second floor. The poverty of their new surroundings did not bother the women; they were happy to be near the Sisters, and during the day they would try to help with some of the work insofar as they were able.

Because of the increase in work, Sister Leonarda felt obliged to write to Steyl and ask her Superiors for more Sisters. Her request was answered, and on August 30, four Sisters came. Among them was Sister Borromea, who was appointed Assistant to Sister Leonarda.[15]

With the increase in personnel, Sister Leonarda felt relieved and more at peace to tell the Sisters that they had been assigned to take over the "little red school-house" near St. Joseph's Home, and that two of them would have to be the teachers. It was an opportunity eagerly seized, even though the Sisters had more domestic work on their hands than the group could handle. However, this new venture meant work among children, and this would give them at least a taste of the missionary work they longed for. The beginning of September saw the Holy Spirit Missionary Sisters from Steyl starting their first teaching mission in the United States.

The school was a little red brick building with two small classrooms. Sister Alexia and Pauline Happ were the first teachers. Sister Leonarda gave lessons in piano and violin and would have taken the upper-grade classes except that she was away from home for several months at the beginning of the school year.[17]

In order to perfect herself in the American language, especially idiomatic English, Sister Leonarda went to Joliet, Illinois, and stayed with the Sisters of St. Francis. There she not only could have American teachers but could be in daily contact with Americans. The Franciscan Sisters were extremely kind and helpful to Sister Leonarda.[18]

When she returned home, her Sisters were overjoyed to see her. It was as if their strength had come back and warmth had come to their home again. Did they need strength and warmth? Oh, yes! These pioneers needed both spiritual and physical strength, spiritual and physical warmth. Of course, they were well aware of the power of prayer, and Sundays would find them in the chapel communing with their God. The casual visitor at the convent may have wondered at seeing a Sister or Sisters carrying a chair from one room to the other. The truth is there was only one chair for each person in the convent, so that if a Sister wanted to go to chapel to sit and meditate, she would usually have to get her chair from the dining room and carry it to the chapel. This was a small inconvenience compared to the joy of a few quiet moments with their God.

But though the Sisters relished these moments of prayer, human as they were, the Sisters also needed someone to whom they could talk, face to face. That someone they found in their Superior.

Sister Leonarda was always easy to approach and had a keen psychological understanding of people. Hence, her Sisters felt at ease with her because she seemed to know each one individually; she had the intuition of a loving mother. The Sisters needed someone to encourage them in these first difficult years; yet they had little time actually to speak to Sister Leonarda. In fact, because of the circumstances they found themselves in, work occupied most of their time, and they lived a very broken community life.[19]

Washdays at St. Joseph's Home were a twenty-hour affair. The Sisters rose early and were bending over the wash tubs at four in the morning, and only at midnight would they be rinsing the last tubs of wash. There were no washing machines or dryers. Everything was done by hand, which meant that they had to rub and rub the clothes, especially those of the small boys who were learning trades in the Technical School and, most of the time, left a week's supply of grease on their trousers and shirts.

Then, too, every morning two Sisters went over to St. Joseph's to take care of the kitchen. Sometimes they would not come home again till late at night—too tired for anything but bed. It was Sister Leonarda who would take care of their personal needs, who would see to it that their habits were washed and ironed, and who frequently took over their post of duty.

Already since the four Sisters had come over in August, there had not been enough room for all in the small convent. But the Sisters ingeniously made a dormitory for themselves in the hayloft of a neighboring barn. Sleeping there was not too inconvenient for the Sisters and could even be fun when the summer breezes cooled their tired bodies after a warm day of unceasing work over wash tubs or hot stoves. The coming of winter, however, presented a different scene, and that first winter was a severe one. The wind and the snow had free access through the wide spaces between boards, and the barn became an icy sleeping chamber. Try as they would, the Sisters could not sleep. They shivered from head to toe. At last they could stand it no longer, and in the darkness of night, they trudged toward their convent dragging their straw sacks and blankets behind them. Inside their home, they threw their sacks around the one stove in the house, and that in the dining room, then threw themselves on the sacks and fell asleep without any struggle.

The rest of the house was not much warmer than the barn, and frequently Sister Martina found a layer of snow on her sewing machine, which had been generously donated by a kind benefactor.

Word came from Steyl that the Reverend Founder had appointed more Sisters for Shermerville. The news was a joy to the Sisters, but it also presented its problem. Sister Leonarda laid the situation before Father Superior Peil and explained that something must be done to give the Sisters more room. Father Peil understood the plight of the Sisters. He was always kind to them and wanted to help them as much as he could. He saw that an addition had to be made to the cottage and appointed the Brothers to carry out the task.

When the Sisters arrived in March, Father Peil met them in Chicago; and during the train ride home, he delighted their imagination with attractive descriptions of the new addition to their convent, so that the Sisters could hardly wait to see the magnificent brick building their fancy had constructed from Father's lavish description.

Sister Johanna, one of the five new arrivals, was shocked to speechlessness when she finally arrived at her new convent. In place of the beautiful brick building she had imagined, stood a rather weather-beaten frame house. For a moment she forgot the joy she had so long anticipated: namely, meeting her former novice mistress; she also forgot the speech she had prepared to give.

In a very short time, however, the Sisters regained their composure and laughed good-naturedly at their own fanciful folly.

During their first year in the United States, the Sisters had been blessed with kind friends from Chicago and the neighboring vicinity, who took an active interest in the welfare of the Sisters.

What a thrill it was for Sister Leonarda when she received the first gift of five dollars for the Sisters from Mr. Boltz!

There were Mrs. Happ, Miss Gaesfeld, and Mrs. Hornburg who scouted the neighborhood collecting necessary pieces of furniture for the Sisters; and there were Sister Borromea's relatives, who lived in Chicago and helped the Sisters with their charity. They had had tangible proof of the Sisters' poverty when they had visited Sister Borromea once. The Sisters served lunch, but could not eat their own lunch because the only dishes in the house were being used by their guests. The visitors noticed this, and the following day, a carton of dishes and cutlery appeared at the Sisters' back door.

These kind benefactors were a consolation to Sister Leonarda, who frequently reminded her Sisters to pray for these generous friends.[20]

At the beginning of the summer vacation, Sister Leonarda considered it a necessity to go away once more in order to improve in the language. Although it grieved her to have to leave her Sisters, she was obliged to go because she felt that knowledge of the language and its proper use was of prime importance for any Sister who wished to work in the country. This time her place of study was the Dominican Sisters of Sinsinawa, Wisconsin. To these good Sisters, too, Sister Leonarda was forever grateful.

Her return home in August was a sad one. Some weeks before she had received a letter with the news: "Sister Perpetua is not well and cannot continue her duties in the laundry at St. Joseph's Home." Sister Leonarda wrote back immediately: "Let Sister Perpetua remain at home and rest." Now a second letter brought the startling news that Sister Perpetua was in a critical condition. Sister Leonarda hurried home only to find that the sick Sister was dying. Two nurses had been called from St. Elizabeth's Hospital in Chicago, but they had gone back with the hopeless statement that there was nothing they could do for the Sister. The pain of a ruptured appendix made the last hours of this young Sister almost unbearable, but she lay quietly, bathed in perspiration, her will accepting pain and death since she knew there was no more anyone could do for her. She had worked in her mission field scarcely four months, but who can know the why and wherefore of death no matter when it comes? Sister Perpetua died calmly, in the arms of Sister Leonarda on August 23, at four-thirty in the afternoon. She was buried in the Sisters' garden until a plot of ground was later consecrated as a cemetery.[21]

The death of Sister Perpetua was a severe blow to Sister Leonarda. She said nothing, but her face showed the deep anguish that the loss of this first Sister meant to her, the spiritual mother.

Before the year 1902 came to its end, God had a singular blessing planned for Sister Leonarda. On the Feast of the Great Saint Teresa of Avila, October 15, Sister Isidora with two companions came to join the ranks of the American pioneers. She was a blessing for the American foundation that only God, at the time, in His Omniscience, could relish. Her life would be from this time on an unending life of prayer and work. She would be the comfort of a Superior whose duties were sometimes onerous and thorny. Sister Isidora, who had consoled Sister Leonarda upon her appointment as novice mistress in Steyl, was once again the happy soul who could cheer anyone by her simple humor. She lived and worked in the U.S. province for more than fifty years; and when she died, no one could recall so much as an impatient inflection. She was a person at peace with God, with others, and with herself; and it gave her an aura of tranquility so that others also felt at peace in her presence.

Just before Christmas, Sister Leonarda told her

community of sixteen Sisters that Reverend Father Peil would conduct their annual retreat from December 26 to January 1. She added with a pleasant smile: Sister Isidora, Sister Carola, and Sister Aquinas, since you have already been fortified by the graces of a retreat at the Motherhouse, you will have to be the Marthas for us while we are the Marys.

In the tranquil silence of a spiritual rejuvenation, the Sisters closed behind them the hardships and blessings of a year well spent.

1. Letter of Mrs. Schroeder (former Sr. Alexia, one of the first five Sisters to the U.S.).

2. Howard Mumford Jones, *Strange New World American Culture: The Formation Years* (New York: The Viking Press, 1952).

3. Jones.

4. Mother Leonarda's Diary.

5. Chronicle of St. Ann's Home.

6. Hermann Fischer, S.V.D., *Life of Arnold Janssen*, pp. 403-406.

7. The League of Women Voters of Northbrook, Illinois, *Northbrook Profiles* (Chicago: Clarke-McElroy Publishing Co., 1951), p. 32.

8. Chronicle of St. Ann's Home.

9. Diary of Mother Leonarda.

10.-21. References are all from St. Ann's Home Chronicle.

Chapter Five

Bringing Christ to everyone and everyone to Christ is the apostolate of the missionary Sister. This is her domain of work but, exhaustive though it is, she must do more. Only when she is doubled and tripled over and over again in countless others who will carry Christ to the world can this great task be carried on. Therefore she seeks others to help her, for as the Constitutions state, "a Sister benefits the Congregation more by her ability to instruct others than if she alone excels."

—Diamond Jubilee Book of S.Sp.S.

Shermerville lay asleep under the soft darkness of night. From nearby fields the sweet smell of fresh spring clover scented the air, the chirping crickets carried on their nightly metallic conversation. Lights in and around the village were out showing that the inhabitants of Shermerville were already resting for the night. Only one light burned in a room on the first floor of the white framehouse. A dim gas lamp cast enough glow to light up the lovely, but tired face of Sister Leonarda. Her eyes shone as always with peace and kindness, but there was a third dimension now—weariness. She sat down at the wooden table in the room and for several minutes let her head rest in her hands. The clock on the table showed twelve midnight. She had been up since 4 a.m., but her day was not over yet.

All day she had been teaching in school; after school she had helped the Sisters with the laundry work at St. Joseph's Home, and now she could finally look through the day's mail on her table, prepare her lessons for the following day, and write some official letters that demanded attention. There was nothing extraordinary about this schedule. For over a year already she found it necessary to do her own work after the other Sisters had gone to rest for the night. It was impossible for her to take care of convent business matters during the day. She had to be with her Sisters for some time, at least, and this was only possible by joining them in their work.

Here in the silence of her room she had time to think through the problems that confronted her as Superior. There was the building of St. Ann's Home for the elderly. This occupied much of her time. True, the construction work for the Home was all under the management and direction of the Society of the Divine Word. As yet, the Congregation of Sisters was still connected with the Society in financial matters, and the Sisters had little, if anything, to say about the construction of buildings or their management. It was the priests who did all of this, and the Sisters merely took charge of the work. This was all in accord with the wish of the Founder. Nevertheless, Sister

Leonarda was deeply concerned about the building.

The Sisters' plans to establish an orphanage had long since been abandoned; and when the Founder, Arnold Janssen, had ordered the Sisters to undertake a home for the elderly, none of the Sisters spoke anymore about an orphanage. Sister Leonarda realized that this home for the elderly was their first work of charity in the United States, and, in addition, it would be their first real convent; so she watched its construction with anxiety and interest. How they needed a real place to live! The weather-beaten framehouse was slowly living out its last days, and Sister Leonarda was anxious to get her Sisters out of it, before those days were over. She was happy that soon the Sisters would have a real convent and more room. They deserved it!

How frequently she encouraged her Sisters in accepting the sacrifices and inconveniences that were so much a part of the beginnings in the United States. Spurred on by her own zeal, inflamed as it was by her great love for the Holy Spirit, she would jot down her thoughts on tiny scraps of paper and then offer these thoughts to her Sisters in her little talks to them.

In these short inspirational messages and advice, her spirituality was in keeping with the thought of the day. This was a time when masters of the spiritual life stressed such teachers in spirituality as Thomas A'Kempis in his *Following of Christ*; St. John of the Cross and Catherine of Sienna; the writings of such "Greats" as Alphonsus Liguori, St. Bernard, St. Therese of Avila; the three Jesuit youths: Stanislaus Kostka, John Berchmans, and Aloysius Gonzaga—all exemplars of humility, penance, and prayer.

It was a time when Thomas Aquinas and Duns Scotus were held as masters of theology and philosophy.

It was also a period of great devotions: to the Sacred Heart since the apparitions to St. Margaret Mary; devotions to Mary after the apparitions to Bernadette at Lourdes; and now with the advent of Arnold Janssen and his three religious Orders, it was a time of awakening to the Holy Spirit and His special mission in the world.

The pure melodies of Gregorian Chant were the Church's official music, and the emotionally filled songs to Christ and Mary gave feeling to the devotions.

It was a time that spoke of heroic virtue, humility, mortification, charity, penance. In the religious life, one was given the Baptist's maxim to follow: "He (Christ) must increase." Rather than assert oneself, the religious was told that silent acceptance, "blind obedience" was a way of becoming more Christ-like. Bearing inconveniences, practicing small acts of self-denial and sacrifice, accepting humiliations and slights—all added up to a purified soul, a strong will, and perfection. A rule of silence was strictly enforced in most religious Orders, so that the soul might be always attuned to the Holy Spirit.

Today with hindsight it is quite easy to show both the value and the shortcomings of such spiritual formation. However, at the time, it was considered the correct method to follow in "striving for perfection." Today's spiritual formation is based on the past. It is simply a continuous process of growth, a "becoming," an evolution of the spirit. It is only when the person is open to God, cleared of its egoism, by a spiritual cleansing of the soul in the practice of the basic virtues: charity, humility, mortification, that the person can safely enter the humanistic era of today and another phase of spiritual formation: seeing oneself in an intimate relationship with God, others, and self on the level of a spiritual, eschatological love.

Although Sister Leonarda's messages followed the spirit of the time, she was not inflexible nor was she a rigid disciplinarian. On the contrary, she would have fit as well in the latter half of the twentieth century as she did in the first half. She understood "change" and could evaluate it. Hers was an open mind.

In the beginning years when there were so many inconveniences, so much work, and so little time, it seemed, to do it all, Sister Leonarda would try to encourage them to go on with hope. In one of their first months here, she told them: "Most people usually get frightened when they hear of sacrifices and self-abnegation, but we in the convent ought to rejoice over them. When we were in the Motherhouse in Steyl, there was nothing that made mission life more attractive for us then the hardships and sacrifices connected with it. Now we have the opportunity to see our wishes realized, and now, too, we can find out whether our love is that genuine love we formerly believed we possessed. Is our love, perhaps, something like that of St. Peter's who solemnly declared to be ready to die with Jesus and then shortly afterwards denied his Master?" (Conference, 1901)

On another occasion she endeavored to explain to her Sisters, who were, perhaps, somewhat discouraged by their constant toil and their inability to carry out any of their own mission works, the value of these initial sacrifices not only for the development of the Congregation but for their own personal spiritual growth. She tells them: "We all know the feeling of happiness we may experience in convent life. This is often the case in the beginning of convent life. Then God leads us, as it were, by His hand and helps us to overcome the first difficulties so that we might not give way to discouragement. But, when our will is somewhat strengthened and directed more firmly toward the good, then He will, at times, let us walk alone on our way. Then He will apparently hide just to see whether we really love Him." (Conference 1901)

Thus she spoke and encouraged her small community of Sisters. But who was there to encourage her, to lighten her burden, and to guide her? She turned to the Holy Spirit. Time and again, she wrote in her private notes her complete submission to the Divine Spirit: "O Eternal Love, God Holy Spirit, to whom I have dedicated my entire life, in order to prove to you my consecration and my fidelity, I offer myself to you entirely as a holocaust of love." (Personal notes)

Does anyone speak of being a holocaust for God—today? Yet, the holocaust, the whole burnt offering, mentioned in the Old Testament was very real to her. Love to her meant a constant giving and a constant being open to—a love so intense that it could be realized only as a holocaust, an entire submission of oneself to God.

Thus she continued her life of total love in the old frame house, working under the light of the gas lamp, far into the early morning hours. The little book lying at the far corner of the table, almost hidden by the school papers she was correcting, was her second guide. The very first article of the Book of Constitutions clearly defined the aim of each Missionary Sister, Servant of the Holy Spirit. Her aim must be "self-sanctification for the greater glory of God in imitation of Jesus Christ and His Blessed Mother." This, then, was Sister Leonarda's program, to carry out that aim—a life of joyful service during the day and even at night.

As she cleared the table of the school papers and books to look at the day's mail, her face lit up in a smile. A glance at one of the papers had revealed the name Martin Levernier. "Poor dear boy!" she said to herself. "He had a hard time with his violin today." Martin took violin lessons from Sister Leonarda. There wasn't much time for a farm boy to practice violin with chores and what not to be looked after; still Martin was determined to learn. But all through today's lesson, his violin had only squeaked some horrible sounds; and Martin was uncomfortable and unhappy. In fact, he was so miserable, he began to cry in utter disgust. When he finally composed himself, he was surprised to see that Sister Leonarda's eyes were also wet. She felt sorry for him. Years later, in recalling this incident, Martin Levernier, now a distinguished business man, humorously added: "I never asked her whether she was crying out of sympathy for me or whether she was crying because I played so badly."[1]

Well, that was Martin! She put his paper in with the rest and took up the day's mail. She slit open an envelope postmarked "Steyl." Her eyes filled with grief as she read just one line: "Mother Josepha died." Both Foundresses of the Holy Spirit Missionary Sisters were gone, and their spiritual daughters were left to carry on the work.

Sister Leonarda knew that the Sisters would feel very bad when she told them the next morning that Mother Josepha was dead. They were, indeed, grief-stricken.

A month later, however, good news came that Sister Theresia was elected Mother General. The choice could not have been better.

May 30, 1903, was set as the day for the laying of the cornerstone of St. Ann's Home. For the first time since their arrival in Shermerville, the Sisters were privileged to have a Church dignitary visit them. His Excellency, Archbishop Quigley of Chicago, officiated at the ceremony. He was glad that the Sisters were beginning a home for the aged, and he wished them God's blessing in their work. After the ceremony, the Archbishop chatted a while with the priests and then expressed his wish to go to the Sisters' convent and visit with them a little. He was greeted at the door by a somewhat surprised and embarrassed Sister Borromea who was home alone tending to matters in the house while all the other Sisters, including Sister Leonarda, were at St. Joseph's Home busy again at their daily work in the laundry and the kitchen. The Archbishop was impressed by their simplicity and diligence and would not call them from their tasks.

Although a Home for the Aged was not in Sister Leonarda's plan as an initial project for the Sisters to undertake in the United States, in fact such a Home was farthest from her thoughts—still as soon as the

Sisters admitted Mrs. Janssen, appeals from elderly people kept coming in. Something had to be done for them and for the Sisters too. St. Ann's Home was the answer. Father Peil, S.V.D., was instructed by the Founder to take charge of the construction, and Father Hoenderop, S.V.D., was selected as the architect. Work on the building commenced at the beginning of 1903.

St. Ann's Home looked like a red brick giant in a surrounding wilderness. The Home was built on a plot of land directly across the road from the Sisters' "cottage in the green." There were five stories to the building: a basement, three floors, and an attic. The entrance was situated on the east side of the building. Broad stone stairways led from the basement to the attic. The dining rooms and workroom, kitchen, bakery, laundry, ironing and mangle room, and a supply room were on the basement floor. The next three floors contained private rooms for the elderly people. Dormitories for the Sisters were on the third floor, and the chapel was on the second floor. This was almost a palace for the Sisters in comparison to what they had.

In the early part of September, the building was still far from completion, but Sister Leonarda gave the laborers a pep talk to speed their work. She told them she had an extremely difficult mathematical problem to solve, and only they could solve it for her. She told them nine more Sisters were expected from Steyl by the 24th of September, and the little cottage was already full to overflowing. Not one more Sister could sleep in that house. Furthermore, she told them, who could tell what that shaky little frame-house would do if it took in nine more occupants. It might even collapse from the strain.

The workmen were won by the cheerfulness of her kind appeal and worked as speedily as possible to complete at least one dormitory for the new Sisters. They attained their goal, and when the Sisters came, Sister Leonarda happily led them to the new dormitory.

The arrival of this group of Sisters was a special event for Sister Leonarda and the other Sisters because the newcomers brought with them the first American postulant, Pauline Heinemann, from New Jersey, who had met the first missionary Sisters when they came two years ago. Pauline's entrance meant that an American novitiate would soon be established thereby sinking the roots of this foundation deeper and more firmly into American soil. It was a joy for Sister Leonarda and her Sisters, a joy that seemed at the moment to blot out all memory of what the previous years had meant in hardship and sacrifice. They would be able to develop now and expand and, perhaps, someday send out missionary Sisters of their own to foreign fields.

Young Pauline was welcomed by the Sisters with the customary greeting: "May God the Holy Spirit bless your entrance." She was a quiet and refined young woman, eager to begin her life of service and willing to accept the privations of the pioneer Sisters. She had her first taste of convent life that same night when, for the first time in her life, she came in contact with a straw sack instead of a mattress on her bed. Sleeping on the straw sack demanded real skill. Whenever she turned from one side to the other, she found that she had rolled her sack and was hanging on the under side of it with all her strength so as not to crash to the floor. It was something like walking on a barrel, only the straw sack didn't turn but stayed firmly in place. The art of sleeping on this round, stuffed sack consisted in being able to turn left and right and still remain on the top of it. Pauline didn't acquire this art the first night. She had to learn the hard way, and her first convent days were well tattooed upon her arms in black and blue bruises. It was, of course, all in the bargain for her and if convent life meant sleeping on those straw sacks, she would see to it that she acquired the knack.

November 10th was general moving day for the Sisters. There was not much to move from the cottage to St. Ann's Home; the Brothers carried over the heavier pieces of furniture, and the Sisters carried their own belongings on their indispensable straw sacks. Carrying the straw sacks up three flights of stairs was tiresome work until someone thought of a shorter and easier system to which all agreed. The sacks were pulled up by a rope through the dormitory window, and in no time at all the Sisters were happily engaged in getting their new dormitory alcoves arranged.

At last they had a suitable convent. Yet, the memories wrapped up in those first years in the cottage could not be forgotten. "We lived in a peaceful unity," wrote Sister Coletta, "such as there was in Nazareth, even though our work, humanly speaking, was much too heavy and too over-burdening."[2] This unity and love were carried with them into St. Ann's Home.

With the opening of the Home, a new period begins in the life of Sister Leonarda. Heretofore, she seems to be the silent clay in the hands of the Divine

Sculptor, the Holy Spirit. He had work for her to perform, and He chiseled away the rough spots in order to mold her into a fit instrument for His service. In those first years, He deepened her soul considerably. He knew that in the future only the light of Faith and trust in God would give her strength to carry on the duties assigned to her. Nothing was ever too difficult for her if she knew it was for the welfare of others. Her faith found its outward manifestation in her zeal to follow the prescribed liturgy of the Church and to cultivate devotions to the Holy Spirit, the Blessed Trinity, the Virgin Mother Mary, St. Joseph and the Holy Angels. In this she was one of the most faithful followers of the Venerable Founder whose spirituality centered around these devotions.[3]

How deeply she was impregnated with the virtue of faith reveals itself in her words of advice to the Sisters who came to her seeking counsel. Sometimes she would write these short sentences of encouragement to the Sister, at other times she would give them to the Sister during the course of their conversation. "Faith," she told one Sister, "is the greatest gift God has given us. Do we value it sufficiently and show our gratitude by living it?"[4] Again she writes: "Our soul would be at peace if we would take every trial, great or small, as coming from Him. He will use it for our sanctification. Thank Him for all."[5]

Once the Sisters and the five elderly women were in St. Ann's Home, Sister Leonarda faced another problem. They had a spacious building now and were not wanting for applicants, but how was she going to equip those rooms? According to the original plan, the Society of the Divine Word took care of the financial upkeep of the Home, decided what fees were to be charged of the residents, and received the money. The Sisters were in charge of all the work, but they also had to provide the furniture for the rooms although they received no salary or any kind of remuneration and had no other source of income.

Almost a century later, one wonders how this could be. How could the Sisters be responsible for furnishing all the rooms if they themselves received no income from anywhere or anyone? Again we can only marvel at the way Sister Leonarda managed to handle the situation.

Since the rooms in their present condition were of little use, Sister Leonarda in her simplicity and kindness went to those people who had already befriended her. These generous benefactors whose names will always be linked with the beginning of St. Ann's Home came to Sister Leonarda's rescue. The chapel necessities were provided by Mr. John Daleiden who donated a monstrance and a ciborium; Mrs. Mary Schillo who gave a chalice and Mr. Brandesher who contributed a large statue of the Blessed Mother. Mrs. Janssen, that little old lady who wouldn't take "No" for an answer when she asked to stay with the Sisters, showed her appreciation by giving the first sanctuary lamp, a censer, and a large, beautiful tower bell.

With the help of these kind friends, the rooms in St. Ann's Home gradually became cheery little homes for the elderly people even though the rooms possessed but the minimum necessities: a bed, a chair, and perhaps, a table or dresser.

The names of the Schillo, Birren, Bongart, Daleiden, Becker, and Happ families are indelibly imprinted in the memories of the Holy Spirit Missionary Sisters and are included in their daily prayers; for it was these outstanding benefactors who, by their material aid, helped the American branch of the Holy Spirit Missionary Sisters to grow and develop.

Whenever a new chapel was opened, Sister Leonarda was never at rest until the Blessed Sacrament reposed in the tabernacle. And once the Blessed Sacrament was placed in the tabernacle, Sister Leonarda was again anxious until a day of adoration could be held. Her love for the chapel was exceptionally striking. Nothing could ever be too good for the chapel. Her intimate love for her God gave her no rest until His Home was adorned as beautifully as circumstances allowed. Yet, she was not only concerned about its exterior adornments, she was far more sedulous about the worship of God in that chapel. No sooner had the Sisters moved into St. Ann's than Sister Leonarda organized the Sisters into a community choir. She loved music, and it was her lifetime task to see to it that the music and singing in the chapels of the various houses she founded was the best. She herself directed the choir in St. Ann's Home.

Days of adoration of the Blessed Sacrament, Sunday High Mass and Vespers, more elaborate liturgical celebrations on Church and Congregation feastdays—all these became the heritage of the American Sisters to be enjoyed and relished by the Sisters down through the years and long after her death. Where the worship of God was concerned, Sister Leonarda demanded of her community the best they had. Half-heartedness and mediocrity in the worship of God were not tolerated by her as many of the Sisters who sang in the choir under the direction of her vigorous baton could testify.

But she demanded whole-heartedness from the Sisters in other things, too; and, most of all, she demanded it from herself. In fact, she was stringent in the demands made on herself, but in the demands on the Sisters, she displayed an admirable psychology, rather, more correctly, a sagacious understanding of the human person, of woman. Whatever she asked of them, whenever she corrected them or wherever she placed them, the Sisters knew that her motive of action was that of love—love for them—a spiritual love which desired only their union with God.

Total strangers who came in contact with her sensed a genuine sincerity in her personality and often remarked that when they spoke to her, her attention was so complete that it seemed she had no other interest in the world but to be of assistance to them. Years later, the great philosopher and existentialist, Edith Stein, a Carmelite nun, would be quoted as saying: "In dealing with man, the spiritual need of our neighbor sets aside each commandment. Whatever we do is but a means toward an end. But love itself is the end, for God is Love." This was, truly, the epitome of Sister Leonarda's dealings with all who came in contact with her.

When Mary Delort of Chicago, the second American postulant, entered in December, 1903, she left behind a sick mother and only the assurances and insistence of her father gave her the courage to leave home. Mary's first meeting with Sister Superior Leonarda eased the heavy grief which lay upon her. "She took me so gently by the arm" writes Mary, "that a wonderful peace came over me. My eyes were filled with tears and many of the Sisters thought I was homesick already, but good Sister Superior told them that I had made a sacrifice in leaving home and that they should all pray for my dear mother. How can I express the warmth and comfort of her soft words and kindly smile? She was all that a mother could be, and I felt that in an hour's time she already knew me and understood me. Never have I known another with such a depth of understanding of the individual soul."[6]

A typical example of the variety of souls in convent life was humorously, and yet beautifully, illustrated in the first two American postulants. God loved variety in His creation, and He loves variety in His convents, too. Pauline and Mary were opposites in almost everything except their one burning desire to become Missionary Sisters; and each one reached that goal in her own characteristic way and lived that life beyond fifty golden years. Pauline was stately, dignified, pleasant in a quiet way; her humor was subdued, but she was always amiable and cheerful. She could sit for hours sewing one thing after the other without showing the least signs of fatigue or restlessness.

Mary was always spilling over with mirth. She liked a hearty laugh, and if there wasn't anything to laugh about, she saw to it that there would be something soon. She had to be up and doing all the time.

"Sister Superior," she once confessed to Sister Leonarda, "I really admire Sister Heinemann; but honestly I just can't sit there and sew all day. Anyway, I was never good with a needle. Maybe I'd better go home. I'm also getting into some kind of trouble always. I like to have fun." Sister Leonarda knew this young live-wire before her and only smiled.

"Sister," she said, "you must get a little wiser. You must know who appreciates your fun and who is annoyed by it. Now, if you are wise, you will save your jokes for those who appreciate them. As for your work, you won't always be in the sewing room. When you get to work in the kitchen, you'll have so much running to do, that you'll be glad to sit down a while and sew. Then there'll be other things to do later on. A missionary Sister must learn to do everything."

"And," remarks Mary, "she sent me to the chapel to say a prayer without making one reference to my going home. I was glad. I didn't want to go anyway. After that, whenever I had a good joke, I'd be sure to tell her. She was the most appreciative audience I had and would laugh tears at my mimicking or at my performance of the Irish jig."[7]

Mary stayed on and so did Pauline, and both worked hand in hand with the Sisters. Although the Sisters were in a large roomy convent and no longer had to contend with the inconveniences of the small cottage, they were still overburdened with work and could not follow a regulated community schedule.

The Sisters who went to work in the kitchen of St. Joseph's Home left early in the morning and came home only at night, sometimes after eight o'clock. Since they seldom had a chance to speak with their Superior, she went to them every Thursday for the noon meal. The Sisters looked forward to this day, and were always livelier and happier when Sister Leonarda was with them. She would prolong their recreation hour during her visit because most of their recreation periods were spent at work; and some of the Sisters didn't get the fresh air they needed since there was no time to go outdoors. Still the Sisters were happy and anxious to follow their leader. Sister Johanna writes: "Good Sister Superior Leonarda was always first in bringing the sacrifices. She helped the Sisters over their difficulties and did her own work in the evening. Late at night she would be sitting in her room doing her work."[8]

Christmas, 1903, was celebrated with a splendor that dazzled even the old people. The Sisters had hungered for the customary celebrations which accompanied Church feasts, and Sister Leonarda was ready at the first opportunity to introduce the lovely customs of the Congregation. Before the Midnight Mass, the Sisters and the clergy walked in procession through gayly lighted and decorated halls to the room where the Christ Child lay in satin splendor. From there the Infant was carried to the crib in the chapel. Symbolically the procession represented Christ's coming down from the Heavenly Father to dwell among His people on earth. The Christmas procession was such an impressive event that many of the old people were inwardly stirred to sentiments of great love and devotion. A solemn High Mass followed, the first to be celebrated in the Sisters' chapel. Christmas day was a day of great peace and contentment for the Sisters and satiated some of their thirst for these beautiful liturgies.

*****

In the early part of January, 1904, Sister Leonarda was approached by Father Peil with another request. He asked for a teacher to instruct some of the boys of St. Joseph's Home. The boys, seventeen of them in the beginning, went to the Sisters' old home, the little cottage, for their lessons. Classes were held here for two years until the house was too dilapidated for use. Some of the boys of St. Joseph's Home who attended these classes caused the Sisters not a little difficulty. It seems that, contrary to the original plan, boys of various degrees of refinement and morality were admitted so that at one time the priests themselves were alarmed to learn that their technical school was putting on the appearance of a reformatory judging from the type of youngsters under their tutelage. Naturally the Sisters, too, had their share of the less tractable boys, but these conditions did not last long for the Founder was not in favor of his priests engaging in this kind of educational work, and in a few years' time the technical school was closed.

At St. Ann's Home there were many applicants. So many people were seeking admission to the Home so that they might live out their years with the Sisters. The latter were kept occupied in fulfilling their needs and in making those years comfortable and happy. If the work among the old people was tiring, it also had its joys, and these were some of the most rewarding joys any missionary Sister could desire. They saw some of their charges close the final chapter of their life on earth with a smile as through the waters of baptism they entered eternal blessedness.

Just a few months after the Home was opened,

Mrs. Picard, one of the residents, became seriously ill. Feeling that her end was near, she expressed her wish to die a Catholic. Father DeLange, S.V.D., prepared her for Baptism immediately since her condition was so poor. She died happily and at peace with God the following day. There were other similar blessings among the residents, and each one added more happiness to the lives of the Sisters.

Before the year 1904 came to an end, there would be another very singular grace in the life of Sister Leonarda. On September 8, 1904, which is the feast of the Nativity of Mary, Sister Leonarda and Sister Borromea had the great joy of pronouncing perpetual vows. Seven years had passed since Sister Leonarda pronounced her first temporary vows, and all this time, even as the Superior in the United States, she was only in temporary vows. Now on September 8, she and Sister Borromea could pledge fidelity forever to their Lord. As a symbol of this perpetual pledge each Sister received a silver ring with the symbol of the Holy Spirit engraved upon it.

Once again the Sisters could witness the inspiring profession and clothing ceremony, for the two postulants, Pauline Heinemann and Mary Delort, also received the blue and white habit of the missionary Sister. The chapel was festively decorated for the occasion, and the entire ceremony from the first chant of the choir: "Prudent virgins, trim your lamps, the Bridegroom is coming; go out to meet him" down to the final words of the priest who placed a ring on each Sister's finger saying: "Receive this ring of fidelity, the seal of the Holy Spirit, that you may be called a spouse of Christ, and after serving Him faithfully, may be crowned by Him for all eternity."

The entire day was a celebration day for the Sisters. Friends called to congratulate the Sisters, and Mr. Sheringer surprised the Sisters with a fourteen-branch candelabra for the chapel.

Next day work began as usual, but for Sister Leonarda it meant just a little more. In addition to her many other duties, she was also made the novice mistress since there were now two novices in the community and no Sister was free to take the responsibility.

St. Ann's Home kept growing rapidly, and soon there was a shortage of space again. A two-story addition had to be built in order to provide more rooms for the new occupants. Whatever free time the Sisters had after finishing their regular duties was spent in painting the rooms of the house. Sister Leonarda wanted very much to have the chapel artistically painted; and she was happily surprised when she learned one day, from Dr. Peter Latz, the house physician, that a famous German artist, Mr. Paffrath of Cologne, offered to paint the chapel. After one half year of work, Mr. Paffrath changed the sooty black walls into a veritable heaven with the patron saints of the Congregation.

Although every Sister had enough work to keep her busy all day long, Sister Leonarda still felt that her Sisters were not carrying out the principal aims of the Congregation. She wanted her Sisters to become more familiar with the use of the language; she wanted them to become better acquainted with the history and geography of their new country; and above all, she wanted her Sisters to become efficient and capable teachers so that they might carry out the activities of the Congregation to the very best of their ability.

Consequently, she contacted Professor Francis Tschan, a Jesuit from Chicago, and made arrangements with him to give classes to the Sisters. During the school year, Father Tschan came out to St. Ann's Home once a week and gave classes, but during the vacation months, he conducted classes daily. Professor Tschan also became one of the benefactors of those pioneer days; his kindness towards the Sisters was outstanding.

Thus a year passed by and almost another year and still Sister Leonarda was not yet satisfied. She still felt that they should be doing more as missionary Sisters. And, then on a warm day in August, 1906, Father Heick called upon Sister Leonarda and opened new horizons for her.

1. Letter of Martin Levernier.

2. Document 56.

3. Document 55.

4. Personal notes.

5. Document 58.

6. Reminiscenses of Sister Josepha, S.Sp.S.

7. Reminiscenses of Sister Josepha, S.Sp.S.

8. Reminiscenses of Sister Johanna, S.Sp.S.
Ann's Chronicle of St. Ann's Home (1901-1906)

Chapter Six

I have a dream . . .It is a dream deep rooted in the American dream . . .I have a dream that one day in the red hills of Georgia, sons of former slaves and the sons of former slave owners will be able to sit down together at the table of brotherhood.

—Martin Luther King

Nestled in the bend of the Bight of Biafra (Gulf of Guinea), skirted by the countries of Nigeria and Rio Muni, lies the small island of Fernando Po. Perhaps few people even know of its existence, but in the sixteenth century it was shaping the fate of American society that would have its repercussions far into the twentieth and possibly even the twenty-first century.

Fernando Po was discovered by the Portuguese in the fifteenth century. Then for centuries, between 1472 when it was discovered, until 1968, it was tossed back and forth among the English, the Spanish, and the Portuguese.

The inhabitants of Fernando Po are the Bantu, a gentle and peace loving people and a happy people.

It was a sad and unfortunate day for them when their small island home was discovered by the Portuguese trading ships. For a few shiny baubles a trade was made: glass beads for human lives. The Portuguese would transport the Africans to Cape Coast, keep them in dungeons in a heavily guarded Portuguese fortress (still standing and open for inspection); and so the Africans would wait in these dingy, musty, dark underground cells until a Portuguese or British ship would come into harbor. Then these unknowing Africans were herded through the undersea tunnel, raised aboard the ship and taken to their destination: slavery in the colonies of the newly found continent of the Americas. History simply refers to this trade in "human raw material" as the three-cornered trade: rum, tobacco, slaves. Humankind today calls it a catastrophe, a grave wrong against a human person and total lack of respect for the dignity of the person.

Thus was the slave trade started in the future United States. When the first footsteps of the Blacks imprinted themselves on colonial soil, they set up an echo that would reverberate in sadness, frustration, anger and revenge for centuries.

In 1863, President Lincoln in his Emancipation Proclamation made the slaves free people. Yet, a speech, a declaration, a piece of paper does not suddenly bring back a lost dignity, laughing eyes, a special racial culture preserved best in its own soil. The Proclamation was a giant step forward, true, but it was not enough. Thirty-five years after the Proclamation, the Negroes in the United States were still no better off than they had been on some Southern plantation.

Again it took a people with a bigger heart than politics or business or trade to see the plight of these people and to recognize their needs. It took someone who saw the human spirit not the material beneft.

Father Heick of the Society of the Divine Word went to Mississippi to get a picture of the land, its people, and its possibilities. He viewed extreme poverty, educational barrenness, and needs too plentiful to list. His idea hinged on schools. Education was the key word. These people had to learn to read and write; they had to know who they were and where they were going. It was a slow uphill task. Slow, because education was needed on both sides—both sides had to realize the humanity in each other and respect it as such.

Father Heick with a few Brothers had to face tremendous obstacles as he set about trying to find ways and means to help the Negro attain his rightful place in society.

So it was that on a warm day in August, 1906, Father Heick came to see Sister Leonarda. "You have prayed well," he told her, "and I have come to thank you for all, for your prayers, your constant encouragement, your help in general. It is largely to you that I owe the success of my work, but now I have come to you with another request. I need Sisters."

Sister Leonarda eagerly listened to Father Heick as he told of his many experiences in opening a mission for the Negroes in Mississippi. The difficulties he had encountered were almost insurmountable, even to the point of risking his life; but he had kept pushing on. If he was not accepted in one place, he moved to another until, finally, in Vicksburg, Mississippi, he could set up a small church and offer Holy Mass in it for a very small congregation of Negro Catholics. This tiny spark of success set him making plans for a larger church, a school, and Sisters to staff it. Ever since he had first gone South on his mission expedition, he had found Sister Leonarda his staunch supporter, and her words always brought encouragement. Now he was back to ask her to give him Sisters for his school.

The opportunity for mission work could not be dropped inspite of the fact that almost every Sister was needed at home. Sister Leonarda told the Sisters of the mission work in Vicksburg and Father Heick related some of his experiences to them. The enthusiasm among the Sisters was alarming; everyone wanted to go, and Sister Leonarda realized that here was another manifestation of her Sisters' loyalty. Of course, everyone could not go, and only three, Sisters Bertranda, as Superior, Sister Maria, and Sister Sebastiana, were selected as the fortunate home missionaries destined to open the first school of the congregation for the Negroes of the South.

September 17 was set as the day of departure, and Sister Alexia accompanied the three Sisters to their new convent in Vicksburg. She returned home to St. Ann's with tales of poverty, hardship, and sacrifice which was the lot not only of the Sisters but also, in the majority of cases, of the poor people among whom they worked. Nevertheless, her stories were so saturated with descriptions of the vast amount of work to be done for souls in this area and the joy the three Sisters already experienced in being able to carry out what was then but an infinitesimal part of the work, that the zeal of the Sisters at home was overwhelming, and Sister Leonarda herself could hardly refrain from sending all her Sisters to work among the Mississippi Negroes. But zeal had to be checked for the moment, or at least put away in reserve, until such time when more Sisters could be spared from the duties at home.

*****

Darkness of a thousand nights
All cast in one.
Hopeless longing for the minute past
The second gone.
Useless sighing for another word from lips
Just closed in death;
Blackness of a thousand shadows
Of the past—
What are they all but light;
For darkness of the soul alone is night!

A. G.

At the very time when Sister Leonarda's little community was expanding so peacefully and her own external life seemed so tranquil, almost complacent, she was in reality carrying a heavy cross, a severe trial. If she told her Sisters time and again to be stalwart and courageously bear up under trial, then she surely had to practice her own words now.

While Sister Leonarda was faithfully carrying out the wishes of the Father Superior of St. Joseph's Home, she was also bound to carry out the obediences of her superiors in Steyl and the regulations enjoined upon her by the Constitutions. Fully aware of where her duty lay, she had already tried, to some extent at least, to fulfill the obligation imposed upon her of carrying out the work characteristic of the Congregation. With this in mind, she had organized a system of study for the Sisters to equip them as teachers and educators; she had begun summer classes for the Sisters, and had sent her Sisters South to begin their first mission school. As more postulants entered, her plan was to take on more schools, and eventually open hospitals. Teaching and nursing—these were the main activities of the Congregation, as outlined clearly in her book of Constitutions. Social work would be a natural branch stemming out of the two, and in time, catechetical work and the foreign fields could be undertaken, for, indeed, the very special aim of the Congregation was to "assist in the propagation of the Faith."

The plan was clear enough, but she had to meet with some bitter opposition in fulfilling commands which were actually part of her vow of obedience. Through a misunderstanding or misinterpretation of the aims of the Congregation, there were some who thought that the Sisters' work was chiefly to take care of the kitchens and laundry in the seminaries. Hence, they concluded that the Sisters had no right to study or teach, and that Sister Leonarda was wrong in obliging some of her Sisters to engage in school work. Words began to be rumored back and forth that Sister Leonarda was not obeying the wishes of the priests until, finally, the misunderstanding carried into the community itself. The Sisters were torn between two loyalties, and they did not know which was the one to follow. Since opposition toward Sister Leonarda was becoming quite severe, many of the Sisters concluded that she must be wrong and chose to follow the wishes of the Superiors of the Society of the Divine Word. It was a time of bitter suffering for poor Sister Leonarda, who stood almost alone with just a few Sisters who, inspite of all they heard, considered her the Superior and approved of her plans to expand the activities of the American community. Although she was the legitimate Superior, her orders were not heeded.

She, however, preferred to remain silent until time would bring about the solution to this problem. Yet, though she went about her usual duties silently and cheerfully, her heart was heavy with grief, and those who faithfully followed her saw that her smiling eyes were shining with unshed tears.

In her mind, too, she tossed the problem over and over. Could she be wrong in arranging plans for the Sisters to study? Were they not obliged as missionary Sisters to establish schools and to teach? She read and re-read the first few pages of her Book of Constitutions where the aims of the Congregation were explicitly enumerated in such concise legal form that their meaning could hardly be misconstrued. She, herself, had been on the teaching staff in Steyl; the Founder's words regarding the education of teachers for the schools of the Congregation were still fresh in her memory, and she well knew how important he had regarded the establishment of the normal school in Steyl. He had once written to Mother Maria: "The mental work of the Sisters, as the studying of Spanish or music, is much more important than the manual work, and, therefore, I ask you to give it first place. The folding of paper, for example, is good, but it is much more important that the Sisters fit themselves to serve God in the missions. Therefore, I ask you to see to it that more time is devoted to studying Spanish."[1]

The Founder had expended great efforts in formulating a curriculum for the missionary normal school for the training of teachers, and it was his wish that every Sister attend some classes. Even the Sisters who were appointed for household duties had to attend language classes so that all might be prepared to work in mission countries.

All these thoughts ran through her mind, and she blamed herself for her incapability as Superior.

For several years, the situation remained unchanged and though it was incredibly difficult for Sister Leonarda to administer the affairs of the community according to her lawful office, she had two "weapons" to use in the struggle: prayer and penance. During this period, she began her long nightly vigils prostrate on the floor before the tabernacle in the chapel. The chapel was frightfully cold during the winter nights, but she would continue to pray, her arms outstretched as her Crucified God on the cross, for hours at a time, sometimes throughout the night. When she did go to bed, it was not for comfort, but for more penance. In her bed she kept a cross made of sharp metal points which she kept beside her during her rest. Most of the Sisters knew nothing of this aspect of their Superior's life. Perhaps no one would have ever known about her penitential cross or the discipline, except a little act of charity which brought to light these modes of mortification used by Sister Leonarda.

She had asked Sister Coletta one day to bring her

a clean pillow case. Sister Coletta, knowing how busy her Superior always was and also knowing the heaviness of her heart those past months, wanted to do more than bring the pillow case for her. She went to the dormitory, where the Superior had her bed in a little alcove, just as every other Sister had. Sister Coletta wanted to put the clean cover on the pillow. As she lifted the pillow, she was abashed to see the blood stained cover and the metal cross and discipline beneath the pillow. Somewhat embarrassed at having unwittingly discovered part of her Superior's hidden life, she left everything as it was and kept the secret until it could be revealed many years later.

Despite the saddening circumstances prevailing at the time, Sister Leonarda continued her work as usual and showed no difference whatever in her attitude toward the Sisters or others. With the opening of a mission in Vicksburg, a new task devolved upon her, that of a yearly visitation of the mission. Since she, too, was still teaching in the little parish school, which was later named St. Norbert School, she was compelled to make this trip during the Christmas vacation. But the trip was a joy for her because what she saw in the poor and humble covent and mission school encouraged her to go on with the work she was doing for the glory of God, the salvation of souls, and the good of the Congregation.

In beginning this Negro mission, Sister Leonarda was doing pioneer work in the field. There were not many congregations of Sisters engaged in working for the southern Negro. Mother Katherine Drexel was another pioneer. She played an important part in helping the Divine Word Fathers establish their missions. Two years after the establishment of the mission in Vicksburg, a red brick school building was erected with her financial aid.

The close of the year 1906 brought with it some hope that affairs might be settled as far as Sister Leonarda and the work of the Sisters was concerned. On December 12th, Reverend F. Bodems, S.V.D., arrived at St. Joseph's Home for the General Visitation of the Society in the United States. He was also appointed to make his visitation of the Sisters' convent. When he came to them, he immediately recognized the extreme difficulty under which Sister Leonarda was forced to work. She herself said very little of the matter, but there were her faithful Sisters who felt that the Superiors in Steyl should have a clear view of the conditions and spoke unhesitatingly to Father Bodems. He was glad of their sincerity and loyalty and said, "Things must be better! Sister Leonarda is the Superior. Sister Leonarda has suffered so bitterly these past years that it is no wonder she could say nothing; her heart is too heavy."

He, then proceeded to explain to the Sisters the purpose of the visitation which was primarily to lay down specific and definite rules concerning the business relationship between the two Congregations. Thus far, there had been no clarity in the matter. When Sister Leonarda had asked the Founder what the Sisters should do later on to support themselves, he had merely answered, "If you work for the Society of the Divine Word, that Society will take care of you."

This absolute dependency was a severe hindrance to the development of the Congregation of Sisters. Even Mother General could never say anything definite about the expansion of the Congregation of which she was the head. How destructive this dependency was manifested itself in an unfortunate way in the American foundation where Sister Leonarda was completely hindered from branching out into different fields of activity by the constant drain made on her Sisters to help with the Society's needs and projects.

Father Bodems saw, too, that far greater havoc could result from this state of affairs such as the disruption of the necessary harmony and unity among the members of the community simply because all were at a loss whom to obey. He wanted, by all means, a financial separation of the two Congregations so that each could develop independently of the other even though the Sisters were enjoined by rule to "assist the Society in the propagation of the faith."

Father Bodems, therefore, set down some regulations for the two Congregations, but nothing much could be done until the highest authorities in Steyl gave their approval; and so conditions remained similar to what they were before. However, Father Bodems continued to work for this separation.

1. Sister Assumpta, S.Sp.S., *The Life of Mother Maria Stollenwerk and Mother Josepha Stenmans,* trans. Servant of the Holy Spirit (Techny, Illinois, 1921), pp. 57-58.

All other facts in this Chapter were compiled from interviews with some of the very early Sisters: Sister Maria, Sister Josepha, Sister Joanna, Sister Foureria, Sister Bertholda, Sister Dulcissima, Sister Anthony.

References for the paragraphs on Fernando Po:

Conversations with "Auntie" the Cook for the Sisters in Ghana (Accra). She came from Fernando Po.

Personal visit to the Portuguese fortress in Cape Coast; information regarding slaves given by the African soldiers at the Fortress.

Chapter Seven

In order to be truly human we must offer to God all that we have and are, that is, all that we have been given. We must place ourselves in the service of God's over-all purpose. If we do this we shall glorify God through our own lives, and we ourselves shall become the honor and joy of creation, and we shall make our own contribution to the fulfillment of the purpose of the whole universe. Nature has indeed no other end except that of creating the necessary conditions for the birth and growth of the spirit. When the created spirit fulfills its final vocation in God, nature too will have fulfilled her own vocation . . . .

—Ignace Lepp as in *The Challenges of Life*

A quiet spring evening was settling over the St. Ann's community. The freshness of new spring grass cleansed the air. Above a dazzling sun was bowing offstage to give the sky to the stars and moon. Inside the house in one small dining room

Mother Leonarda was eating supper with her friend Mother Katherine Drexel. It was April 9, 1907. Early that morning Sister Leonarda and Sister Borromaea had gone to Union Station in Chicago to meet Mother Katherine Drexel who was stopping off to visit them enroute to some of her missions.[1]

It had been through the opening of the Vicksburg mission that the two women met and became friends. Mother Drexel had given financial help to the Divine Word Missionaries when they began the mission in Vicksburg, Mississippi. Now she and Mother Leonarda had much to discuss regarding their work among the Blacks in the South.

They were not the first religious women to do mission work in the United States. The Church had always looked to its nuns for help when new countries were discovered and new lands opened. In 1790, the first nuns came to this new country. They were four cloistered Carmelite nuns, and because of them, it is good to know the country began with prayer. These cloistered nuns inundated the new country with their prayers. The Carmelites were followed by three Poor Clare nuns who founded schools for girls in Georgetown. Then came the Visitation nuns. In 1809, Elizabeth Seton, now St. Elizabeth Seton, (canonized in 1975), founded the first native sisterhood, the Sisters of Charity, who opened Catholic elementary and secondary schools.

There were also two religious Orders of Black women: the Oblate Sisters of Providence, founded in 1829 in Baltimore, and the Sisters of the Holy Family, founded in 1842 in New Orleans.[2] In the final decade of the nineteenth century, Mother Katherine Drexel founded her Order of Sisters of the Blessed Sacrament for Indian and Black people. Katherine Drexel was the daughter of a wealthy Pennsylvania banker who, upon his death, left an immense fortune to his two daughters. Katherine chose to use her fortune to finance the missions established by the Order she had founded in 1891.

There were other nuns who came from Europe to settle here and establish schools, orphanages, and other charitable works. One such group was the Sisters of St. Joseph from Le Puy, France, who were brought here by Bishop Verot for the exclusive purpose of ministering to the Black people.

Yet, even with the various sisterhoods working in schools among the Negroes, the work of the Church among the Black people in the United States was sadly deficient. Perhaps this inadequacy goes back, at least in part, to the failure of the second plenary Council of the Roman Catholic Church in the United States in 1866 to set up a viable, comprehensive program for evangelization as well as for the social adjustment and educational preparation of the four million freed Blacks. The Bishops at that Council, for the most part, displayed an almost tragic lack of understanding for the Black people and the problems their freedom engendered.[3] Today, the Bishops' attitude at the time is seen as a loss for the Church and a tragedy for humanity.

Thus the work of the Church among the Blacks remained largely a missionary effort on the part of some priests, Brothers, and nuns. This was the situation when Mother Leonarda and Mother Katherine sat discussing their missionary work in Mississippi on that April evening. Both were women of vision and both had a keen perception of human nature, and it surely occurred to them many times as they planned their work among the Blacks that the present approach to the Black problem of setting up separate schools for them could not add up to the best way of helping the Black adjust to a free society and find acceptance in it. Yet, this was the only avenue that the nuns saw open to them just then, and they set about mapping out excellent educational programs in schools, staffing the schools with well-prepared teachers, and turning out some very fine educated young people who could take a place proudly in society.

The two Foundresses sat discussing their plans, their hopes, realizing quite clearly the obstacles that had to be overcome—in some cases the animosity and even treachery of the whites; in other cases the suspicion and doubt of some of the Blacks. Yet, both women knew it was a necessary work, a work they must struggle and fight not only to continue but to better. As they sat in that small dining room discussing what was already then fast becoming the number one problem of the country, there was no flamboyance or grandiloquence in their plans or voices. They conversed in a subdued and quiet manner and carried out their tasks in the same way—calmly and quietly but with tenacity and invincible strength.

In a way, but in an entirely different way, these two religious women joined the ranks of other women in the United States at this time, women completely different from them in life style, methods, and background, but having much in common regarding purpose: to respect the dignity of the person; to treat each person as a human being.

The time in which the two Foundresses lived was

one of social and economic unrest throughout the world, and all people whether Religious in convents or people living in the mainstream of the world were greatly influenced, as always, by the history of the time. Since the mid nineteenth century and decades into the twentieth, working people began and continued protesting their terrible working conditions and low wages, showing their dissatisfaction in strikes and in the formation of Labor unions. The latter, however, were not yet as powerful as they would eventually become. In fact some laborers were even suspicious of the Unions. Among the striking factory workers, miners, and other laborers there was a large number of immigrant Catholics. Many felt lost, confused, and looked to their Church for answers.

But in the United States, the Catholic Church at the time was conservative and wary. From the time the country came into being, the Church had had to fight for its existence. First, there were the "No Popery" slogans of the pre-Civil War days, the lynching of dozens of Catholics, the burning of Churches and Convents; then there was the "American Protective Association" after the Civil War, an organization in which members swore never to vote for a Catholic, never to hire a Catholic if a Protestant were available, and so on down through the Immigration Restriction Laws aimed primarily at curtailing immigration from countries predominantly Catholic.[4]

The Catholic Church had to be constantly on the defensive, constantly protecting its faithful, and from this need to defend and protect arose the elaborate well organized parochial school system as we know it today as well as orphanages, homes for the elderly, and hospitals. All started as protective measures to insure the growth of the Church in the United States.

If the Church seemed aloof from social problems and hesitant about going into the mainstream of politics, social problems and labor, it was only because years of defending its right to exist as Catholic made the Church extremely cautious.

Yet, the Church was not totally silent. There were a few but powerful members of the hierarchy and clergy who spoke out for the laborer and social reform. Bishop John Lancaster Spalding, named by President Theodore Roosevelt in 1902 to the commission which arbitrated the country's first industry-wide strike when anthracite coal miners walked off their jobs, was one of them.

There were also Father John J. Curran of Pennsylvania and Father Peter C. Yorke in California, two priests who emphatically fought for social reform.

Perhaps the most prominent clergyman was Father John A. Ryan, who gave a bold nudge to Catholic conservatism and its social conscience by his book, *A Living Wage*.[5] The nudge aroused a conservative hierarchy into some involvement in social issues later on.

What exactly was Rome's thought at this time? Already in the last decade of the nineteenth century Pope Leo XIII in a masterful stroke boldly set forth the rights and responsibilities of labor, capital, the State, employer, employees, free enterprise, individual ownership, child labor—in his brilliant encyclical *Rerum Novarum*, which became the blueprint for many of the labor and social reforms of the twentieth century. Leo XIII stated his ideas so clearly, developed them so logically and so much in harmony with the basic needs, aspirations, and genuine desire of the human person that even his enemies did not refute the basics in that encyclical. It answered the cry of the people.

Pius X, who followed Leo XIII, was little concerned with the relationship of the Church in the modern world, with politics, or the growing trend toward democracy. Pius was the simple, warm parish priest, the Pastor, a man of gentleness and good humor. He gave his people the decree on frequent Communion and early Communion for children; he gave them also the important *Motu Proprio*, a decree on the reform of sacred music.[6] He did not regard strikes and labor reform his concern, as such.

Thus the Church responded to the times.

In the United States strikes and protests among laborers continued, and one group that was perhaps the most vocal of all the groups, was the working woman. There is a truth that is often forgotten or overlooked. One tends to evaluate a woman according to her physical "weakness" as compared to the physical "strength" of the male, and hence one disregards her true power and strength in crises.

The truth is a woman can carry an immense emotional, physical, or spiritual burden, even a combination of all, and still plod on. The instinct of self preservtion is powerful within her but does not end with herself; it reaches out in protection to her children and finally to all human beings.

This was shown in such women as Clara Lemlich, an eloquent speaker even in her teens, who got the women in New York's rodent-filled garment factories to strike—120,000 strong—for better conditions;

in Pauline Newman, a fearless and vocal striker; in Mary McDowell, a union organizer in the Chicago stockyards, and in other courageous women of the time.

The early twentieth century glows with women who fought against tyranny in the factories, the mines, the stockyards. They fought against the very poor, if not downright ugly working conditions: dirt, disease infested, damp, dark factories and holes; against the inhuman working conditions especially for women and children. They marched, they protested, they spoke at meetings and rallies. They were lifting the working person.

In that small dining room at St. Ann's Home, the two Foundresses were keeping in step with the rest of the world. They, too, were answering a need, championing a cause, trying to remedy a social need. Mother Leonarda and Mother Katherine Drexel were quietly planning their program to lift a people to its feet to walk with heads erect and confident. The Clara Lemlichs and Pauline Newmans were loudly proclaiming the dignity of every person and the right of each individual to be given a living wage, decent work conditions, and respect as a human being. The Religious women were opening doors, offering all people opportunities for advancing and belonging, carrying human dignity beyond the human to the divine. Both the cause of workers and the cause of the educators would take time, but the latter was the more challenging, the more sensitive, with greater possibilities for misunderstanding and erroneous interpretation and far less recognition and appreciation.

The two women just finishing their evening meal

were not in the least concerned about recognition or appreciation. It was something farthest from their minds.

Mother Leonarda set down her cup of coffee. She had that look of happy reminiscence as she said: "I went to Vicksburg last December, and what I saw surprised and shocked me, and at the same time made me happy and filled with such a desire to open more schools that I could hardly tear myself away from the South. When I told the Sisters about the poverty I found in Vicksburg and about the friendliness of the people who now have become more confident in the Sisters, I had a hard time restraining my community from packing up and going to the South. I see the work as a beautiful apostolate in this country."

Mother Drexel nodded and her face lit up. "I know what you mean, Sister; yes, this is a much needed apostolate in this country, and I am afraid it is already late in coming. Still, we are fortunate to be here at this time; at least maybe we can give some impetus to a work that must be done."

The two Foundresses continued talking. As they were about to leave the dining room, Mother Drexel exclaimed, "I was really surprised to get your letter, Sister Leonarda. It was postmarked 'Techny.' For a moment I couldn't imagine from where it had come."

Sister Leonarda gave one of her hearty laughs. "Oh, I should have explained. It seems that the United States Postal Service considers our place to be large enough to be raised to the status of a postal station with its own Post Office and name. The Divine Word Missionaries chose the name Techny as reminiscent of the first technical school they opened here. Actually it was in February, 1906, that postal service was granted to us. Right now Techny includes only St. Joseph's Home, St. Ann's Home, and three private homes. One of the Brothers is the Postmaster.[7] In time I think this shall grow to be quite a little city in itself."

Mother Drexel agreed: "Yes, I see it that way too."

The visiting Foundress planned to stay the night at St. Ann's Home and then continue her journey to one of her missions.

In the morning as she said good-bye, Mother Katherine Drexel extended an invitation to Sister Leonarda to stop at Cornwell Heights (Motherhouse of the Blessed Sacrament Sisters in Pennsylvania) whenever she had to travel to the East. That invitation to Sister Leonarda would be accepted on at least two occasions in the future.

The two women remained friends until the death of Mother Leonarda in 1937. Mother Katherine Drexel died in 1955. In the future years, when the Holy Spirit Missionary Sisters opened a mission in Ghana, West Africa, they were always cordially welcomed by the Sisters of the Blessed Sacrament in New Orleans during the time Missionary Sisters waited for the freighter, which would carry them and their boxes to Africa, to load at the dock before setting out for Africa. Usually the Sisters would stay at the Sisters' Convent near Xavier University, founded by the Mother Drexel Sisters, and wait until they were allowed on board and ready to sail. Mother Katherine Drexel's Sisters followed their Foundress' cordiality and continued her friendly relationship with the Holy Spirit Sisters. It was one of the many friendships that Mother Leonarda opened up for her community.

In October, 1909, the Divine Word Missionaries opened a mission in Jackson, Mississippi, and Mother Leonarda followed, opening a school. Sister Cyrilla was appointed Superior, and Sisters Johanna, Josepha, and Willibalda were chosen to go with her as pioneers in this new mission. Soon Holy Ghost School, Jackson, was growing as rapidly as St. Mary's School in Vicksburg. Both missions had both an elementary school and a high school, and St. Mary's also had a Kindergarten.[8]

With the opening of another school in the South, there was a heightened spirit of good feeling among the Sisters. It raised the hopes of some that their desire for mission work might be fulfilled.

Yet, even at St. Ann's, the Sisters did have some of the joys and satisfaction of a missionary. Among the elderly there were some men and women who realized in their waning years the love and truth of a living God. They saw the Holy Spirit at work among them, and they believed. Some were death bed conversions.[9] Some enjoyed the peace of faith in their last years. In her Diary, Mother Leonarda mentions that Gertrude Jones, one of the residents, received the Sacrament of Baptism on May 12, 1907, in St. Ann's chapel, and the whole house rejoiced.[10]

There were countless ways for the Sisters to be true missionaries to the elderly in their care: showing understanding, practicing a selfless giving and great, sometimes even heroic patience with the elderly whose age and physical disabilities made them irritable, forgetful, and dissatisfied on occasion; encouraging the elderly to accept each day's sufferings and disabilities with fortitude; being a friend to a lonesome senior citizen.

Indeed, the work had its assets and its drawbacks. Mother Leonarda knew that, but there was so much more to think of. It is true that at the beginning of the twentieth century the United States with twelve million Catholics in a population of seventy-six million was still considered a mission country. But the Catholic population was growing with the swelling number of immigrants from Eastern and Southern Europe. Mother Leonarda knew very well that Father Arnold Janssen had sent the Sisters to the United States not only for mission work but also to set up a training center and a novitiate for American girls who felt called to be Holy Spirit Missionary Sisters.

What the American region needed was vocations —more native vocations. So far, every year, sometimes twice or three times a year, Mother Leonarda would have to ask Steyl to send Sisters. The work was increasing, but the number of Sisters to take on the added work lagged behind. Steyl complied and kept sending Sisters; Mother Leonarda was grateful but hoped that soon the Congregation might be more firmly rooted in American soil by professing more native Americans who would not only carry on the work in the United States but would be sent to overseas missions as well.

With only a Home for the Elderly and two mission schools in the South, and a small school in Techny, the Sisters were not that well known. That was one very big disadvantage for getting recruits. The Order needed to establish itself in a work that would get the Sisters in contact with young women among whom there might be missionary vocations.

Even though Father Bodems had promised to work for a separation of the two Religious Orders, he did not succeed immediately in obtaining this separation. The Sisters continued to work in the laundry and in the kitchen of St. Joseph's Home. When Sister Barbara came from Steyl, she was placed in charge of the new bakery. From then on she baked all the bread, cakes, etc. for the three hundred or more people in St. Joseph's, for the residents of St. Ann's, and for the Sisters.[11]

As the years went on other tasks were assigned to the Sisters by the Divine Word Superiors.

When the Society of the Divine Word in the United States began publishing its two periodicals: *Katholischen Familienblatt* and the English, *Christian Family,* the Sisters were given another job: the responsibility of folding and mailing the two periodicals as well as folding, stapling, gluing, and mailing other small publications for the Society. The Sisters also took care of all the correspondence involved in the publications, mostly "begging" letters. In one month, December, 1908, the letters sent out by the Sisters came back with answers in the neat amount of $12,000.00 for the Society's needs.[12]

The Sisters seemed to have a lot of luck in getting action and answers to the letters they sent out for the Society; yet, ironically when the Sisters received permission to take up a collection in Iowa so that *they* might build a larger chapel at St. Ann's Home, they met with little success and had to give up the project for the time being.[13]

There was still another task assigned to the Sisters. The Brothers in charge of the farm for St.

Joseph's requested the Sisters' help again. This time it was farm work. Two Sisters had to take care of the milk. Every day they carried the huge milk cans from the farm to St. Ann's Home. One part of the engine room was changed into a milkroom. Here the Sisters separated the milk and cream and churned the butter.[14]

For most of the Sisters, separating milk and darning men's socks and ironing white shirts was a far cry from the missionary work these women had anticipated. It was, therefore, to give her Sisters hope and confidence to push on—in spite of the non-missionary work they found themselves obliged to do—that Sister Leonarda wrote in one of her short conferences for the Sisters: "Happy those religious who are animated with the spirit of faith . . . .Let us often think that our dear Lord is standing right before us seeing all we do . . . .Thus gradually we shall acquire the spirit of faith. We shall never become insensitive to suffering, hardship, and annoyance, but accepting them in the spirit of faith, they will fill our souls with happiness and peace."[15]

If she wrote to encourage her Sisters, she wrote to encourage herself, too, perhaps even more so, because she had to bear with and try to rationalize the struggle within her between carrying out the aim of her Congregation regarding missionary activity and the actual work they were obliged to do here for the Society of the Divine Word.

Some of the Superiors in Steyl recognized the problem that existed here for Mother Leonarda. The Sisters still had no financial income whatever but worked purely in the interest of the Society of the Divine Word.[16]

At one time, in 1907, Sister Raphael, assistant to Mother General Theresia in Steyl, recommended that Sister Leonarda look somewhat ahead and see if somewhere here in the States the Sisters might take over or establish a hospital so that the income therefrom might be a financial foundation for the Congregation in the United States.[17]

As yet, however, the Society demanded the Sisters' help in all their undertakings, and so long as the highest authorities of both Orders in Europe were not issuing any changes or directives with regard to the independence of each Order, no one down the line could do anything about it here, and Mother Leonarda was not free to look for an activity solely for her community.

Hence she continued to guide and supervise the growth of St. Ann's Home, but the Society of the Divine Word continued to have complete financial control, receiving payment from residents and any donations, and also interviewing and admitting all applicants for the Home.

The Sisters' inability to branch out into activities that would make them better known; the un-missionary-like flavor of most of the work they carried on now in the States were, to be sure, obstacles to vocations, especially since the Order called itself "missionary" Sisters. There was yet another obstacle in this country: language.[18]

The greater number of Sisters in Techny were from Steyl. In that beginning decade of the foundation here in the United States, the Sisters were so badly needed for the increasing work load, that as soon as they came from Holland, they were put immediately in some work area. There was little time for learning the language, getting to know the country, adjusting to the newness of a different culture—not extremely different—but different. Thus from sheer necessity, the Sisters conversed in their native German. People heard and concluded erroneously that one had to be German to enter the Order and one had to speak German.

From the very beginning Mother Leonarda tried with determined effort to give all the Sisters classes in English and in other studies. It has already been seen that in doing this she had to fight great odds. Her greatest opponent at one time was Father DeLange, who succeeded Father Peil as the Divine Word Superior in Techny. Father Peil had been a kind man, demanding much from the Sisters, but realizing the burden of work the Sisters carried. Father DeLange was an extremely strict man to the point of painful eccentricity; not only the Sisters but also members of his own community felt the effects of that severity. He was known to come in while the Sisters were recreating (their one hour a day) and stop the recreation hour so that the Sisters would do their work. He even forbade the Sisters working in the kitchen and laundry at St. Joseph's to go over to St. Ann's for dinner on the day of Mother Leonarda's namesday celebration, something that had been a customary event from the beginning.[19]

Yet, in spite of a Father DeLange and opposition from some members of her own community, Mother Leonarda managed to work out a course of studies for her Sisters and kept on fighting to get her Sisters into higher education to get degrees. During all her terms in office she saw to it that many Sisters were given an excellent education.

She also insisted on using the language of the country—English—at work, recreation, prayer. Her directive was later confirmed by the First Provincial Chapter in 1909. Because so many of the Sisters were from Germany, two days a week were allowed to be "German days" when the Sisters could converse, etc. in German. This rule held until 1942, five years after Mother Leonarda's death. That year fourteen postulants, a large number for the Order at the time, entered the Convent in Techny—all Americans of several nationality backgrounds and not one spoke German. Sister Leonore Scholter, the postulant directress at the time, did not require the postulants to use the community German expressions, and the two "German days" were dropped. The expression "Gott Vergelts" was substituted by "God bless you." English, the language of the country, was considered the language to use at all times; but German was the language of the Founder and the Foundresses and the language of the Order's origins, it was held in respect, and the Sisters were encouraged to learn it and use it. The Order was now becoming a part of America, U.S.A.

If Mother Leonarda felt disappointed that so few young American women chose to be Holy Spirit Missionary Sisters, that so few entered the Order in Techny, then she felt, indeed, saddened when some left the community.

Whatever their reason for leaving, Mother Leonarda saw a number of Sisters and postulants, both Americans, and Germans who had come from Europe, leave the convent in the first decade. In her diary, Mother Leonarda notes the name of the Sister and the day of leaving. For each entry in her diary she concludes with: "The farewells were very difficult." Knowing her sensitive nature, one can almost see the faint wetness of her eyes as she made the entry in her diary. Sometimes the Sister entered another community, as, for example, Sister Baptista who left the Missionary Sisters to enter the cloistered community of Poor Clares.[20] Others simply left the religious life altogether.

The one farewell which was undoubtedly the hardest to take because it was so very close to Sister Leonarda was the leaving of Sister Clara, one of the four Sisters who came with her in May, 1901. In her diary, Mother Leonarda wrote briefly: "August 7, 1908. Sister Clara left the convent today. She went to see the Poor Clares in Cleveland. I accompanied her to the train which left Chicago at 8:25 A.M. We took leave of each other. The Sisters were very surprised."

The farewells when Sisters left were actually painful; the death of a Sister was even more so. Five times Mother Leonarda stood at the death bed of one of her Sisters, comparatively young Sisters, in a new province in those first early years.

In some of these cases, the utter inability to help the seriously sick Sister made the death even more tragic. Had medical science progressed just a bit more and had there been more medical help available sooner, chances are, some of these young lives might have been saved as in the case of Sister Perpetua, a young nun in her twenties, who died of untreated appendicitis because there was no way to get her to a Chicago hospital. For Mother Leonarda, a woman with an intense love for all people, and so much more for the Sisters in her religious family, each death hurt like a mother's loss of a child.

There was yet another loss she must sustain from those early difficult years. And this loss she would have to carry with her in sadness into her grave. On January 2, 1908, a day after the close of the annual retreat for the Sisters and a day after the Profession ceremony, a young nun, Sister Raymunda, went into a convulsive emotional shock from which she never recovered. Her mental disease was irreversible. She would not get better; she would only get worse. Sister Leonarda suffered intensely not only in seeing the mental affliction of this young, capable Sister, a life stopped in its vibrant twenties, but also in having to bear much from the Sister herself, who, in her completely deranged mind, caused the Superior great inconveniences and heartaches by her frequent vengeful and mean actions toward the Superior. Sister Raymunda outlived Sister Leonarda, but the former could never again take part in community life. During the next six decades the sick Sister was cared for in a loving manner by her Sisters in an area designated for the senile in St. Ann's. As the Sister advanced in years, she gradually became more subdued. Sister Raymunda's commitment to God by her vows had truly been that "holocaust," the consummation of her whole self. When God had called her, he asked for *everything*, indeed. By her vows she had said, "Yes, Father!" And he took her at her word.[21]

As Mother Leonarda bore each loss, pain was quietly etched on her peaceful face. She did not complain. Only in her diary, her small notebook, in which she penned in her tiny even German script the day to day entries does she show the stress of years, and here one realizes what inner strength this extraordinary woman possessed.

In spite of all, though, the Region was growing and in 1907, the General Council in Steyl raised the North American foundation from a region to the status of a province with Sister Leonarda named the first Provincial Superior.[22] In the new province there were eight professed Sisters in perpetual vows; thirty-six in temporary vows, two novices, and one postulant.

At the same time that the news regarding the raised status came, two other directives came from the Steyl Motherhouse. Both were received with much joy by Sister Leonarda and her sisters.[23]

The first directive had to do with the vows. It was ordered that the original period of seven years' waiting before perpetual vows should be shortened to six. Thus instead of taking temporary vows for seven years and then perpetual, the Sisters would now take vows each year for three successive years, then for a period of three years, and at the end of three years, perpetual vows.

The second directive from Steyl was concerned with Sisters' birthdays and feastdays. How does one celebrate these special days in everyone's life in a community of thirty, forty, a hundred or more religious? The Founder and early Superiors in the Order were not without cleverness in the matter of celebration. They gave the three Orders founded by Arnold Janssen, a unique day to be celebrated each year; it was called Family Feast. Everyone's birthday and namesday would be celebrated together in community on a special day chosen each year according to circumstances. This was the birth of a custom that became dear to each Holy Spirit Missionary Sister in all the years to come and in all parts of the world. It was one very special day of the year when the Sisters could forget work and problems and even try to forget pain and let themselves go just enjoying the day and life: playing games, perhaps table tennis or tennis, softball or volley ball; maybe a bit of square dancing, a long leisurely walk, or just a restful day with a book or paints; even a good conversation or time in prayer. The Sisters engaged in the kitchen saw to it that much was prepared beforehand; the Superiors usually sent extra help to these departments for the day.

Family Feast always began with a beautiful morning liturgy in the chapel establishing the theme of community and unity.

The Feast became a dearly loved custom in the community and an important one. In order not to miss out on Family Feast, there would be times that Sisters even re-arranged traveling schedules just so as to be in their community for Family Feast. Each mission celebrated its own Family Feast. The songs, the poems, the skits, the games, the extra special meals, the liturgy celebrations during the day—all added up not only to a birthday celebration but a celebration of community and life. And what a display of talent! Family Feast was that respite from the many things that concerned one on every other day of the year, from the daily work and hour to hour schedule every day. It was the day of preview of eternal joy and made one want to exclaim: "Lord, it is good for us to be here." (Mark 9:5)

Sister Leonarda gave herself as wholeheartedly to the Family Feast celebration as she did to her work and prayer. She always enjoyed a good joke, an amusing skit; she loved to sing the German hiking songs, and knew how to have fun. She wanted, above all, that her Sisters enjoy these days, too, and did her best to see that they did.

As the months went on, the number of residents at St. Ann's Home grew, and soon the building was too small again. A new wing for St. Ann's was begun in 1908. Together with the annex, a large chapel was planned.

It was in the Fall of the same year that a friend came to St. Ann's to stay and become one in a line of delightful personalities that graced the Home. The residents had a justified complaint about the road leading from the Home to the train station. It was a gravel road which made walking difficult for the senior residents. One day an elderly man came to live at St. Ann's. He was Caspar Roehrig, a rough old soldier who had fought for his country in several battles in the Spanish American War. It was Caspar who solved the problem of walking to the station. He had brought with him a horse and buggy and placed both at the disposal of the Home; many of the residents enjoyed a ride with old Caspar. His rough and gruff external manner hid a sensitive heart and caring ways. He liked St. Ann's and spent many years in the Home; in fact, Caspar became one of St. Ann's loved legends.[24]

The year 1909 entered reality in a calm, subdued way. The Society of the Divine Word was in its 34th year of existence. The Congregation of Holy Spirit Missionary Sisters was in its twentieth year. The Congregation of Holy Spirit Sisters of Perpetual Adoration was in its thirteenth year. The three Orders had already branched out from Europe into North and South America, New Guinea, Asia, Africa. The Divine Word priests and Brothers went first followed by the Holy Spirit Missionary Sisters, and then by the Sisters of Perpetual Adoration. The Founder had watched it all grow. He was there with every priest, Brother, and Sister as a guide and confidante, a director and administrator, a teacher and leader. God had let him see his three Orders rise from a seedling into mighty trees with strong branches. Arnold Janssen had been a prolific writer and had given his communities as well as individual members of the communities words of advice, encouragement, perhaps at times admonition. However, in the last years, he felt his strength waning, and a tiredness possessed him. He had lived a fruitful life, and he knew it would soon be time to place the administration of his communities into other hands. On January 15, 1909, God called him by name. He had done well and deserved his rest and reward. The news of Father Arnold's death brought grief to all the members of the three Orders he had founded, and all his spiritual sons and daughters round the world mourned his passing. He had been a severe man on occasion; he had also been gentle and understanding. With the preciseness and exactness of the scientist and the mystical depth of a St. John or a Teresa of Avila he had formulated his communities, established them, and guided their growth. He gave them, above all, a unique spiritual depth in the Divine Word and the Holy Spirit. In this he was a man with a vision far ahead of his times.

He was gone now and only one comfort remained: He was a powerful intercessor for them among God's blessed. They knew he would never abandon the great works he had brought into existence. Rather it was for his priests, Brothers, and Sisters to continue his work, to see to it that it grew, developed, and expanded so that one day they might hear him speak again: "Well done, good and faithful sons and daughters."

The death of Arnold Janssen ushered in a new phase in his communities. Father Nicholas Blum was appointed Superior General for the Society of the Divine Word pro tem.

One of his first acts as Superior General was to issue a decree on April 19, 1909, for a General Chapter to be held in December in Steyl. Soon after, the Holy Spirit Missionary Sisters would have their first General Chapter.

This meant the coming together of members of the Society of the Divine Word and later members of the Holy Spirit Sisters from as far away as China and New Guinea. These new Religious Orders now had a degree of experience which would be used effectively in studying and evaluating the Book of Constitutions (Holy Rule) and Customs as to their relevance to the present day and future and the need for change or abrogation.

1. Diary of Mother Leonarda (April 9, 1907).

2. Thomas Bokenkotter, *A Concise History of the Catholic Church* (New York: Doubleday & Company, 1977), pp. 347 ff.

3. James Hennesey, S.J., *American Catholics, a History of the Roman Catholic Community in the United States* (Oxford: Oxford University Press, 1981), pp. 161 ff.

4. Hennesey, pp. 210-211.

5. Hennesey, p. 211.

6. Bokenkotter, pp. 364-365.

7. Chronicle of St. Ann's Home.

8. Chronicle of St. Ann's Home.

9. Chronicle of St. Ann's Home.

10. Diary of Mother Leonarda (May 12, 1907).

11. Chronicle of St. Ann's Home.

12. Chronicle of St. Ann's Home.

13. Chronicle of St. Ann's Home.

14. Chronicle of St. Ann's Home.

15. Chapter Conference of Mother Leonarda (September 16, 1909).

16. Chronicle of St. Ann's Home.
Document 14, an account of Sr. Joanna.

17. Chronicle of St. Ann's Home.

18. Chronicle of St. Ann's Home.

19. Document 14.

20. Diary of Mother Leonarda (April 13, 1907).
Document 14.

21. Chronicle of St. Ann's Home.
Diary of Mother Leonarda (January 2, 1908).

22. Chronicle of St. Ann's Home.

23. Chronicle of St. Ann's Home.

24. Chronicle of St. Ann's Home.

Chapter Eight

The characteristic spirit permeating our educational institutions comes from the Holy Spirit; truth and love. From the Holy Spirit as from a divine Fountain the school should imbibe science and wisdom and pass it on to others. Because it draws from this divine Source the school should be, as it were, a glowing fire of apostolic zeal and charitable works that is forming temples of the Holy Spirit in human hearts.

—Diamond Jubilee Book of S.Sp.S.

It was a rising stretch of land with just enough of an undulating hill to give it a graceful charm. It was called Belleview, and, oh, what colors! All over, the October sun had splattered the trees with brilliant hues. Maples flamed in red and gold; oaks stood in subdued wines and olives; and the elms hesitantly tried on a spot of saffron here, a little russet there. Scattered among the trees were sumac and barberry bushes now revelling in all the brilliant colors that spilled on to them from the October skies.

It was one of those pleasantly warm Fall days with a bright sun and blue skies that poets like to write about. Mother Leonarda surveyed her surroundings, saw the glow of dazzling sunlight around her, the colors, the peace, and once again she was a young girl, one of Herr Abeler's students running home after school along the scenic path through the woods, enjoying the wild flowers, the birds, singing the songs she loved. Then she was among the trees in the Sisters' garden at Freckenhorst—that happy place where the call, lying dormant within her, came to life, a glowing ember that flamed into a consuming fire.

It was this latter memory that was uppermost in her mind when she came to the place where she was now standing. She was a seer and a builder. In this land she saw the reality of a hope she had cherished from the beginning. She wanted to build a school for girls here. She could already see the young, bright-eyed girls coming here to study and becoming aware of so much more in life, just as she had with the Sisters in Freckenhorst.

The place where she now stood was about a mile south of St. Ann's Home and St. Joseph's. There was a good looking and spacious house on the land that would be suitable for her needs and a beautiful stand of trees and bushes. The whole area was slightly elevated in comparison with the lowland of Techny.

She decided to write to Reverend Mother General Theresia that night. In just a month she and Sister Borromaea would be going to Steyl for the First General Chapter of the Holy Spirit Missionary Sisters, and she wanted her request to precede her in order that the Superiors would have time to reflect on it and discuss it with her in Steyl.

That evening in the quiet of her room, she first wrote a letter to Father Auf der Heide in Steyl, who was the Father General Director of the Holy Spirit Missionary Sisters and told him of her wish to establish a school. Then she took a sheet of stationery, dated it October 19, 1909 and wrote:

Dear Reverend Mother:

I have just written a letter to the Reverend Father General Director regarding a matter about which I have already informed you, namely, a school for girls. Your answer to my letter gave me courage to present the matter to the Reverend Father Director. This would not be in a hurry had not a special situation concerning it arisen.

She stopped a moment. What she had to write was a delicate matter to explain. During the past years she had suffered because of the friction between the Society of the Divine Word and the S.Sp.S. Sisters in the United States, and it was not all over yet. The split among her community with some Sisters going back and forth carrying their tales, gossip, and problems to the priests and Brothers was still a problem; and it generated another delicate situation, another problem. A familiarity developed in some cases that was not spiritually healthy and in many cases was divisive to the religious life. The excessive gossiping between some nuns and priests not only resulted in a lot of slander and the undermining of lawful authority, but also caused a greater rift between Mother Leonarda and her Sisters and hence an unstable community life.

Thus Mother Leonarda tried to explain as tactfully as possible why she wanted a place located some distance from the Mission House. She uses the German word, "verkehrs," a kind of trafficking to describe the problem.

> *A house in Techny was called to my attention because of the low price which was asked for it; but on account of 'the trafficking' the place is less suitable. This one that I am referring to is one mile south of the Mission House, a lovely spacious house, on high ground with trees around it. Without too much expense it could be purchased for us, for which the superior general has the option for one year. This amount of time will run out in three months.*
>
> *Everyone is of the opinion that we can hardly find a better place for the aforementioned purpose, and there will be hardly any contact with the Mission House.*
>
> *We have long desired a place like this because it is not far from our convent. Will you please put in a good word for us if it appears good to you? Our Sisters, like Sister Alexia, Sister Romana, Sister Christine, and perhaps Sister Maria, would be well qualified for the school: and certainly later there will be more good school Sisters.*

She added a few other news items: Sister Irmengardis could do light work; she had been ill for quite some time. Sister Raymunda was fairly well and had been quiet for some time, but since "the day before yesterday, she again became agitated."

In her ending paragraph she mentions the South. "In the South all goes well." A few more words and she signed her name, put the letter into an envelope, addressed it, and dropped it into a tray on her desk.[1] She had requested something that would be just for the Sisters—a work they would take up because they wanted it and needed it.

It was getting late. As from the very beginning so now she still kept later hours because the volume of work and the necessity of her being available to the Sisters when they needed her or wanted to talk to her or when the residents wanted her made it necessary for her to postpone administrative matters and correspondence to the late evening. Today she was exceptionally tired. Ever since the Provincial Chapter in August, she had been busy with matters of the province as well as in preparing for the General Chapter in Steyl, and then there was always laundry work that needed extra help, and the never ending work in the canning room.

She looked at her calendar on the desk to see what appointments were scheduled for tomorrow when she noticed today's reminder. She had second shift on night duty! How could she have forgotten! The number of sick and infirm residents in the infirmary had been increasing from week to week so that several months ago it had become necessary for the Sisters to begin night duty. Every night two Sisters split the night watch. Mother Leonarda never gave her Sisters a task which she herself would not do. Hence she put herself on the night duty schedule with the rest of her Sisters.[2] Night duty was simply an addition to daytime duty. In the beginning there was not enough help to separate the Sisters into day and night shifts.

It was after midnight. In a couple of hours she should be relieving the Sister on duty. She looked at her desk; there were still important letters to answer. As was her wont so many times, she sent the Sister on duty to bed a couple hours earlier and simply began her watch two hours sooner.[3]

After making the rounds of the infirmary and the house, she sat at the desk in the hall and continued her correspondence at the same time answering the needs of the sick and infirm.

Usually Mother Leonarda took the first watch. Then it was that she would wake the Sister who was to relieve her two hours or more late. Mother Leonarda knew how hard her Sisters had to work during the day and assuming night duty was an added burden. As for herself she seldom stopped to assess the situation and see that she, too, was already overburdened and that one could not go on indefinitely on less than four hours of sleep at night while carrying on a full load of mental and physical work during the day and half the night. She looked robust and healthy and still had her Westphalian glow of energy, but she asked too much of herself and was wearing herself out much too quickly. As early as 1909, those who knew her well could detect lines of fatigue mingling with the lines of her pleasant smile. She was only thirty-five.

Much had happened in both Techny communities since the Founder's death in January. Very significant for the Society of the Divine Word was the opening of the minor seminary with the admission of six students. The seminary became known as Mission House of the Society of the Divine Word, or simply, the Mission House, as it became popularly known. Over the years the seminary would grow, adding a building for printing and publishing in keeping with one of the Founder's most cherished wishes: to spread the Good News of the Word through the printed word. Other buildings were added and the garden beautifully landscaped until the seminary and its surrounding grounds and farm was a unique microcosm with a communication network of missionary activity that encompassed the world. The Society of the Divine Word left its imprint of greatness in the world from the beginning of its existence. Great missionaries came from this Order as the saintly Father Freinademetz, missionary in China, and Archbishop Henninghaus, another great missionary from Shantung, China. There were famous S.V.D. anthropologists such as Father Schmidt of Germany and later Father Luzbetak of the United States. In the field of science there were distinguished physicists, and there were other impressive figures: exegetes, theologians, liturgists, writers, artists, spiritual directors, retreat masters, sculptors, and musicians, so many more. Many of these priests and Brothers came from Europe and other parts of the world, but many came from Techny from a long continuous line of seminarians dating back to the first young boys who entered the Mission House in 1909.

The Divine Word publications helped to make Techny quite well known in the surrounding Chicago area and surrounding States. People would come from the city and suburbs during the summer to enjoy the beauty and the peace of the Techny gardens.

One of the rich traditions of the Catholic Church is its meaningful, symbolically rich processions. At one time almost every feast had its special procession. The Church took a profound theological doctrine of faith and presented it to her faithful clothed in the emotionally rich symbolism of a procession. There was the Christmas procession at the Midnight Mass, symbolically depicting Christ the Divine Word's descent from the Father to earth as Man. The Palm Sunday procession was a triumphal march for Christ on the eve of His death. Or the Church took a ritual from a nation, a cult, and gave it a Christian interpretation such as harvest festivals. The Church called these Rogation Day Processions to ask God's blessing on the farms and orchards. The Maypole dances became the lovely May Crowning procession in May honoring Mary, the Mother of God.

Father Arnold Janssen, true to his German heritage, loved these beautiful processions and traditions in the Church and urged his communities wherever they settled and built missions to introduce, as soon as possible, these traditional processions.

The Techny communities did just that. As soon as possible the Corpus Christi procession was held on the seminary grounds. The procession was an elaborate external manifestation of love and reverence for God's gift of Himself to His people in the Eucharist.

The Corpus Christi procession in Techny caught fire immediately. On June 21, 1908, an extra train with sixteen cars brought between two thousand and three thousand people to Techny for the Corpus Christi procession. The Sisters had prepared dinner for five hundrd to six hundred people; all the other people were given coffee, sandwiches, currant rolls, candy, and pop. In the late afternoon the thousands of people happily boarded the trains again for home.[5] A day like this in Techny restored peace to lives and strength to face tomorrow. One decorative feature of the procession was the hundreds of little flags that lined the paths along the route. The Sisters made these too. Weeks ahead, recreation periods were spent in making these little flags. On a day such as Corpus Christi, the Sisters did the necessary work in the Home and then between times they tried to help in cooking for the visitors, serving them, and then the inevitable cleaning up afterwards.

Since train traffic to Techny was increasing year to year, on April 16, 1909, the Milwaukee Road made Techny a passenger stop. It was a great convenience for the entire Techny community as well as for visitors to Techny.[6]

Towards the end of June, the annex to St. Ann's Home that had been started in May, 1908, was completed, and at the same time the whole house was equipped with electric lights, a true blessing.

Mother Leonarda was so happy to see that the elderly residents had more room, and now, the convenience of electric lights too.

Whenever she saw the residents of St. Ann's or stopped for a moment in this person's room or that other lonely woman's room or whenever they came to see her just to talk to her or to hear her words of consolation and comfort, Mother Leonarda had before her the image of her own parents. How very strange life is! In answering God's call, she put herself at the service of so many others and separated herself yet farther from those she loved the most and wanted most to help. So it was now. She was able to help so many people at St. Ann's; but for her father who was now seventy, she had to let only a letter do all that she would have liked to do for him. It is at times like this that even the holiest religious may question her choice or may feel a twinge of guilt. Then faith is needed, for faith clarifies love and puts life in proper perspective. It gives meaning to Christ's words: "Anyone who prefers father or mother to me is not worthy of me . . ." (Matthew 10:37)

It was somewhere around the beginning of June that Mother Leonarda had received a letter from her father, and she had been waiting for a free moment to answer it. She took the time one Thursday when she had night duty and the residents were comparatively quiet for the night.

The letter is an insight into her humanness, that part of her which made her so approachable and understanding. She knew how much people disliked writing to the nuns when they knew the letter would first be read by the Superior. At this time in most religious communities, mail for the Sisters was first read or "scanned" by the Superior before it was given to the Sister, a custom which gradually became quite obsolete. Mother Leonarda knew how much her father disliked this custom, and so she begins by saying.:

Dear Father:

As long as you can still do it write. No one sees the letter except myself. This is my greatest consolation. May God reward you a thousand times for your trouble.

As for the wedding celebration, Theodore's wife will be a good daughter to you, I hope, a substitute for Therese. Write to me as to how everything is getting along. You must see to it that Theodore does not expect you to do too much work. I know from former years that you can do too much for him. I would wish that Elizabeth would feel at home immediately.

I can hardly believe, Papa, that you are seventy years [old] already. How time flies!

What do you think about my coming back to Steyl again? I would never have dreamed it. I wonder if I will see you again. In one way, I rejoice, but when I think about the leave-taking, then I would rather remain here. But as God wills . . . .

I am glad you arranged the inheritance . . . .As you have made it, Papa, it is all right, but I would have liked to know it, since after Theodore I am the oldest. I hope that you have kept enough for yourself so that you are not always dependent on Theodore. That I would not want by any means . . . .

Now I must close. Dear Papa, write again soon. Greetings to all brothers and sisters . . . .[7]

In the same letter Mother Leonarda also mentions how hard it must have been for her father to see his youngest daughter, Therese, also leave home to become a religious Sister. She was the fourth girl to leave, but she entered the Franciscan Sisters. Antonia, the only girl who did not become a Sister in the Lentrup family, was a teacher.

No matter how heavily burdened she was, Mother Leonarda never forgot her family. If she could not write, she prayed. And that summer was a busy one. It saw the beginning of another favorite work of charity of the Venerable Founder's. Blessed Arnold believed firmly in the power of the spiritual retreat. By his writings, his directives, his conferences he showed that each human being who wants to live fully and happily must, of necessity, take some time, preferably daily, to look into the depths of the soul and assess one's progress for good on the road of life. It was Arnold Janssen's conviction, therefore, that there was little more wholesome in life than at least two or three days spent in solitude and spiritual retreat, in an atmosphere of tranquil silence and prayer to look at oneself as honestly as possible, and then make a plan for strengthening virtue and deepening communion with God. So from the very beginning Arnold Janssen encouraged the members of his Order of missionary priests and Brothers and missionary Sisters to open their doors to lay retreats. Nothing was dearer to him than to see an ever growing number of spiritually renewed Christians leavening the world with their faith, hope, and love. So now the Sisters in the United States began retreat work. The first lay retreat was held from July 29 to August 1, 1909. There were fifty participants. The Sisters continued retreat work and up to the present the work is flourishing; and it is hoped this great work will go on bringing peace and spiritual comfort to many people.

In the midst of all the activity, Mother Leonarda had to prepare for a very important event: the first Provincial Chapter of the Holy Spirit Missionary Sisters in the United States. The Chapter was held from August 15 to September 8, 1909, and was presided over by Rev. Father DeLange. One of the most important duties of the Chapter was the election of delegates to the coming General Chapter in Steyl. Sister Borromaea was elected a delegate. Mother Leonarda was already an ex officio member of the Chapter.

Shortly after the conclusion of the Sisters' Provincial Chapter, Father DeLange and appointed SVD delegates set off for Steyl and the General Chapter of the Society of the Divine Word. Their first order of business when the Chapter opened was the election of a Superior General as successor to the Venerable Founder. They did this promptly by voting into office the man who had been acting General since the death of the Founder: Father Nicholas Blum. He was a fine administrator, an understanding man, and a fortunate choice for the Sisters, too, since he had had a real insight into the problems and conditions existing between the two Orders in the United States and within each Order when he had come on Visitation to Techny.

The year was gradually unwinding and coming to an end. On November 15, Mother Leonarda and Sister Borromaea left for Steyl and the first General Chapter of the Holy Spirit Missionary Sisters. The farewells were not happy ones. Although there had been considerable friction between some Sisters and their Superior, and it was not all settled yet, the Sisters seemed to realize the burden that Mother Leonarda had carried, and now as they said good-bye, there was a fear that she would not return. Perhaps only now did some Sisters realize their good fortune in having such a woman as Mother Leonarda as their Superior. How many have the silent endurance and kind understanding, and above all, the maganimity and forgiveness that she possessed!

Perhaps some of the nuns who had caused their Superior grief by their petty tale bearing and often slanderous remarks realized now as she waved good-bye that another less holy and forbearing woman as superior would have sent them off packing long ago. Yet here she stood, a smile and handshake for everyone, and no one could see or guess from her demeanor who it was that had grieved her.

Would she return? She had worked hard and under the most trying circumstances; she had suffered in heart and soul, for which there is no "bottled analgesic." Would she return for more? Right now, no one knew.[8] She herself knew only one thing. Her work here in the United States was not finished.

Regarding this farewell, Mother Leonarda notes the following in her Diary: "November 15, 1909: Sister Borromaea and I began our travels to Steyl today at 7:20 P.M. The leave-taking was hard. Sister Assistant and Sister Foureria accompanied us to the train. We traveled with the Erie Line to New York."

Mother Leonarda and her companion were still on the ocean steamer, crossing the Atlantic on her first visit to the Motherhouse in Steyl and to her homeland when things began happening at St. Ann's. There had been a saying at St. Ann's Home among the Sisters from the earliest years that whenever Mother Leonarda was out of the house for a few days, something unfortunate would happen. This time was no exception.

Just four days after she left, on November 19, Mrs. Wolf, a resident at the Home, died. Death among the elderly residents was not extraordinary, but hers was an example of what sometimes happened because the Sisters had no voice in interviewing applicants for the Home and hence seldom knew anything about the residents who were admitted. Whatever financial arrangements were made had been made between the applicant and the Superior of the Society of the Divine Word. Once the applicant became a resident, the responsibility for taking care of the person became the Sisters'.

When Mrs. Wolf died, the Sisters discovered to their consternation, that she was penniless. Now it fell to the Sisters to see to it that she received proper burial and a place to be buried. Not only was she penniless, she was also alone. There were no relatives who could be notified and perhaps could help with the burial expenses. The Sisters, too, still had no income of their own. Once again, it was to their friends that the Sisters turned for help. With the help of friends the Sisters were able to see to it that Mrs. Wolf had a proper burial and burial place in the cemetery with the prayers of the Church, a Solemn Requiem High Mass, and final cemetery services.[9]

When Mr. Bald died on December 2, a problem arose that was much more complicated, indeed. Again, the death was not extraordinary. Mr. Bald was quite old; he had been ill for some time, and when the doctor and the Sisters realized how gravely ill he was, the priest was called on November 28 and administered the Sacrament of the Sick, anointing Mr. Bald with the holy oils to strengthen him either to a renewal in health or in preparation for his final journey. Mr. Bald died quietly four days later. On December 3, the body was to be taken to St. Boniface cemetery for burial. However, before this took place, some trouble arose as to the price for the grave. The Sisters had $50.00 which Mr. Bald left and gave the money for the grave. It was accepted. When it seemed that all was settled, trouble came from a completely unknown source.

The body had already been taken from St. Ann's Home and was to be buried in St. Boniface Cemetery. However, the procession was halted and prevented from proceeding to the cemetery. Mr. Birren, the Undertaker, was informed that the body had to be examined by the Medical Examiner. An autopsy was ordered. Someone called "Austin" was asking for the autopsy because a rumor was circulating that Mr. Bald had been poisoned. The Sisters knew nothing of the rumor until they were informed of all this by Dr. Latz, who had attended Mr. Bald and who was the House physician, and by Mr. Birren, the funeral director. Of course, the Sisters were totally taken aback by the whole thing, and for weeks they had to suffer the painful embarrassment of court sessions, newspaper accounts, and especially the poignant ignorance of who had done this to them and for what reason. Was someone against them? Did someone have a grievance against St. Ann's? It remained a Mystery.[10] It took four weeks before the report finally came out. The Coroner stated that there was nothing suspicious or questionable regarding the death of Mr. Bald. Death came from natural causes.

Although she was not in Techny at the time, Mother Leonarda considered the incident important enough to mention in her diary. She ends her account by saying, "We never knew whose wicked fabrication this was."

In the future there were other incidents where the Sisters had to suffer in some way because of someone's malice or hatred.[11] One looks for reasons—personal dislike? private enmities? religious fanaticism? or does the answer lie again somewhere in the cloudy tangled web of the history of the time?

Was a German-founded community of nuns coming to the United States at the turn of the century considered a welcome asset to the community, the

Church, by everyone? It was just around this very time that the Church itself was wrestling with a nationality crisis that carried on well into the twentieth century.[12]

Two dominant groups in the Church, the Irish Catholics and the German Catholics were lashing out at each other trying to establish their own ideas for the growth of the Church. The Irish had been seeking refuge in this country for centuries fleeing their homeland because of persecution. Gradually, they lost a great deal of their cultural heritage, but they established themselves firmly in this land, and, in the Church, they soon dominated the American hierarchy.

The German Catholics, by 1900, had become the second largest group in the Church. Almost the complete opposite of the Irish, the Germans held tenaciously to the customs and practices of their German heritage. They did not forget their cultural roots, but instead tried to transplant some of these roots in their new land. They established schools with German the language of the school. They brought in their own priests and nuns from Germany to work the German parishes and schools. They firmly believed that keeping their German language was a safeguard for keeping their faith. There were some who believed as the writer in the *Buffalo Volksfreund* that "America is no nation, no race, no people like France, Italy, and Germany . . . .It is no nation, and therefore, it has no language outside the languages which the immigrated people speak in their families."[13]

There was a decided conflict between Irish Catholics and German Catholics, the latter stressing a Church with German cultural strength and pressing for greater German representation in the country's hierarchy; the former urging Catholics to reconcile the Church with modern culture, and prominent clergymen, such as Father Isaac Hecker, stressing the idea that the Church must take on an American mentality if it wanted to make any progress in growth.

At one point Pope Leo XIII stepped in, brought out the true meaning of the Church and its catholicity, and, for a time, both sides calmed down a bit.

However, the antagonism was there, and the problem of many nationalities, many languages and cultures being assimilated into one, not only tested the growth of the country, but even rankled the very catholicity of the Church itself in this country.

It would take two World Wars, and a Second Vatican Council before the Church in the United States could begin to sing in its liturgies, "There is one Lord, one faith, one Baptism . . . ."—in its churches where Irish, Germans, Poles, Italians, Blacks, Orientals,—all races, all nationalities shared the same pew and sang in unison.

The nationality conflict was very real, and in this country, some form of persecution of certain nationalities, races, or religious beliefs was not at all exceptional nor unheard of.

The Holy Spirit Missionary Sisters coming to this country were totally unaware of this conflict. The average immigrant coming to the United States from a country where one language was spoken, one culture permeating all—does not immediately understand the pain and conflict and struggle that has gone into making one country of many cultures and many languages.

Were the Sisters tasting some of the bitterness of

this conflict of nationalities and religion? The Catholic Church was still not totally accepted or tolerated in all parts of this country. Is it possible that the Sisters were the butt of prejudice? If so, they were not the first religious community of Sisters to be the target of malice. There were always those who had to display their prejudice.

By the time Mr. Bald was finally laid to rest in peace, Mother Leonarda had safely crossed the Atlantic, and the other delegates from around the world had assembled in Steyl for the first General Chapter of the Holy Spirit Missionary Sisters. There were extremely important matters to discuss and decisions to be made which would effect the future and the continuance of this Missionary Order of Sisters. First, however, in the order of business, just as it had been with the Society of the Divine Word, was the election of a Superior General. A day after the Chapter began telegrams were sent to the various missions of the Sisters over the world with the words: Mother Theresia. She was elected to a twelve-year term. The Sisters in all the missions reacted with joy and celebration. Mother Theresia had already proved herself an exemplary Religious and a fine administrator and mother. The Order continued in capable hands.

Both Orders, the priests and the nuns, were requesting approval from Rome for their Constitutions, the Holy Rule. One factor was a deterrent to approval: the present financial arrangement of the two orders which made the Sisters totally dependent on the Society of the Divine Word.[14]

An arrangement such as this between an Order of Priests and Brothers and an Order of Religious Sisters was not in accord with the regulations and wishes of the Holy See. Thus Rome withheld approbation of the Constitutions until such time when the Orders would function autonomously.

The Sister's General Chapter, therefore, devoted much time to deliberating on the question of financial separation from the Society of the Divine Word and establishing the total independence of the Missionary Servants of the Holy Spirit. All the details of separation, however, could not be worked out during the time of the Chapter. Some matters had to be settled in the individual missions; thus final arrangements were completed months later.

During the next months the various regulations and directives that had been discussed at the Chapter were promulgated among the houses of the Congregation.

The Chapter itself came to an end in February. Sister Borromaea traveled back to the United States with five Sisters missioned to Techny. Mother Leonarda remained in Steyl. When the news reached Techny, there was a heavy sadness among the Sisters and the residents. They all feared that this was a sign that she would not return. Already in January they had begun preparations to greet her on her arrival. The residents had bought a set of fourteen Stations of the Cross for the chapel as a beautiful token of appreciation to be presented to Mother Leonarda upon her arrival at St. Ann's. The Sisters had scrubbed the house from attic to basement and kept up the decorative Christmas lights and Christmas star in the entrance window. When the Sisters heard of the delayed return, they left everything as it was and hoped that Mother Leonarda would return.

Easter came and still no Mother Leonarda. Then a few days after the feast, March 30, Wednesday, she arrived in Techny bringing with her six more Sisters from Steyl. While the Brothers went to get Mother Leonarda and the Sisters from the station, St. Ann's was illuminated with all the electric lights. There in the front window the Christmas star shone brightly, and the shooting of firecrackers greeted the Foundress. Sisters and residents were happy once again to have their Mother back. Perhaps the most surprised of all, was Mother Leonarda who was completely bewildered by this outpouring of joy and affection at her homecoming. The problems of the past seemed to have been obliterated by the happiness of the moment. She went from the chapel where the choir sang Mary's beautiful canticle, the Magnificat, in thanksgiving for her safe journey, down to the dining room for a little refreshment, and on to shaking hands individually with all the Sisters and residents. The next day a long program was given in her honor.

Just how all this affected Mother Leonarda is revealed in a letter she wrote to Mother Theresia on April 9, 1910. "The good Sisters and all the old people had a very lovely reception prepared. They did more than they really should have done. We were all happy to be with each other again, and the new Sisters rejoiced likewise to have the long journey over with. We arrived eight hours late, so we did not chat long and went straight to bed. Although I was rather tired, I could hardly sleep, and, consequently felt exhausted the next day." Then she adds a sentence so utterly human one can only smile. It is a feeling honestly asserted: "What made it worse was to sit through the many speeches by the Sisters and the old people." She continues: "The old people gave a very beautiful set of the Stations of the Cross for our church. Three days after my return, I assembled everyone together in order to thank them and tell them something about the Motherhouse. They all rejoiced like children. I showed them the picture of our patron St. Ann which I brought with me for a banner, and I told them that you, Reverend Mother, selected it. That made it special."

In the same letter she goes on to thank Mother Theresia for the added days she was permitted to spend in Steyl. She assures her of carrying out the customs of the Congregation as they "are practiced in Steyl"; she talks about the sick Sisters and how each is faring, and mentions a few things to show that, in spite of the joyful welcome celebration, all was not yet at peace in the community. She writes: "....That Sister Assistant sometimes acted independently can in part be the fault of the priest. He told her she had absolute power and she could do what she wanted. My attention has also been called to the fact that there was much visiting going on between the priests and Sisters, but, that since Father Superior returned, it has all stopped.... They have much information about many things, so it appears, information about which I did not inform them or anyone. The frequent visiting and talking brought much to light. Do not worry, Reverend Mother, I will do my duty in every respect, and I intend to keep the good spirit and good relations." (Letter of April 9, 1910)

She had returned! Her first days home she had to fight homesickness for the Motherhouse in Steyl, but she knew very well that it was her task now to build on the foundation she and her faithful companion Sisters had laid in tears, joys, much suffering and sacrifice. She knew the years ahead could be just as if not more difficult, but now she had the added strength of sincere friends—people who had befriended the Sisters and her in particular year after year. They were people who seemed to be always there when she needed them; someone she could rely on.

There was much to be done. When she returned from Steyl, she had brought with her a sample of the material that was now being used for the habits. At the General Chapter it was decided that the light blue habit and white veil chosen by the Founder, though attractive, indeed, was rather impractical when one considered the work the Sisters had to do and all the traveling and the kind of traveling they did especially in the mission lands—in bulla carts, sampans, lorries, etc.... The color of the habit was changed to dark blue including the veil and a mantle. Over the scapular, each Sister wore a cross with the emblem of the Holy Spirit, a dove, suspended on a red ribbon. The novices wore a white veil.

Mother Leonarda set about at once trying to match the blue material here and then had the new habits sewn. It could not be done at once, of course. Some Sisters worked in the sewing room, but, by far, not enough. It took several months to get the habits made, but by December, they were finished, and the Sisters began wearing the dark blue habits on the first Sunday of Advent. Residents and visitors missed the lovely light blue and white habits, but for the Sisters, the change was a gainful practicality.

As more Sisters came and more were engaged in school work, Mother Leonarda was concerned more and more that the Sisters were educated and well prepared for their profession as teachers. During the course of the years, she re-vamped the entire teaching plan, added to the curriculum of summer courses, and brought in a piano teacher from Chicago. She herself taught some of the summer courses. With her onerous administrative duties, her constant "being on call" for the Sisters—listening to them, counseling them—and being also "on call" for the residents; her task in directing the choir and the Gregorian chant schola; her time spent conferring with salesmen, business men, architects, contractors; her night duty watch; her help in the laundry and basement; and then her trips to the South to visit schools and convents there, one wonders how she managed to work out such a thorough plan of education for the Sisters and even teach some courses. But she did!

The great task that she faced, of course, when she returned from the General Chapter was working out the financial separation of the two communities, the S.V.D. and the Sisters, S.Sp.S. She worked hard on this, and as the Chronicler for St. Ann's writes: "Most of the work of transition was done by Sister Provincial Leonarda herself; a young Sister helped with the correspondence."[15]

In exchange for a definite sum of money, St. Ann's was to be transferred by the Society of the Divine Word to the Holy Spirit Sisters.

On April 25, 1910, Mother Leonarda informed Mother General Theresia that the final act in the financial separation is about to take place. She writes:

Today I mailed a letter to Rev. Fr. Director General in which I wrote him regarding some points which I would also like to bring to your attention in this letter.

Effective May, we will begin our own bookkeeping. If I am not mistaken, we will have to assume a debt of $90,000.00. Does this frighten you? Now no one can say: 'In America they are rich and do not need any support.' We will be burdened with this debt as long as we live and will not be able to undertake anything new.

Then between the period of the last sentence and the beginning of the next sentence, her missionary zeal, business acumen, and her awareness for future growth take over so suddenly that she writes:

Nevertheless, I must tell you of a proposal that was made to us by a Mr. Nagel from Santa Fe, New Mexico. He wants to donate to us 150 acres of land, a house with 16 furnished rooms, stables and barns if we are willing to open a sanitarium there. We were told that the land is very fertile and good for planting fruit and vegetables. There is also good water from a well and beautiful grounds surrounding the house. We will have to investigate to make certain everything is so as it was presented to us . . . .

She goes on to give five reasons why the Sisters should accept this proposal. Then she asks Reverend Mother for her opinion.

She also writes of another offer.

We also had an offer of a Parish school in our vicinity, only twenty minutes distant on the way to Chicago. Our priests often visit the school. The Sisters would be able to change off coming home on Fridays and return Monday morning. If I remember right, it was decided that we should not accept Parish schools. However, we thought an exception might be possible in this case because the school is so close. . . . .It would be easier for us to take over this school because we would not be bound to it and we would have no expenses but an income from the beginning. Most of all we would perhaps gain a better reputation as teachers.

In regard to the girls' school, we may not open the school for another year due to our debts. So much good remains undone because the means are missing . . . .

(Letter of 4-25-1910)

So the girls' academy that she had hoped to open a mile down the road still could not be realized as she mentions in the letter. She would just have to delay the fulfillment of her dream a bit longer.

Year after year Techny became better known, but strangely enough and unfortunately for the Sisters, people in general associated Techny with the Society of the Divine Word, seldom with the Sisters. As the Techny community of priests, Brothers, and students increased; and as visitors, tourists, retreatants, and sightseers increased, so did the Sisters' work increase and greater demands were made on the Sisters' time with regard to cooking and washing dishes. Yet, people in general were quite unaware of the Holy Spirit Missionary Sisters working "behind the scenes" in Techny. It was not that the Sisters wanted any special attention; they simply wanted to be better known so as to be able to attract young women into their ranks.

At the beginning of another school year in September, 1910, the Divine Word Fathers opened two more stations in the South: Meridian, Mississippi, and Little Rock, Arkansas. Three Sisters were appointed for Meridian: Sister Romana, Superior, Sister Praesentata, and Sister Lamberta. They arrived in Meridian on September 17 and were very much surprised to find a beautiful large new building with a chapel, school, and Sisters' home all in one. The people were very friendly toward the Sisters.

The new mission in Little Rock, however, was the very opposite of Meridian. Little Rock was extremely poor. For quite some time the Sisters here lived in great poverty.[16] There was little to eat, and at one time, the Sisters had to satisfy their hunger with a few stewed prunes at meals—something they found hilariously funny in later years as they looked back. Added to the lack of material necessities was the somewhat hostile attitude of the people. The beginnings of this mission were very difficult. Discouragement soon pushed its way into the small community of Sisters. Sisters Bertranda, Johanna, and Louise held on, but their letters to Mother Leonarda revealed their frustration and depression in trying to get this mission started.[17] Mother Leonarda encouraged them as best she could by letter and visitation. Finally, she invited the Sisters to come to Techny and spend part of the summer at St. Ann's to build up strength and courage.

The following year in June, 1911, in a suburb of Little Rock called Harrington Addition a new school was opened, and the Sisters were asked to take over. The school was one hour's distance from the center of the city. It was the Negro section of the city, and there were twenty children who needed to go to school. However, the children were very mistrusting and wary of these strange women and were not too eager to become friends with the Sisters. The latter summoned their courage and hope as they left every morning and returned in the evening by street car. In time the people's distrust turned into a trusting friendship, and even the extreme poverty was mitigated by the caring people. Once the Sisters and their work became known, the mission went ahead with renewed hope.

At St. Ann's the year 1910 would end with a loss, a special loss. That very willful lady who came to the Sisters on that summer evening in 1901 and practically forced them into accepting her as a boarder, who, we might say, made St. Ann's happen by her dogged determination to be cared for by the Sisters for the rest of her life and wouldn't take no for an answer—this woman, Mrs. Janssen, had lived with the Sisters almost ten years.

On November 27, 1910, she was found dead in her bed at 7 A.M. She passed peacefully into eternity and, in all probability, only a few minutes before the Sisters came to wake her since her body was still warm. Father Gruhn was quickly summoned, and he anointed her with the holy oils. One wonders what were her thoughts through the years as she saw St. Ann's established and grow—grow into quite a large structure—all because she wanted to live with the Sisters. Surely many of those who had come to St. Ann's to live out their years in peace blessed her in their hearts.

It is about this time and the following years that Mother Leonarda mentions in her diary the names of some Divine Word Fathers who were giants in their priestly lives, and who did much good spiritually for the Sisters and for the residents.

Father Fred Gruhn was the chaplain appointed for the Sisters; Father Aloysius Loechte was appointed the Sisters' confessor. Father Gruhn was a deeply spiritual man, matter of fact, a no-nonsense type of person, who preached or bellowed a sermon but always left one with a provocative good thought. When he sang the Preface of the Mass—as it had been done in a time of elaborate solemn liturgies—his congregation would watch the candles on the altar as they vibrated from the power of this man's voice. Everyone waited to see one fall, but one never did; and maybe some were just a little disappointed. Father Gruhn was one of the few aware of Mother Leonarda's sufferings of the time and aware also of the gossip and its evil. In fact Father Gruhn was also the subject of slanderous gossip. There was little he could do, but in his sermons and advice he gave encouragement and hope. Father Gruhn was connected with the Sisters for many years. His sister became a member of the Congregation of Holy Spirit Missionary Sisters and was connected with St. Ann's for many years.

Father Loechte was the thinker, the exegete, the apologist, theologian, moralist. He argued and proved, but so calmly and so logically, it was an intellectual pleasure to listen to him. He had been appointed the Sisters' confessor, and he also gave a retreat to the Sisters, which led Mother Leonarda to remark in her diary: "Father Loechte's retreat was the best one I ever made." He, too, understood the mettle of Mother Leonarda's soul. He was well apprised of the problems she encountered.

There were other S.V.D. priests and Brothers at the time who did much for the Sisters. Mother Leonarda was ever grateful for good priests and Brothers who dispensed their spiritual aid and good advice with holiness and intelligence, and, yes, good humor. Prayers for priests and Brothers were always included in the Sisters' community prayers as well as their private prayers.

As the year 1910 drew to a close, there were "eighty professed Sisters including thirty in perpetual vows and four postulants at St. Ann's." In recording these statistics, the Chronicler ends with a final sentence for the year: "Techny is not known enough. So far only German aspirants or those of German descent."

In the middle of March of the following year, Mother Leonarda went South for her Visitation. It was the second day that she was gone, a Thursday evening, and all the Sisters were gathered in the chapel for a holy hour of adoration and night prayers. Suddenly, there was a deafening noise and a frightening impact shook the whole house. The walls trembled; the Sisters knelt fixed in terror; the choir abruptly stopped singing, and the organist added to the fright by accidentally striking the open diapason. A second blast followed immediately, and now the floor under their feet seemed to give way. Everyone expected the floor to open up and swallow them, for they thought this was an earthquake. Gradually the tremors subsided, and the fear lessened somewhat. Slowly the Sisters began praying again while a few Sisters went out to try to find out what had happened. The news came to them in a telephone call. A large powder factory in Kenosha,

Wisconsin, had blown up, and the area as far south as Chicago was affected by the tremors—a distance of some seventy to eighty miles.

When it was over, the Sisters exchanged silent messages which said, "Mother Leonarda isn't home. Something had to happen!"

For the past few years there had always been some building going on at St. Ann's—additions to the original structure, renovations, remodeling, etc. Nothing much had been done to the surrounding grounds, and Mother Leonarda had been hoping right along that St. Ann's grounds could be landscaped. There had always been something more urgent needed, but now with the Home growing as rapidly as it was and with so many people coming out to Techny to visit or just relax, something had to be done to beautify the outside area.

Father F. Hildebrand, a Divine Word Father, drew up a plan for embellishing the grounds. Roads, paths, flower beds were laid out; trees and bushes planted and sod laid. Later on little shrines, the Stations of the Cross, and a Lourdes grotto were put up. Two men had been hired to do the landscaping, and they did a fine job. When June came around, the Corpus Christi procession weaved its way from the seminary grounds to the newly ornamented garden of St. Ann's.

At the same time that the grounds were landscaped, the Sisters also acquired a small poultry farm. Three hundred chickens, some ducks and geese, and a small pond for the latter were added to the Sisters' care.

In June, 1911, Father DeLange called the Sisters together one day in the conference room and read to them the new elections for the American province. Sister Leonarda was once again elected Provincial Superior; Sister Alexia, her Assistant; Sister Borromaea, Sister Martina, and Sister Isidora, members of the Council.

A special celebration was planned for the fifteenth of June. On that day the Sisters would renew their Vows according to the new Constitutions which they had just received from Steyl, and the newly elected officials would be installed. It was to be a day of joy for all the Sisters and was anticipated with a happy expectancy. Yet when the day came, it brought with it a taste of bittersweet sadness.

Sister Macaria, who had been ill for some time, took a turn for the worse. On the eve of the celebration, the death struggle set in. All through the night Father Loechte and Sister Superior kept vigil beside the dying Sister. In the morning at the first liturgy celebration, the Sisters renewed their vows according to the new Constitutions. At 8 A.M. a solemn Mass began in the chapel, and 8:10 A.M. just as the community was singing the beautiful hymn for Corpus Christi, Lauda Sion, the bell began tolling the death of Sister Macaria. Mother Leonarda had been at her side—happy in the renewal of vows, sad in the loss of another Sister. Her new term of office began with grief. It was as if every happiness in her life would be always tinged with some sadness.

One happiness, though, which she had so longed to realize did finally reach fulfillment. The little white house on the very, very small hill called Belleview, surrounded by trees and green fields, about a mile south of St. Ann's was converted into a home economics boarding school for girls. Thirty-two acres of land had been purchased from the Society of the Divine Word including the house, barn, and stables; and the Sisters went about immediately converting the house into classrooms and living quarters for the boarders. On September 18, Father DeLange blessed the place which was now known as Holy Ghost Academy. On the following morning the first Holy Mass was said in the new academy. Sister Alexia became the first Superior, and the school officially opened with seven pupils. The curriculum provided for domestic science and academic subjects.

Holy Ghost Academy was by no means a wealthy boarding school for girls. As a matter of fact, the school was reminiscent of the Sisters' first convent. Sleeping quarters for the girls were in the attic. Soon a little wooden house was built next to the old house affording a bit more room. There were many difficulties in the beginning. In fact, some of the girls did not feel at home at all in such primitive surroundings.

Since the Sisters did not have the staff nor the equipment to make Holy Ghost Academy an independent house, all the baking, washing, and sewing was taken care of by the Sisters in St. Ann's. Everything was conveyed back and forth, up and down the small hill, about a mile in distance, over snow and ice in a small cart. The first winter was very cold, and to make things worse, the steam heat apparatus did not work. Both the Sisters and the girls suffered much. Pipes froze. With everything else, water, too, had to be conveyed from St. Ann's; and as if those troubles were not enough, the snow that winter was so high, the priest could not come for daily Holy Mass. In fact, even the Sisters who worked at the Mission House in the kitchen and the laundry were stranded there and could not get through the snow to go back to St. Ann's.[19]

But the winter did come to an end, and gradually the situation at the academy improved. The pupils, too, became more and more familiar with their new surroundings, and whatever hardships they endured in those harsh beginnings, they were always very loyal to the Sisters and even helped with the work.

Now that the Sisters had two activities going in the State of Illinois, it was necessary that Mother Leonarda take steps to have the community incorporated under the laws of the State especially for the lawful transaction of business. It was in the Fall of 1911, that Mother Leonarda took the initial steps toward obtaining these rights and the deliberations were completed on December 11, when the Sisters obtained the Charter. The name of the Corporation was written as "Servant Sisters of the Holy Spirit." The directors of the Corporation were the Sisters of the Provincial Council with Sister Provincial Leonarda, the President.[20]

Two days later Mother Leonarda wrote to Mother General Theresia in Steyl. First she wishes Mother Theresia all the joys of the Christmas season and mentions the promotions that came for the Sisters to make vows.

In one paragraph she speaks about the situation with Father Regional DeLange. She writes: "Reverend Father Regional is again friendly and good to us, at least outwardly. Our confessor talked to him on our behalf; since then he again communicates with us and will resume his conferences to us. I do not know how he really feels toward us. I expect more trouble and difficulties, but I am ready and calm. I can bear external difficulties easier so long as the Sisters are good. It is a great consolation for me to know you understand me and bear everything with me. May the Holy Spirit reward you!"

Later in the letter she poses a question for Mother Theresia: "What do you think, Reverend Mother, who of the Sisters should I train to assist me with my work: Sister Ursuline, Sister Bernardine, or later Sister Marysia? At present I do everything myself because no Sister can be spared. However, it is too much. The Sisters require so much of my time. Yet, if the Sister does not know English well, it will not be of much help."

In a closing paragraph, Mother Leonarda mentions another matter which shows that she still had problems concerning the independence of the Sisters' community. She writes:

> *Sr. Afra wrote me that Rev. Father Regional De-Lange told her that it was not certain that the Sisters from the South would go to Techny for their vows next summer. How shall I respond to this when he notifies me? It is my belief that it is much better for these Sisters to come here, even necessary for them, because among the nine Sisters who are to make vows, I think there are some doubtful vocations.*
>
> (Letter of 12-13-1911)

The decision to call the Sisters to Techny was rightfully hers, and she could have bluntly stated this to the Regional Superior at the Mission House. However, she always tried to carry out the duties of her office tactfully and prudently.

If the good of the community or the good of an

individual Sister was at stake, or if she believed something was wrong, she would not hestitate to act immediately. If, however, her authority or if she as the Superior were by-passed or embarrassed, she preferred to wait and see or, if only she were affected, then to accept it and try to forget.

She was always aware of the fact that the religious life she had chosen was a life of perfection, and that sufferings of whatever kind are very much a part of that life. This thought is reiterated time and again in her Chapter conferences and in letters and notes to individual Sisters.

One Sister who was accustomed to having a brief weekly chat with Mother Leonarda regarding the Sister's spiritual life, work, difficulties, etc. was the recipient of many short thoughts written by Mother Leonarda for the Sister's spiritual growth. These handwritten thoughts show us also the soul of the woman who wrote them.

At one time she tells the Sister: "Misunderstandings and trials are the best means on our way to perfection. Our Heavenly Mother is our model and protectress."

Another time she writes, "Why do we worry? Everything is in God's Hands, and He expects us to do our duty and leave the rest to His providence. This is the means to keep the soul in peace."[21]

To another Sister she writes: "Just picture to yourself that our Lord is looking upon you every moment of the day, and He counts all your trials, your energy, your good will, and also your failings . . . .He loves you, otherwise He would not put such crosses upon you. Try to do all you can to avoid friction . . . ."[22]

Constantly living in such openness to God, such trust in Him, such acceptance of the good and the bad in life, being always "in His presence" and adhering to God with utmost strength, gives a person an indescribable serenity—deep in the soul and overflowing to one's exterior.

Those who live simply on the surface of life—enjoying in a superficial way its pleasure, seeking its conveniences, bogged down by its materialism and sensuality—perhaps can never really understand the serenity and strength of the person steeped in God. There may at times be a ruffling of the spirit, a time of depression, a period of doubt, but in the very core of the soul there is God and peace.

So it was with Mother Leonarda.

1. Letter of Mother Leonarda to Mother General Theresia (October 19, 1909).

2. Chronicle of St. Ann's Home.

3. Document 29.

4. Chronicle of St. Ann's Home.

5. Diary of Mother Leonarda.
Chronicle of St. Ann's Home.

6. Chronicle of St. Ann's Home.

7. Letter of Mother Leonarda to her father (June 15, 1909).

8. Document 14, an account of Sr. Joanna.

9. Diary of Mother Leonarda.

10. Diary of Mother Leonarda.

11. Two incidents: Gunshot through the library window in the late evening. Sr. Leonore was working in the library. Incident occured around 1940. Arson of the pergola in the late evening.

12. Thomas Bokenkotter, *A Concise History of the Catholic Church* (New York: Doubleday & Company, 1977), pp. 352-358.

13. Crosby, *God, Church & Flag*, p. 12 as in James Hennesey, S.J., *American Catholics, a History of the Roman Catholic Community in the United States* (Oxford: Oxford University Press, 1981), p. 195.

14. Chronicle of St. Ann's Home.

15. Chronicle of St. Ann's Home.

16. Chronicle of St. Ann's Home.

17. Document 14, an account of Sr. Joanna.

18. Chronicle of St. Ann's Home.

19. Chronicle of St. Ann's Home.

20. Chronicle of St. Ann's Home.

21. Document 75, excerpts of M. Leonarda's letters to Sr. N.

22. Document 76, excerpts of M. Leonarda's letters to Sr. Genevieve.

Chapter Nine

Besides the education and instruction of youth, other works fundamental for our co-operation in the missions are the works of Christian charity, for what 'counts is faith that expresses itself in love' (Gal. 5:6). *These works are carried on in hospitals, orphanages, asylums, and in social work.*

Concerning this work conducted by Sisters, Pope Benedict XV said that Religious in orphanages, hospitals, asylums, and schools have, according to the designs of Divine Providence, an incredible mystical power for spreading Faith. This power comes from Christ at work in His co-worker, for He also gave His apostles the injunction "Attend the sick . . .make lepers clean . . . .Gratis you have received; gratis you must give."

—(Mt. 10:8-9)

(Diamond Jubilee Book of S.Sp.S.)

The warm June air was heavily scented with honeysuckle, violets, and lilies of the valley. Tiny colorful humming birds, spiralling nervously, darted in and out of the honeysuckle bushes searching for sweet nectar while somewhere in the garden a brown thrasher was amusing himself and his listeners with his cheerful mimicking calls. As if not wanting to be outdone in song, a bright red cardinal, like a crowned king surveying his domain, sat high in the branches of a maple calling "Ma a-ree, Maa-ree." The bird families had already established themselves as permanent spring-summer residents of the Techny gardens and seemed to have taken out bird rights for themselves and their progeny, for they returned to Techny year after year after year. Of course, there were always sparrows, always the robin, and though rather unlikable fellows, there were also the raspy starlings. Sometimes an oriole or a red winged blackbird passed through, or canaries and a bluebird now and then. A few woodpeckers spent a short summer in the garden, and the early hours of dawn were punctuated with the melancholy cooing of the mourning doves.

Birds, trees, flowers would always be a very beautiful part of Techny. An exceptionally lovely day was beginning at St. Ann's. There was a distinctive, pervading peace in the atmosphere, so much a part of Techny already.

That magic of the early summer brought a feeling of good cheer and new hope to the elderly residents as well as to the Sisters. Only too soon the days would begin to get hot and humid, the sticky weather of the Great Lakes region. Those muggy days were difficult for the elderly residents, especially those with respiratory problems, but today the June day was perfect.

The morning cleaning had already begun. Sisters were busy with their regular chores on the floors. They had help from some young high schoolers. For some time it had become customary for high school girls from the Chicago area and young women to spend their vacation time at St. Ann's. During their stay they would help the Sisters with little jobs around the Home, something the Sisters appreciated very much.

On this particular day two girls were cleaning around the inside entrance area, and at the moment from the corner of their eyes they were watching an unrehearsed dramatic vignette unfold before them. They had seen Mother Leonarda cleaning the stairs at the entrance; she was always somewhere helping with whatever morning cleaning had to be done. They knew that. What held their attention now was a business man entering the Home. The girls heard him ask Mother Leonarda, who was bent cleaning the stairs, if he could speak to the Superior of the House. Mother Leonarda straightened up and smiled. Her face was flushed from her bent position, her habit was pinned a little to keep it from sweeping the floor, and, of course, she wore an apron. She said to the man, "Please wait in here" and directed him to a small parlor. Then she went into the cloister area nearby. In a very short while she came out, apron off, habit straightened, and face a bit rosy but relaxed and smiling. She went into the parlor and with gracious composure said to the man, "I am Sister Leonarda. Now, tell me, Sir, what can I do for you?" The man opened his mouth, momentarily forgetting to close it, when he realized the Superior was the very same nun he had seen cleaning the stairs; then taking his cue from Mother Leonarda's smiling face, he smiled, too, and stated his business. Mother Leonarda had just a hint of a merry twinkle in her eye.

Later on the salesman, for such he was, referring to the incident, told another Sister that he was greatly impressed at the combination of utter simplicity and the professionalism of a capable administrator exquisitely melded in this fine woman.[1]

Indeed, Mother Leonarda was a woman whose personality was many faceted. She was equally at home with the ordinary or the great. She could sweep stairs or scrub the basement floor as well as conduct a business meeting of architects, contractors, and bankers or direct the choir. She could listen patiently to the complaints and whims and problems of the elderly residents who regarded her as a mother, even though she was the younger person; and she could likewise listen to and counsel her Sisters of all ages in the religious and spiritual life. She could also give a well-deserved rebuke and a necessary correction.

She was there when the Sisters needed her in the laundry or in the butchering room, the kitchen, anywhere. She was also there at a Sister's bedside soothing her in time of sickness or comforting her as death approached. She had a brief word or a little note for a Sister going through a spiritual ordeal or a time of discouragement or family problems; or for a resident suffering a setback or depression. She had words of advice and wisdom for a teacher with a question or a problem; she was an efficient and capable teacher herself. She gave of her experience and perception in meetings with lawyers and business men. She gave herself richly and generously to anyone who needed her.

Years before—perhaps when she said her first "yes" to the Holy Spirit in Freckenhorst—she had immersed herself in Christ and in the love of the Holy Spirit—she had experienced the flame kindled and burning—and now this deepening intimacy manifested itself in the radiance of the mature personality. The psalmist sings, "Look to him that you may be radiant with joy." (Ps. 39) That is what she did! This immersion into Christ and His Holy Spirit gave Mother Leonarda the special relationship she had with God, with her Sisters, with all people, and with the world. It permitted her to show a profound sensitivity, to be moved deeply, to be aware of problems, to listen and be open, to advise and counsel, and yet to remain even minded and balanced, self possessed and serene, a very real part of the world she lived in and yet interiorly calm and poised and properly distanced from the world to be able to view it dispassionately and objectively.

It was this mature personality that Father Arnold Janssen had recognized in Mother Leonarda from the earliest years of her religious life, and hence he laid upon her the burden of founding a new province. The years proved him correct in his judgement. Mother Leonarda had, indeed, established the Order of Holy Spirit Missionary Sisters in the United States. It was a foundation begun in extreme poverty, almost superhuman work, but courageous love.

In 1912 that love was still growing stronger and settling the foundation deeper in American soil.

The boarding school "on the hill" was developing very well into the kind of school Mother Leonarda had wanted. Actually, it was not what she had originally planned, which was a Home Economics School similar to the one she had attended as a young girl. She had learned through trial and error that such a school, popular as it still was in Europe, was not the type of school parents wanted for their girls in this country. They wanted an academy with classes which were preparatory for higher education, and that is what she gave them.

Less than four months after the academy opened, the girls were already giving a Christmas-New Year program including a play called *Echoes of Bethlehem* to the residents of St. Ann's. It was the first play in what would become one of the most enjoyable extracurricular features of the academy: celebrating just any feast or occasion with a dramatic presentation.[2]

A notable amount of talent emerged from those plays and programs presented by the girls. It was an unpolished natural talent, but it delighted captive audiences of senior citizens at St. Ann's, the Sisters, and, of course, the parents and friends of the young actresses. There was a newness also in the school play; it was beginning a new trend in school entertainment.

Across the country, too, new forms of art and literature were emerging. The Victorian age and romanticism in the arts was giving way to new modes of realism and naturalism. In the literary world such notables as Mark Twain and William Dean Howells had just about written their last great work, and new names: Theodore Dreiser, Jack London, Frank Norris, Hamlin Garland, Stephen Crane were beginning to make an impact in literature although the naturalism of Dreiser was still too strong at this time for the general American public.

In poetry, American talent was coming into its own in a new poetic genre. Poets such as Edwin Arlington Robinson, Vachel Lindsay, Edgar Lee Masters with his *Spoon River Anthology*, Carl Sandburg calling Chicago "hog butcher of the world," and Robert Frost, the bard of New England, were all appearing as giants on the American literary horizon together with the imagists: Amy Lowell, Ezra Pound, and T. S. Eliot.

In music, the American people were beginning to stomp their feet and sway to the rhythm of ragtime and later jazz, and, in contrast, for contrast is so much a part of American culture, the American public was showing a renewed appreciation of the classics; the opera was becoming popular. Then there was the new popular music of Irving Berlin and George M. Cohan who got the American people on their feet singing: "Oh, How I Hate to Get Up in the Morning" (Berlin) and a few years later "Over There" (Cohan).

The world of American art saw the rise of American impressionism and artists such as John Marin and Charles Demuth, followers of Van Gogh and Cezanne, presented their work to a somewhat shocked public.

In architecture Louis Sullivan and Frank Lloyd Wright were beginning a movement which gave a functional and social meaning to forms of architecture.

And rising straight as an arrow from the swarming throngs of citizenry and the bustling activity of New York and Chicago rose the huge steel structure so uniquely American, the skyscraper, a true symbol of a country that, by 1912, was on its way to the top as a leader.

Rounding out the sphere of the arts was a very new art form—the motion picture—and somewhere around 1915, a small California suburb, Hollywood, also became, for better or or for worse, a symbol of the United States.[3]

Back at Holy Ghost Academy, the girls who put on their plays may have been doing what girls all through the years would do at one time or another, dream of this glamorous place called Hollywood and mimic the exaggerated gestures of their favorite stars. It was the fantasy of the young girl's life, and it made life all the more interesting. There were some girls, however, who saw an entirely new life open to them: the life of the missionary Sister, and they knew what choice they would make in life. Mother Leonarda had been right. A number of girls who had been students at the Academy became Holy Spirit Missionary Sisters.

As the first months of 1912 rolled away, it could be said that the Academy was progressing well, and St. Ann's was running smoothly, that is, almost smoothly.

One day in early February the Sisters detected a gas smell in the kichen and store room area of the Home. When a check of all the external equipment showed nothing amiss, no jets opened, etc., the Sisters reported the matter to the Brother in charge of the building and equipment so that he might examine everything in greater detail.

For some reason, one cannot understand why, the Brother in searching for a gas leak in the pipes in the store room lit a match. The explosion was terrible. The Brother himself barely escaped with his life by jumping through a window. David, one of the workmen who was with him, was seriously injured on one foot and needed hospitalization for several weeks. The entire storeroom was destroyed as was the classroom above. Had the Sisters adhered to the schedule they ordinarily followed at this time of day, then at least six or seven Sisters would have been studying in this classroom at the very time of the explosion. As it was each Sister was either detained or changed her customary practice that day for no apparent reason, and only two Sisters were near the room at the time of the explosion. One Sister had gone to the classroom, but contrary to her practice, she did not sit at her desk. Instead she sat in the far corner of the room, the only area which escaped destruction. A second Sister had decided to study in another room because of the gas smell. A third Sister was detained and never got to the room. Several other Sisters were occupied longer than usual at their work and were late in getting away to study. When they all saw the total destruction—tables, chairs, desks, floor, ceiling of that classroom and that ordinarily they would have been sitting directly above the explosion, they all had a mighty good reason to thank God and His Angels for protection.[4]

In spite of tragedies and misfortunes and problems, each year also brought its quota of joys and blessings. This year the special reason for rejoicing was the visit of Mother General Theresia to the United States.

Since the Congregation of Holy Spirit Missionary Sisters was growing as it was and spreading its mission activities farther and farther over the world, it became necessary for the Mother General to travel extensively to the various missions of the world where the Sisters worked. She had to keep in touch with her Sisters, see to it that the aims of the Order were being carried out, observe the kinds of circumstances in which the Sisters had to live and work, and, of course, see if they were happy and healthy.

Correspondence by letter was one way of keeping in touch, but the Mother General had to see her Sisters, talk with them individually, and actually see the places where they worked. Thus she undertook periodic visitations to the Congregation's missions around the world. This year marked the first such visitation of a Mother General to the United States Province. On March 20, Mother Leonarda met Mother Theresia in New York. The S.S. Potzdam docked punctually at 11 A.M. With Mother Theresia came Sister Tiburtia and six postulants. The latter were immediately put on a train bound for Chicago. Mother General and Mother Leonarda went to Cornwell Heights in Pennsylvania to see Mother Katherine Drexel.[5] This was one of the times Mother Leonarda took up her friend's invitation to visit Cornwell Heights.

The visit was short, and they left the next day for Chicago. They reached Techny on March 23.

The visitation of a Mother General or her representative always had a double effect. It was, of course, an honor, a reason for celebration, but it was also something awesome and made some Sisters a little apprehensive; others, somewhat timorous. Mother Theresia was a beautiful, simple soul; it was not difficult to talk to her, and this is exactly what the Sisters did as the Superior General conducted her visitation in St. Ann's and in the South and East.

Although almost all the Sisters found it easy to

talk with their Mother Leonarda, it was always good for the Sisters to be able to talk with a Sister outside the Province. This, of course, was one of the reasons for the Visitation. The outsider would be able to view things in a more objective way. However, the Visitator was at a disadvantage also. Viewing a place, a situation, etc. in a very limited time did not give one the needed time to get the feel of the country and its people, its customs and aspirations, to understand a people's uniqueness.

A wise Visitator took this into consideration. She would question, look, prudently make recommendations. The Holy Spirit Sisters were quite blessed in their Mother Theresia. Her closeness to God gave her a rich understanding of human nature.

As Mother Theresia was approaching the last two months of her visit in the United States, Reverend Nicholas Blum, Superior General of the Society of the Divine Word, arrived in the United States. It was May 10, 1912.

For about two months both Superiors General were in the United States at the same time. It afforded a fine opportunity for the superiors of both Orders to meet and plan further developments of the Orders and their combined work and try to settle problems.

A final memorable occasion was July 18 when the Sisters celebrated Family Feast and a Farewell to Mother Theresia. Three days later Mother Leonarda accompanied Mother Theresia to New York. Just as the steamer bearing Mother Theresia was ocean bound, the ship, Regedom, was coming into the harbor bringing four more Sisters from Steyl for the North American province. Mother Leonarda waited for the newcomers, took care of all the necessary business, and then hurried home with the four Sisters because she had another task ahead, and she had to make some last preparations.

She was introducing another innovation: the first teacher conference for the Sisters of the Province. Father Gruhn presided over the conference which began on August 3, and which turned out to be a complete success. As a result of the many discussions held during the course of the week, it was decided that similar conferences on a smaller scale should be held regularly during the school year.

Other changes were being made in the house. Some time ago Mother Leonarda had sent Sister Mathia, a talentd Sister, to study art with the Notre Dame Sisters in Longwood, Illinois. Now that she had completed her studies and was returning to St. Ann's, Sister Mathia was given one room in the house to be her art studio. Mother Leonarda had planned that Sister Mathia would work together with the, as yet, small department for the making of Church vestments and embroidery. The work was undertaken as a source of income.[6]

The excellent artistry and creative design—painting, embroidery, crocheting, etc.—that came from this department defies adequate praise. The exquisite work with silks, satins, brocades—the best of materials for vestments used in the worship of God—became greatly sought after by people throughout the country: Church dignitaries, parish priests, seminarians, relatives of priests, etc. For many years the Sisters filled the orders for the J. P. Daleiden Company of Chicago, the large Church Goods Company.

The comparatively few Sisters who worked in this department, for one had to possess exceptional talent to create the splendid art work called for, were almost always working late. It seemed they were always making deadlines. Truly, they created beauty. Some of the intricate, minute, detailed stitching used in the outlining of Faces of Christ or the Saints was the talent of only one or two Sisters, and they used that talent day in and day out until age weakened eyes, and they no longer possessed the vision needed for such work.

Before the year's end, Mother Leonarda had sent her Sisters to two other stations. The Divine Word Missionaries had branched out into the East and had opened a Mission House in Girard, Pennsylvania. Their land site was in a very beautiful area, a place of green hills and acres of vineyards. In Fall the air was heady with the fragrant vintage of so many vines hanging heavy with clusters of the rich purplish fruit.

In the first few months students took care of the housework in the Mission House, but as the number of priests, Brothers, and students increased, the work became too much for them to handle, and once again the Divine Word Missionaries asked for the Sisters. On September 4, 1912, Mother Leonarda accompanied three Sisters to Girard, and the Sisters took over all the domestic work for the S.V.D. in this Eastern house.[7]

She was always looking for more activities that would be in accord with the Sisters' missionary calling, and, of course, for some activity that would enable them to be financially stable. An opportunity presented itself when she was asked to take over a hospital in Granite City, Illinois. On November 26, Mother Leonarda went with Sister Borromaea to look over the hospital.[8] She discussed plans for taking over the hospital.

She had no sooner returned home than she set out once again, this time for Girard to see how the Sisters were faring there and to settle some problems. She returned to Techny on December 14, and two days later she traveled with Sisters Borromaea, Domitilla, Bertha, and Rita to Granite City to take over the hospital. Thinking all the while that there would be a short transition period when the Holy Spirit Sisters would take over the hospital from the nuns working there at present, Mother Leonarda and her Sisters were utterly surprised to find a vacant house when they arrived on December 16. They were told the former Sisters had already left very early that morning and simply left the sixty patients in the hospital to wait for the new owners. Mother Leonarda was taken aback to find all that she did find or did not find. The sixty patients were without breakfast, and hence the five Sisters first of all had to feed the patients. They worked feverishly with some of the employees who remained at the hospital to prepare the food and serve breakfast to the patients. Mother Leonarda stayed in Granite City for eight days helping the Sisters with all the work to be done and getting the hospital in working order.

She came home on Christmas eve only to be greeted with the sad news that Sister Konrada was leaving the Order that very day.

There was also another piece of tragic news. One of the residents had somehow removed the heavy wire grating from his window and had fallen two stories to the ground. The doctor was immediately summoned as were his relatives. And a priest came. In a very short time his relatives were at his bedside. The man lived only one and one half hours after the fall. He had been given the Sacrament of the Dying and had been anointed and given absolution. While his relatives, the Sisters, and the priest surrounded him, the man slipped quietly away.

One man died; another man came to begin living at St. Ann's. The man who now came had been a shoemaker by trade. When he was asked if he would like to continue his trade at the Home, he was only too glad to set up shop there and take care of the shoe repair. This meant that another Sister was freed for other work because up to this time, the Sisters had also taken care of all the shoe repair in the house.

One day at the very beginning of the new year, Mother Leonarda received word from the Mission House that the American region of the Society of the Divine Word had been raised to the status of a province. Father Burgmer was appointed the first Provincial Superior. He succeeded the Regional Superior Father DeLange, who was now appointed for the mission in the Dutch East Indies (now Indonesia).

During the year Mother Leonarda was asked by the Pastor of a parish in the small village of Kickapoo, Illinois, to send Sisters to his parish. After she saw the place and made the necessary arrangements, Mother Leonarda sent Sisters Willibalda and Amata to Kickapoo. Shortly after the Sisters arrived, the Pastor, who had invited them and who was favorably disposed toward the Sisters, was transferred by the Bishop to another parish, and for three weeks the Sisters had to carry on in the parish as well as they could.[9]

It was another difficult beginning but very little has come down regarding the Kickapoo mission. Several Sisters were, in turn, appointed for Kickapoo during the next months. Among these Sisters was Sister Bernardine who, later in life, when she held the office of Directress of Studies and Provincial Superior, would inevitably laugh and shake her head when she told stories about those first months in Kickapoo. The Sisters had to be everything: teachers, pastor-priest, counselor, etc. It was a rather short venture all in all. Difficulties mounted and the work, too, was not exactly that which the Sisters counted among their missionary activities.

However, Mother Leonarda was not one to give up without giving it a chance, and so she kept the Sisters in Kickapoo for some time.

At St. Ann's, work was going on as usual. Ever alert to the educational needs of her Sisters, Mother Leonarda had made arrangements, during the course of the year, for Sister Clemenza of Holy Name School in Chicago to come to St. Ann's every Saturday to give the Sisters courses in Literature, History and Reading. Sister Clemenza became another lifelong friend of Mother Leonarda's.[10]

Ever since she came to this country, Mother Leonarda tried to send Sisters with a particular talent or skill to a place of learning where that talent could be nurtured and developed. She had sent Sisters with a desire for and interest in nursing to hospitals and schools of nursing in the area for training; some she sent to schools of music; others, schools of art; and still others to seminars and workshops on household management and dietetics. This year she opened the way for her Sisters to study at the Catholic University of America in Washington D.C. by sending Sister Dominica as the first Holy Spirit Missionary Sister to study and graduate from that University.[11] Many Techny Sisters would be future graduates of this prestigious institution of learning.

Along with all the positive developments of the Order in this country, one misfortune seemed to plague the Sisters with an almost yearly visit: fire.

This year just the day before the beautiful Marian feast of the Assumption, fire again destroyed a part of the Sister's property. Lightning struck the barn, and, although the barn was not yet so large, the destruction was complete. The barn would have to be re-built.[12]

Just a few months later in January, 1914, fire broke out in one room of Holy Ghost Academy. This time the Brothers from the Mission House came so quickly and worked so fast that the school was spared any notable destruction. The Brothers certainly prevented a great loss.[13]

Toward the end of 1913, Mother Leonarda had another problem to take care of. The taking over of St. Elizabeth's Hospital in Granite City had been a shaky ordeal from the beginning. Problems connected with the hospital began to mount higher, and a little over a year after the Sisters had taken charge, December, 1913, Mother Leonarda had to withdraw her Sisters from St. Elizabeth's Hospital.[14]

However, she would not let the loss of this undertaking stand in her way in carrying out what she considered a real aspect of missionary work: the care of the sick in hospitals. Simultaneous with her making preparations to withdraw from Granite City came a request from a group of people in Watertown, Wisconsin for the Sisters to take over the hospital there. She accordingly sent Sister Borromaea and Sister Martina to Watertown to look over the hospital.

The Sisters were favorably impressed. About three weeks later Mother Leonarda herself went with Sister Borromaea to see the hospital. The Sisters encountered no special difficulties in the business transaction, and around the middle of December the bill of sale was settled.

On January 5, 1914, Mother Leonarda went with five Sisters to take charge of St. Mary's Hospital in Watertown.

How different from St. Elizabeth's in Granite City! Here in Watertown everything was in order. The entire hospital was clean and orderly. The nurses had stayed on until the next day. There were eight patients. The Sisters examined everything from room to room, and Mother Leonarda saw in their faces that they were pleased with the purchase.[15] She was happy!

It was the beginning of a fine relationship of service and friendship between the Holy Spirit Missionary Sisters and the people of Watertown which continued for more than forty years.

Having settled the Sisters in Watertown, Mother Leonarda went back to all the work calling her throughout the Province. Pages of her diary read like a train schedule. From Watertown she traveled to Girard to see about some matters there; from Girard to Washington D.C., thence back to Techny where she had some last business to settle with Granite City, and then she was on her way to Watertown again.

Through the hospital in Watertown she became acquainted with the Order of Redemptorists, and they petitioned her to have some of the Holy Spirit Sisters to take charge of the domestic responsibilities in their Sacred Heart College. She sent three Sisters there.

In spite of all her traveling back and forth, she did take time to write a sentence in her diary: "Our white horse died, the best horse we had."[16] She was still the efficient manager as she was when she directed her Grandmother's farm in Ahlen. She was aware of all that was going on in the management of her household.

She was very much aware of another great need. The Province was growing, activities were multiplying, and the double use of St. Ann's Home as a Home for the elderly and at the same time the Central House of the Order was proving to be very impractical and very limited in space. The Sisters needed a separate Provincial House in the United States.

The Girls' Academy was also growing, and it would be necessary to build a larger school.

Thus Mother Leonarda again petitioned the Generalate for permission to build. In a letter dated February 11, 1914, she writes:

> *. . .I enclose a drawing giving you an idea of the plan. This year we will build only the Academy with its own entrance, also the boiler house. The Provincial House we will build later.*
>
> *Two weeks ago Mr. Happ transferred 18 acres of land to us on which we will pay him interest for life. We plan to build on this land. It is opposite the present academy. Alongside the land there are the Stations of*

the Cross. Mr. Happ also indicated later he intends to donate all his remaining property to us, 20 acres of land and two houses. Both he and his wife suffer from heart trouble and have no children. They do anything for us. Mr. Happ also promised to assist us with our building project, that we obtain good and reasonable contracts, etc. He is a capable business man and is acquainted with many people.

. . .Recently I talked to him (Father Provincial) regarding our plans and intention to build. He was very much in favor of our moving farther away from them, leaving the Home for the Aged where it is.

. . .In the beginning I was afraid we would not get along with our project without the S.V.D., but we will succeed if the Holy Spirit is the Master Builder . . . .

A month later she sent another short note with the plans. She writes:

Enclosed we are sending the plans for the new Academy. We did not anticipate the cost to exceed $30,000.00. However, Mr. Gaul, the architect, estimated the cost at $60,000.00. If we did not trust in Divine Providence, we would have reason to be scared. It will be impossible to borrow such sum on Notes. If the Society of the Divine Word would transfer the title of ownership of our property to us, without mortgage, we would be helped. We would then assume a mortgage on St. Ann's and gradually liquidate it by taking up smaller sums of capital. The payments of interest would not be too difficult . . . .

We recommend this urgent petition to St. Joseph, also the approval of our building project.

(Letter of 3-3-1914)

Finally on April 20, 1914, she sent a formal application for the erection of a Central House. It stated:

The Provincial Council, after long and mature deliberation, finds it necessary to establish and build a Sisters' Mission House combined with Novitiate, Postulancy, and an Academy. This house will be the Central House of the Congregation in the United States, Techny, Ill. . . . The present building will be a Home for the Aged.

The new Central House (Convent) of our Congregation is deemed necessary for the promotion of apostolate in this country. For reasons, evident to every person acquainted with this area and the country, we have often been advised to establish ourselves at a greater distance from St. Joseph's.

We submit this application to the General Council for approval.

The application was approved on May 13, 1914.

On May 22, the Provincial Superior Father Burgmer surprised the Sisters with the news of the election and re-election of Superiors for the Province. The Sisters thanked the Holy Spirit and cheered as they greeted Mother Leonarda on her re-election as Provincial Superior.[17]

In a couple of weeks she was on the road again, this time heading for Washington D.C. to attend the graduation of Sister Dominica from the Catholic University. The ceremony over, both Sisters went to the South to give courses to the Sisters who had stayed in the South for the summer and had gathered in Vicksburg.

It was while she was in Vicksburg that half way across the world a shot was fired in Sarajevo assassinating the heir to the Austrian throne, and the world was plunged into the bloodiest international war in the history of the world. First, Austria declared war on Serbia; then Germany declared war on Russia, then on France, then Belgium; and finally Britain declared war on Germany.

The United States remained neutral. With its heavy immigrant population, sympathies were divided between the Allies and the Central Powers. In general, however, it was difficult for the American to know just exactly what were the reasons for the war; in fact, the neutral countries did not know what the war was all about.[18] History began to give reasons and causes much later when this frightful World War was looked at from the objectivity of distance.

However, on that August day in 1914, when Germany plunged headlong into war, the Sisters in Techny, most of whom were from Germany, were not interested in reasons and causes or the politics of war. They only knew that many of their loved ones would be either fighting in the thick of battle or would in one way or another suffer because of the war. With overseas communication slowed up or stopped, they waited anxiously to hear news of their families.

It was a time of new trials for the Sisters, personal trials. Mother Leonarda knew her brothers and nephews would be called upon for some duty. She knew only one way at present to help: prayer.

But life had to go on. Even in war there are lights, momentary periods of joy. For the Sisters there was a very special day—December 8, 1914. It was the 25th Jubilee Celebration of the Missionary Congregation of the Servants of the Holy Spirit. The day began with a solemn liturgical celebration. In the afternoon there was a procession through the Home in which the girls of the Academy were dressed in long flowing white robes. Mother Leonarda read a beautiful prayer dedicating the province to the Holy Spirit, and then all the Sisters renewed their Vows. In the evening there was a celebration honoring the Holy Spirit, the Reverend Founder and Foundresses and the Immaculate Conception. A memorable and happy day![19]

It was December 21, the Third Monday of December. Every third Monday of the month was specially dedicated to the Holy Spirit, and the Sisters had certain prayers for the day and usually adoration of the Blessed Sacrament all day. Mother Leonarda knelt at her place in the chapel waiting for the priest to come out for the afternoon devotions. Her mind wandered to the new Academy which was now in the process of being built, and then, inevitably, her thoughts went to Mr. Wallish. She flinched a bit and prayed for him as she had so often since that fatal accident. Mr. Wallish had fallen from the roof of the new building and died almost immediately. She remembered the periods of questioning and the grief-stricken wife who would not be consoled. Of course, she would take care of the family, but how does one compensate such loss?[20]

Then she thought of the letter she had just received from a certain Sister Mary Antonea in Dubuque, Iowa. Sister Antonea told her there was a Dr. Schilling in a small town in Iowa called New Hampton who was anxious to find Sisters who would be willing to build a hospital in that town. It seemed like another opening for the Sisters. She must get in contact with Dr. Schilling.[21]

Some people thought she was imprudent, lacking in business acumen, experience in economics. She was rash, they said, to build at a time like this. What would they say if besides building an Academy and a Provincial House, she would also begin building a hospital?

It did not matter. She quietly went on doing what she knew had to be done. How could they know or understand the unflinching trust, the total abandon she had in the Holy Spirit, the "Master Builder."

Suddenly she heard the priest say: "The Spirit of the Lord has filled the whole world . . . ."

The Third Monday devotions had begun.

1. Document 41, an account of Sr. Natalis.

2. Chronicle of St. Ann's Home.

Link, S. & William B. Cotton, *American Epoch, A History of the United States Since the 1890's* (New York: Alfred A. Knopf), pp. 40-48.

4. Chronicle of St. Ann's Home.

5. Diary of Mother Leonarda.
Chronicle of St. Ann's Home.

6. Chronicle of St. Ann's Home.

7. Chronicle of St. Ann's Home.
Diary of Mother Leonarda.

8. Diary of Mother Leonarda.

9. Diary of Mother Leonarda.

10. Chronicle of St. Ann's Home.

11. Chronicle of St. Ann's Home.
Diary of Mother Leonarda.

12. Diary of Mother Leonarda.

13. Chronicle of St. Ann's Home.

14. Chronicle of St. Ann's Home.

15. Chronicle of St. Ann's Home.

16. Diary of Mother Leonarda.

17. Chronicle of St. Ann's Home.

18. David A. Shannon, *Twentieth Century America* (Chicago: Rand McNally & Company, 1963), pp. 154-158.

19. Chronicle of St. Ann's Home.
Diary of Mother Leonarda.

20. Diary of Mother Leonarda.

21. Account #80, a New Hampton Hospital File.

Chapter Ten

Will you end wars by asking men to trust men who evidently cannot be trusted? No. Teach them to love and trust God; then they will be able to love the men they cannot trust, and will dare to make peace with them, not trusting in them but in God.

For only love—which means humility—can cast out the fear which is the root of all war.

Thomas Merton

As 1915 entered history on a cold winter morning, it brought no abatement to the war in Europe. Rather, this year would mark the use of a new weapon in warfare: the submarine. So long as Germany and Britain and their European allies carried on the war within the limits and framework of traditional military operations, the United States saw no reason to enter the war. However, once Germany challenged the control of the seas, neutrality on the part of other nations was also challenged.[1]

Unfortunately, as is the case always in time of

war, propaganda was rampant. Since the United States counted as Americans, people from all nationality backgrounds, there was naturally a split in loyalties. Living here in comparative safety and with only limited news reports to go on, each person sided with his own homeland.

Even Mother Leonarda wrote to Mother Theresia in Steyl on August 12, 1914:

> *How will you now fare during the hard times of the war, and how will our houses fare in Germany and Austria? We were all very sad because of the many relatives that had to go to war. All my five brothers probably had to go; I wonder if they are still living. . . .The local English papers do not give true accounts and Germans cannot get information because the cables have been destroyed. We can hardly imagine how it really is. Daily, we say the Litany of the Saints for peace and for victory of the German homeland . . . .*

If she wanted victory for her homeland, she was not alone. There were those, such as Colonel House in the United States, who may not have wanted Germany to be victorious, but at the same time did not want German power destroyed because he considered Germany a natural European bulwark against Russia.[2]

However, on May 7, the tragic sinking without warning of the British liner, the Lusitania, off the coast of Ireland by a German submarine in which more than 1,200 non-combatants including one hundred twenty-eight Americans were killed, forced President Wilson to meet Germany's challenge to freedom of the seas by issuing an ultimatum.

Still, he as well as most Americans were opposed

to entering the war, and he succeeded by messages, ultimatums, and pledges in remaining neutral for another two years.[3]

With little news from home to go on, Mother Leonarda continued to pray for her brothers and her whole family. There was little else she could do for them. There was little else any of the Sisters could do for their families. Never is the feeling of helplessness more painful than when an ocean lies between loved ones and it is impossible to reach out one's hand in so much as an assuring touch.

For Mother Leonarda and for a number of Sisters at St. Ann's the final week of 1914 and the first day of 1915 were spent in the quiet and solitude of the annual retreat. Mother Leonarda needed to get away from the all-encompassing activity of work and business and the inevitable conflicts of life to take a quiet and penetrating look at God and herself. For the Religious Sister whose life and love are God and whose work for others must always be seen in this relationship and in this perspective, the eight day or six day retreat is a necessity.

Mother Leonarda was no exception. The year had seen her bustling around with activity, opening new missions, building *new* homes. It had also seen her in great physical pain for in September of 1914, she had to be hospitalized.

Sister Borromaea, who was at St. Bernard's Hospital in Chicago at the time, furthering her studies in nursing and particulary surgery, gives an account of her Superior's ordeal in a letter she, Sister Borromaea, wrote to Mother Theresia. The letter is succinctly to the point.

. . . Today I must send you an unexpected message.

About three weeks ago our good Sister Superior Leonarda noticed that she had a tumor the size of an egg on her right side. She had some pain and the swelling spread inward. The matter seemed a little suspicious and she showed it to the doctor. He thought the best thing would be to go the hospital and have it further examined. This she did.

Because it was cancer, our good Sister Leonarda was operated today at ten minutes to eleven. The whole right breast had to be removed. It was good that she did not know how dangerous the operation was. Because I have been here at the hospital for already three months with Sister Clementina learning more about nursing and surgery, especially in the treatment of festering wounds, I was present at the operation. I could not stand seeing it. It took longer than ten minutes before she fell asleep. The doctor made a biopsy; it was cancerous and ready for surgery. That was enough for me. I left the operating room and went to the Lord in the chapel. The operation was done in twenty-five minutes.

As I write this letter, Reverend Sister Superior's mind is clear again even though she has much pain, especially in her right arm. She will not be able to write soon. If you, dear Reverend Mother, so wish I will let you know about her condition . . . .[4]

Mother Leonarda herself does not mention her mastectomy at any time. There is no reference to it in any letter she wrote nor does she even mention it in the personal notes of her diary. No one hears of her sufferings or perhaps her anguish over the physical and psychological pain of such surgery—nor the aftermath of fear which somehow gnaws its way in after cancer surgery. The Sisters only knew what the

Chronicler wrote for September 14, 1914: "Mother Provincial Leonarda went to St. Bernard's Hospital in Chicago for a painful operation. She returned after two weeks. The Sisters thanked God."

That had been almost four months ago. After a short convalescence she was hard at work again. Now she was in the last days of her retreat. Once the retreat was over, she knew she would return to the problems of the new Provincial House being built. It would seem that the difficulties generated by the war now going on, the financial problems which always plagued the Sisters, and the dozens of hindrances of all kinds in obtaining materials for building, etc.—all this would have been enough to overcome. However, she found herself again in the middle of conflict between the Divine Word Superiors in Techny and the Generalate in Steyl. This time it was over a name for the new Provincial House.

When the Order of Holy Spirit Missionary Sisters was founded in Europe by Arnold Janssen, the Order became immediately recognized as primarily a foreign mission Order. There had already been a number of teaching Orders and nursing nuns, etc., but Father Arnold Janssen wanted a missionary Order of Sisters for foreign mission work. Their rightful title and duties as missionary Sisters was acknowledged by the Divine Word Fathers and Brothers as well as by the people in Europe. In time everyone knew the "Steyler" Sisters and knew they were missionary Sisters.

Not so in the United States, though. Somehow the missionary aspect of the Sisters was lost here, or perhaps it is more correct to say, it was generally not acknowledged by the Divine Word Fathers. Why? It is difficult to say, but very probably it was because from the very beginning the Divine Word Fathers in the States needed the Sisters not in the capacity of missionaries but as domestic help. How far some priests of the Society went in ignoring the Sisters is brought out in a letter Mother Leonarda wrote to Mother Theresia:

> *. . .Here I would like to mention something else. It is strange that the SVD do not mention us in their publications. They wrote an English biography about our founder under the title Father Arnold Janssen, Founder of the SVD. Not a word is said that he is our founder too. People who know us find that strange and ask us about it . . .The new mission calendars do not mention us at all. We asked Reverend Father Markert to announce our jubilee for December 8th. Later on we sent him a report on the celebration. The report was so shortened, dry and changed that we couldn't recognize it. The enclosed announcement shows how the SVD keep us from rising as a mission house . . . .*[5]

When the new Provincial House was being built, Mother Leonarda wrote the Generalate and asked for the following title for the new House: Sisters Servants of the Holy Ghost—Holy Ghost Mission House and Academy. Correspondence that flowed back and forth across the ocean show what a problem the name provoked.

> *Dear Reverend Mother, lately when Reverend Father Director General asked for the title of the new house, we answered that the following would be put over the entrance: 'Sisters Servants of the Holy Ghost' and above that, 'Holy Ghost Mission House and Academy.' The Generalate agreed on this title.*

Reverend Father Provincial wished that we omit 'Mission House' for two mission houses in one place would be confusing. I tried to persuade him that this would not be a problem but he did not give in and said he would write if we would use the title. This is why I thought it better to give in and to leave off 'Mission House' . . . .

(Letter of August 21, 1914)

The following answer came back to Mother Leonarda from the Generalate in Steyl:

You will see that we are not quite willing to give up the mission title. I would advise you to never change things that the Generalate approved—unless there is an urgent need—but to first ask or make other suggestions. It is not within your competency to change things that are approved from here, and consequently no one can take it amiss when you leave the matter undecided . . . .

(Sept. 13, 1914)

The very next day another letter was written to Mother Leonarda by Mother Theresia's secretary, Sister Raphaele. The letter comments on the yearly report submitted by Mother Leonarda, but the last paragraph is again about the title:

In a letter to Reverend Mother you mentioned the change of the title for the house. The Generalate did not like the title and decided that one of the following replace it:

Servants of the Holy Spirit, Mission Sisters' House, Holy Ghost Academy

or:

Holy Ghost Convent and Academy of the Mission Sisters, Servants of the Holy Spirit.

By no means may the word 'mission' be left out of the title. You yourself may see which of the titles sounds best in English. We like the last one best.

(Sept. 14, 1914)

In the next six months four more letters were exchanged. Finally Mother General Theresia herself wrote a forthright letter to the Reverend Superior General Nicholas Blum expressing the hope that the matter would have a favorable outcome.

Enclosed is Sister Superior Leonarda's letter for your examination. About a month ago, Rev. Father Regional (Techny) suggested to you, Rev. Father, that you give the new Sisters' Convent the name of 'Holy Ghost Institute' and to entirely omit the word 'mission'. We, however, did not agree with this. We asked you . . .to call it 'Holy Ghost Academy and Provincial House of the Mission Sisters, Servants of the Holy Spirit.' To this you consented. . . . Rev. Father Burgmer (Techny) objected to the word 'mission' and complained to you, Rev. Father.

Sister Superior is right when she says the words 'mission sisters' do not mean much in this country because of the many immigrant orders that call themselves this. However, there are no Sister Mission Houses, and as you can imagine, we would like to have this. I think it would be wonderful since the Society founded the first mission house in North America, and we would have the first Sisters' mission house. Our Reverend Founder also called our house here 'Sisters' Mission House' and up to this time, this title has not caused any confusion.

The enclosed notice is from the February issue of the Familienblatt. *Here you see that no one pays attention to our wishes and statements regarding the title of the provincial house. They simply publish a title that suppresses our mission endeavor and mission character and with which we cannot be satisfied. We ask you, Rev. Father Superior General, to step in and to guard the rights of our congregation . . . .*

(Steyl, Feb. 26, 1915)

Superior General Nicholas Blum answered her in a few days as follows:

I gladly give you permission to call the new house in Techny 'Sisters' Mission House' or 'Provincial House of the Servants of the Holy Spirit—Mission Sisters.' The title 'Mission House' is not appropriate. . . .Besides, it is also questionable whether a Sisters' Convent may simply call itself mission house because it implies first of all an institute for mission priests. Only 'Sisters' Mission House' is correct and justifiable . . . .

(Steyl, March 1, 1915)

Thus the matter was concluded, but the Sisters maintained their title of Missionary Sisters, emphasizing their principal work in the Church.

At the same time that she was trying to smooth out and settle the problem of a name for the new Provincial House and boarding school, Mother Leonarda was corresponding with Sister Mary Antonea in Dubuque, Iowa. The latter had introduced her to Dr. Schilling in New Hampton, Iowa, who had long cherished a dream for his little town.

The story begins several years earlier, in 1912 actually, on the morning of a violent rainstorm. The Franciscan Sisters who taught at St. Mary's Parish School in New Hampton were leaving the school and returning to their Motherhouse in Dubuque. Sister Mary Antonea, the music instructor, was greatly loved by the people of the parish. One of these, Dr. Schilling, whose son Bernard had been instructed by the nun, was very grateful to the Sisters. When he saw the storm deluging the town the morning of their departure, he went to the Sisters' convent and took them in his car to the train station since the Sisters had no other arrangements except to walk there. As they waited for the train to arrive, Sister Antonea in a sudden burst of gratitude exclaimed impulsively, "Doctor, if there is one thing in the world we can do for you at any time, please let me know."

Dr. Schilling, just as fervently and equally impulsive, replied, "Sister, if you can induce a community of Sisters to build and to conduct a hospital here in New Hampton, you will have discharged your fancied obligation in full."

And so it was. A dream was told, a promise made. The train came; the Sisters left, and several years went by; and it seemed the train station incident was forgotten.

Dr. Schilling had continued his search, but found himself at dead ends. He was about ready to abandon his dream, when on another bleak, dreary day, a duplicate of the train station day three years before, he received a letter he recognized immediately. It was from Sister Mary Antonea who wrote:

Enclosed you will find the letter which we received from Mother Leonarda (Provincial of the Missionary Sisters Servants of the Holy Ghost) in answer to the one that our Mother wrote to her with regard to the contemplated hospital. From its contents you will see that she wishes to hear from you. I hope that at last you will surely be able to get Sisters to take charge of the hospital and I wish you the best of success. I would be glad to hear all about it after you have made the arrangements. I am glad that I was of a little service to you as I certainly owe you a great deal for all you have done for me, and I feel I cannot repay you . . . .

(Dubuque, January 24, 1915)

Dr. Schilling immediately contacted Mother Leonarda. She replied that she would like to meet with representative citizens of the community at some near date. Even though she was still occupied with the building of the provincial house, she went with Sister Borromea on March 4, and met with a number of business and professional men of New Hampton in the parochial school building. The minutes of the meeting were very brief, but the accomplished results were great. A contract was signed wherein the Missionary Sisters Servants of the Holy Spirit agreed to establish, conduct, and maintain an adequate up to date hospital in New Hampton, Iowa, for a period of not less than twenty-five years provided the people of New Hampton give them approximately one fourth of the intitial cost of the building.

Permission had to be obtained from the Archbishop, the Most Reverend John J. Keane. For some reason, not expressly stated anywhere, the Archbishop was initially reluctant to give his permission. However, he did finally give his permission for the building.

The people of New Hampton responded generously and energetically. Societies, clubs, and individuals donated to the building fund. The people undertook furnishing the rooms and collecting necessities. It is to the credit and magnanimity of the people of New Hampton and the determination and hard work and faith in God of Mother Leonarda that St. Joseph's Hospital was finally built, furnished, dedicated, and officially opened on February 6, 1917. The first patient was a maternity case, and a lusty lunged boy filled the new hospital with the miracle of new life. Dr. Schilling's dream not only came true; it was already multiplying into a new dream of life and love.[6]

On July 7, 1937, just about two weeks after Mother Leonarda died, Mr. H. R. Worrall wrote the following article for the *New Hampton Tribune*.

> *We were surprised and shocked to read in your paper of July 1, of the death of Sister Leonarda at St. Joseph's Hospital. Your very short notice of her death made no mention of the fact that it was Sister Leonarda who gave the people of New Hampton this wonderful modern hospital. For the information of the many people who have come to your city in later years, and, who quite naturally think of the hospital and the weather as gifts of nature, may I offer some history?*
>
> *. . .During the year of 1916 the Hospital was built, and the opening was on February 6, 1917. Just two months later, on April 6, 1917, America entered the World War. With the excitement of war, and the subsequent sky-rocketing of prices of foodstuffs and all hospital supplies the responsibility on Sister Leonarda and her loyal and devout co-workers was appalling. When fuel for heating went up six hundred per cent, and a carload lasted only one week, a member of the Hospital Board suggested to Sister Leonarda that closing might be necessary. That good Sister replied: 'No, No, God's work never fails.'*

Following the World War, Iowa was deflated, land went down, and the banks all closed. . . .But St. Joseph's Hospital carried on, thanks to Sister Leonarda and her humble Sisters . . . .

It is impossible to pay a fitting tribute to such a life of sacrifice and service . . . .

The building of St. Joseph's Hospital in New Hampton seems to stand unique among the other building accomplishments of Mother Leonarda. There is a thread of serenity, a beautiful optimism permeating the establishment of this hospital. It was a quiet place, a place of repose; it was a place Mother Leonarda would go to when she sensed her end was near.

Yet, at this time, she still had years of work ahead. She courageously forged ahead building the new provincial house and the hospital in New Hampton between the years 1914 and 1917—a time of war when materials and manpower were limited, and when severe anxiety, worry, and concern troubled the hearts of just about everyone on both sides of the Atlantic. She went ahead as usual trusting in the Holy Spirit.

It was a bright sunny summer day, the nineteenth of June, 1915. Very early in the morning before the heat became too intense, a rather strange procession of horse drawn wagons, one car, and a number of Sisters carrying bags made its way along the road from St. Ann's Home to the new provincial house. It was moving day. Only a part of the community moved to the new home. Not all the Sisters could leave St. Ann's, of course. Forty-one Sisters remained at the Home to carry on the work there: ten of these Sisters worked in the seminary kitchen. However,

Mother Leonarda and her Council moved; Sister Gertrudis, the novice mistress, and her twenty-five novices and six postulants; the Sisters who were teaching and studying, and three Sisters to care for the work in the new convent.[7]

In the afternoon a thanksgiving service was held during which Father Burgmer, the SVD Provincial Superior, blessed the new home. Assisting him were the Rector of the Seminary, Father Aubry, and Father Gruhn. The service began with the beautiful hymn to the Holy Spirit, "Veni Creator Spiritus." As many times as Mother Leonarda had sung this hymn in the past, for the Sisters sang this hymn to the Holy Spirit at the very beginning of the day—it was their very first communal act of worship when they gathered for Morning Prayers,—now at the blessing of the new Convent each line held an even deeper and more personal meaning for her. Her whole being sang—"Come Creator Spirit—Qui diceris Paraclitus" —You who are called the Paraclete—my Advisor and Advocate—You the Most High's Gift to us, to me; You living Fountain ever burning with love—You my spiritual Solace—Comfort of my soul. Divine Spirit, light fires of love in our whole being—senses and soul—Keep from us any enemy and let peace fill this Home. Let all who dwell in this Convent Home be led by You along righteous paths—let them shun all evil. Through you let us come to a true knowledge of the Father and the Son now and forever.

As the procession slowly walked through the building, the Litany of All Saints was sung asking these special Friends of God to add their protection to the new Convent. The ceremony concluded with Mary's Canticle of Thanksgiving: "My soul magnifies the Lord!" Another milestone reached!

The new provincial house still needed much equipment. There was no bakery, no mangle in the laundry, and little furniture. For the time being the Sisters at St. Ann's simply added the new house to their work list. Baking and mangling had to be done at St. Ann's; then baked goods and laundry had to be loaded on Mr. Flanagan's wagon and driven to the new convent. It was not just time consuming but also more strenuous work for the Sisters who had just about enough already.

St. Ann's gave the new house a beautiful chalice for Mass and some statues for the chapel. Their generosity was soon compensated for by replacement gifts from the residents.

Sometimes Mr. Happ, who lived opposite the new provincial house and had been so generous to the Sisters, drove the Sisters back and forth to St. Ann's in his car.

The move to the new house coincided with the return of some of the Sisters from the South for retreat and studies. Since they were in the habit of going to St. Ann's when they came in from Chicago, that is where they went. The Sisters at St. Ann's had a good laugh when they saw the Sisters standing with their suitcases at the entrance. St. Ann's had been home to them for so long, it was a little difficult to change old habits. But they laughed, too, took their bags, and began walking up the road to their new home. The Sisters always walked the distance, about a mile, between the two houses unless they had supplies to carry. Now seventy years later this is somewhat difficult to visualize. Highway 43, Waukegan Road, is a very busy highway with traffic lights on the very corner where the Convent and Academy were built. Willow Road, which runs East and West, has become a much traveled four-lane highway connecting Expressways. But in 1915 and until the 1940's it was a very narrow dirt road with a car or wagon passing along it maybe twice a week at most. The girls of the Academy went sledding down Willow Road with no fear of any passing vehicle. Throughout those early years the road heard the laughter of students and nuns as they went on their hikes and picnics picking fresh apples off the trees which lined the Sisters' property along Willow Road. It was a time of peace "out in the country" as Americans called these as yet sparsely inhabited sections of land surrounding large cities. There was very little noise and no pollution, but a lot of fresh air and peace.

Soon after the Sisters took up residence in the new Convent, St. Ann's Home received a private telephone line which was connected with the new Convent. Heretofore, St. Ann's Home had the same telephone line as the Divine Word Seminary. This caused some embarrassing situations. All that was changed now as the seminary had a private line and St. Ann's had its own line. In time, of course, the necessity of each House having its own private line was recognized, and the Provincial House, too, got a private telephone line.

That year Family Feast was celebrated by the Sisters in St. Ann's and in the Provincial House at the same time. However, all the Sisters wanted to participate in some of the celebrations at the Central House, so it was arranged that half of the Sisters went to Holy Ghost Convent in the morning and half went there in the afternoon.

Having a separate Provincial House was something new, indeed, for the Sisters. The fact that most of the feastday celebrations and other matters concerning community life would be taken care of at the Provincial House was something the Sisters at St. Ann's would have to get used to.

At Christmas the Midnight Mass solemnities were celebrated at the Convent and not at St. Ann's. Some of the Sisters from St. Ann's were able to take part in the celebration. That year it was truly a white Christmas. A heavy snow had fallen, and the Sisters did not have an easy time walking in the snow and finding their way in the dark. Yet, to be able to take part in the inspirational Christmas procession—the young academy girls dressed as angels in long flowing white robes carrying the Christ Child on a gossamer cloud of silk and lace, and then the most Solemn Midnight Mass so rich in rites and symbolism; the rich flowing rhythm of the Gregorian Chant, and the ever lovely Christmas carols—all this more than repaid the Sisters for their walk in the snow and dark.

Before 1915 came to an end, the Sisters would lose another dear friend among the residents at St. Ann's —Mr. Sheringer. He was always doing favors for the Sisters and was always ready to help. In fact, his last act on earth was one of charity. He had gone to the Post Office at the Mission House to deliver some packages of altar breads which had been ordered for the next day. As he was returning he became suddenly very ill, so that a Sister and a student had to support him home. He rallied just long enough to receive the priest's blessing and anointing. By evening he had already gone to his Creator, and the

Sisters were left with another memory of a dear friend.

In Europe the war continued in full force. Very little news came to the Sisters regarding their families. Mail was not getting through, at least not for months at a time.

Adding to the already existing problems was the weather. The summer of 1916 was so oppressively hot that one day one hundred people fell victims to the heat in Chicago. Consequently, many people from Chicago sought respite from the stifling heat of the city in the cooler country air surrounding St. Ann's. At one time sixty such "city refugees" were at the Home in addition to the elderly residents. The work multiplied, and very shortly space ran out. Sisters from the Convent came to lend a helping hand.[8]

The heat didn't stop the politicians who gathered at Chicago for the Republican Convention and at St. Louis for the Democratic Convention. It was a time of confusion, a time of promises, a time of bitter criticism. In the end, though, Wilson was re-elected. And for the time being, at least, the United States continued its neutrality.

Over in Steyl, Holland, six professed Sisters and three postulants were preparing to cross the ocean to the United States. What courage these young women had—crossing an ocean that hid treacherous submarines beneath and warships on top! The Sisters left Holland on the *Rheindam* on Septembr 1. On both sides of the Atlantic the Sisters prayed earnestly for their safe journey. September had always been set aside in the Church as a month of the Angels, and the Sisters gave the Angels no peace until the nine

Sisters reached Hoboken safely on September 19.

It was the first Friday of April, 1917. Early in the day, before the interruptions started, Mother Leonarda sat at her desk trying to finish the Chapter conference she was preparing for that evening. In keeping with the times and with the special day of the month dedicated to the Sacred Heart of Jesus, she chose as her topic "Suffering."

She read her opening sentence: "We all know that suffering is hard, can be very hard. Nobody can deny the existence of suffering." Her thought was interrupted by a knock on the door. So it was beginning already, she thought, but she said, "Ave," the greeting to enter, and the Portress came in. "Sister Provincial," the Sister exclaimed in a rather excited tone, "Reverend Father Rector just called on the telephone to let us know that the United States has declared war against Germany. Now what will happen to us in this country?" the nun questioned with a stammer.

Mother Leonarda bent her head and murmured, "Thank you for coming to tell me, Sister. I don't know what will happen; I only know this is a time when we need faith and trust. We can only pray." The Portress left. Now the whole world was in a bloody war, Mother Leonarda thought. So many more lives lost—dear ones in Europe; friends in her new country. And just a few days ago she had read that the neutral countries still did not know what the real issue of the war was. Pope Benedict XV had tried to intervene, but his proposal was rejected. Neither side trusted him. Yet, two years later Wilson's Fourteen Points sounded very close to Benedict XV's proposal.[9]

The Foundress continued writing her conference: "Suffering on earth is a grace, and we are ungrateful if we depreciate the advantages it has for us. One should rather fear to be without suffering. These kinds of visitation should be made use of in the sense of the biblical talents. Our gratitude for graces of suffering manifests itself best in quiet selfless endurance for whatever afflictions God may have in store for us. Sufferings have an educative, a formative influence upon the soul, pointing unmistakably to noble and beautiful character traits. It is because souls are created according to the image and likeness of God that the Holy One from the cross exhorts us: 'Learn from me.' Fools we are if we so easily forget the truth while thinking: 'I have the biggest cross! Why just me? Why this cross? Why does nobody understand me? Why have I neither rest nor consolation? Why must I walk through life so misunderstood?' Tell me—Are you really suffering as much as your God and Master that you may say like Him: 'My God, my God, why have you forsaken me?' He on the cross was indeed without consolation. You always have had one to console you—Him, God Himself. . . .What shall be our surprise when once the eternal unmistakable truth will dawn upon us that we have not so much glorified God through ability and success as through our acceptance of suffering and the cross . . . ."[10]

She put down her pen, closed her eyes and smiled in a way that said: "I can tell all this to the Sisters, try to encourage them, but in the end it is each individual soul's response to grace, and it is only in the power of each person to choose to accept the reality of the day to day sufferings or not to accept them. Suffering is, indeed, difficult to bear and difficult to understand."

Before the year ended, Mother Leonarda had not only opened St. Joseph's Hospital in New Hampton but had also sent three Sisters to take over the kitchen in Kenrick Seminary, St. Louis, Missouri. She had wanted to get into the St. Louis area to open a retreat house, but this could not be done immediately. Eventually, she did open Little Flower Retreat House, which in time, because of financial needs, had to open its doors to take in the elderly also.

During the war years, both summer and winter brought severe weather. In the summer there was the intense heat forcing people to look for cooler spots in the country. In the winter there was extreme cold. The oldest residents at St. Ann's kept saying they could not remember a colder winter. Snow lay on the ground five to six feet high. Postal and train services were stopped for quite some time. For the first time since they started working in the seminary kitchen, the Sisters were unable to make it even across the road and had to spend the night away from their convent home. Everyone felt the rigors of the weather that winter.

For the sick and infirm the winter was especially difficult. On Christmas Day, 1917, Sister Alderica, a young Sister died. The new year had hardly begun when Sister Ottonia, another young Sister, died in Little Rock; and while the Sisters were yet bereaving her loss, Sister Redemptora, a young nun of twenty-four years, died. She was the sister of Father Weyland, a Divine Word priest.

Each loss was a poignant pain for Mother Leonarda. She had a sensitivity that cried out silently in her soul.

However, the time of sadness and trial was not yet over. Death would claim more victims in the following months. From war-besieged Europe, the Spanish influenza epidemic spread to the United States and traveled the length and breadth of the country, killing thousands. By the beginning of another year, it had already found its way to St. Ann's and some residents died from it. The Sisters, sometimes eight to ten at a time, were sent to the infirmary. One strange factor of this flu was that it seemed to hit the strong and hearty Sisters; the weaker, seemingly sicker Sisters, were not flu victims. During this time a skeleton crew was in operation at St. Ann's. Around the world the flu epidemic took an estimated five to twenty million persons.[11] The war had claimed an estimated six to seven million soldiers.

When the Armistice was signed on November 11, 1918, the war was over; but people the world over were still suffering and burying their dead as the flu epidemic raged on.

For the Sisters, the new year seemed to have as sad a beginning as the whole of the year just passed. Hardly two months had gone by when death claimed another young Sister. Sister Irmengardis had spent practically her whole religious life sick. As her end drew near, Mother Leonarda and the chaplain and a few Sisters circled her bed and the dying Sister pronounced her perpetual vows. It was a happy moment, but very brief for she died soon after.[12]

Mother Leonarda was, as always, traveling back and forth to the various stations, seeing to the Sisters' needs, the circumstances under which they worked, listening to them, helping them in whatever way she could.

On March 12, she took time with the Sisters of the whole province to celebrate a very special day in the Congregation. It was the twenty-fifth anniversary of the taking of Vows—the Silver Jubilee—of Mother Theresia, Sister Gregoria, Sister Andrea, and Sister Scholastica. This was the first event of its kind in the history of the Congregation, and although the celebrating Sisters were all stationed in the Motherhouse in Steyl, Holland, the Holy Spirit Missionary Sisters over the world celebrated this unique occasion with them.

Eighteen years had passed since Mother Leonarda came to the United States and set up beginnings in a small frame house in Shermerville. Now the Holy Spirit Missionary Sisters were totally independent although Father Auf der Heide was still the Father Director in Steyl until he laid down his office in 1922. In the United States, the Sisters had established St. Ann's Home, a hospital in Watertown, Wisconsin, and one in New Hampton, Iowa; five schools thus far in the South with plans to open at least two more schools; the Sisters were working in seminary kitchens in Techny, Girard, and Missouri, and with the Redemptorists in Watertown. They were teaching at St. Norbert's School in Techny, and they were conducting Holy Ghost Academy.

It was June, 1919, and a tense feeling of expectancy pervaded the air. The time of appointments was at hand, and the Sisters wondered whether they would continue to have Mother Leonarda as their Provincial Superior.

On June 28, Mother Leonarda assembled the Sisters in the morning, and in a clear, matter-of-fact voice read the following appointments:

Sister Willibalda—Provincial Superior
Sister Irenaea—Assistant Provincial
Sister Leonarda—Superior of St. Ann's Home

The Provincial Council was made up of the above three Sisters and Sister Isidora and Sister Dominica. At St. Ann's Sister Borromaea was the Assistant Superior.

That evening the Sisters assembled in the conference room to listen to Mother Leonarda's last Chapter discourse. She began with a quote from Christ Himself when He exhorted His disciples just before His agony in the garden on the eve of His death: "Watch and pray that you enter not into temptation."

She was a mother leaving her children when duty called elsewhere, and she wanted to leave them with all the help she could possibly give them. There was one fear she had—that her Sisters weighed down by the overwhelming amount of work under which she knew they lived day after day would let that work become an obsession and supersede their real reason for being a Holy Spirit Missionary Sister, namely self-sanctification and the salvation of souls.

She told them, therefore, "that a missionary's life was full, always working with people. However, such a busy, active life does not have to be a danger to the religious life, rather it offers occasions for greater merit; indeed, there is truth in the fact that some of the best Religious are those who did the most work, for they were constantly coming closer to God in their service of others."

Mother Leonarda goes on to enumerate what the

Religious Sister must be aware of. She asks: "Where then does the trouble lie? First, it is in the seemingly harmless absence from the religious exercises ever so often and the ever so slight deviation, now and then, from the Order of the Day; in other words, the lack of genuine fervor and zeal.

"A busy Religious must, above all, be extraordinarily zealous in her spiritual exercises. It is from her communion with God that she receives the strength for greater work. In a life so demanding in sacrifice so many times a day, the Religious needs to be closely bound to her community and to her God, and she must be always aware of the Good Intention; otherwise she may quickly succumb to weakness and fulfill her duties as a simple employee, not a Missionary Sister Servant of the Holy Spirit.

"Another evil that may tempt the busy Religious is depression, melancholy. Depression cripples the strength of the Sister and prevents the successful completion of work. Depression also shows suspicion and distrust of God Himself. It is an insidious fault, for while the Sister continues to work in the service of God, she is at the same time questioning God's love. On the other side of the spectrum is the Religious who works enthusiastically and tenaciously, seemingly full of zeal, and yet she works alone, isolated from obedience, simply ignoring higher authority and relying solely on herself. Such a Sister works hard but with little merit for she works for own good and esteem.

"Next, the Religious must always work remembering she belongs to a community. She is a part of that community. She needs the strength of the community.

"And lastly, the Religious must always strive for perfect chastity. She cannot become a slave to creatures. Her eyes, her thoughts must be ever on the Lord."

She completed her exhortation and closed with a few words of farewell. "I hope that each one of you," she continued, "will welcome your new Superior in the true spirit of fellowship and as a representative of God. Pray daily for your Superiors.

"I thank you now at this time for the trust you placed in me through the years, and I especially thank the older Sisters for all the sacrifices they had to endure in those early years. The Holy Spirit who sees all will reward you.

"I also beg you to forgive me for the failures for which I was responsible during my administration. I know that I was probably a stumbling block for some. God the Holy Spirit is our Judge. He knows the reason why things happen. It is for all of us now to strive zealously to be genuine Missionary Sisters Servants of the Holy Spirit so that our Founder's motto may be fulfilled in us and through us: 'May the Heart of Jesus live in the hearts of all people.' God the Holy Spirit bless you."[13]

Next day at noon, Mother Leonarda in that self-possessed manner, so much a part of her, escorted the new Provincial Superior and her Council to their places. This was the way it worked in the convent. Another would continue the work she had begun, and even though she may have wished to see other works completed, other ideas put into operation, or perhaps to enjoy for a few more years at least the relatively quiet atmosphere of the Provincial House in comparison with the constant bustle of St. Ann's, this was not to be.

Quietly the following morning, very early before the Sisters were even awake, Mother Leonarda left Holy Ghost Convent and arrived at St. Ann's before Mass began. Only the new Provincial Superior knew of her leaving. Mother Leonarda wanted no fanfare as a farewell or as a welcome. But there was one very happy community of Sisters, and no matter how quietly Mother Leonarda may have wanted to return to St. Ann's, the secret leaked out, and both Sisters and residents at St. Ann's were at the Entrance at that early hour to greet Mother Leonarda and welcome her with an enthusiasm and joy that said: "We love you!"[14]

1. Link, S. & William B. Cotton, *American Epoch, A History of the United States Since the 1890's* (New York: Alfred A. Knopf), pp. 174 ff.

2. Link, p. 175.

3. Link, p. 175 ff.

4. Letter of Sister Borromaea to M. Theresia (September 16, 1914).

5. Letter of Mother Leonarda to M. Theresia (February 3, 1915).

6. Chronicle of St. Joseph's Hospital, New Hampton.

7. Chronicle of St. Ann's Home.

8. Chronicle of St. Ann's Home.

9. Murphy, Francis, *The Papacy Today*, New York: Macmillan Publishing Co., 1981, p. 35 ff.

10. Chapter Conference of Mother Leonarda (1911-1914).

11. 1984 Almanac, p. 297.

12. Chronicle of St. Ann's Home.

13. Mother Leonarda's Final Chapter (June, 1919).

14. Chronicle of St. Ann's Home.

Chapter Eleven

. . . The deepest and essential sign of our Congregation is love of God made visible in an intensive and all-embracing love of neighbor. To persevere in carrying out this idea, one must lead a life of joyous fidelity . . . . The missionary's spirituality is a hidden wisdom that knows the greatness of the worldwide task of establishing the Church but recognizes in humble simplicity the worth of one's own insignificant personal contribution despite the exertion of all one's bodily and spiritual powers.

—Diamond Jubilee Book of the S.Sp.S.

She took up her duties at St. Ann's, and somehow it seemed as if it were just a continuation of what she had been doing all the time. Her four-year interval at the new Provincial House had come and gone—so very fast.

Actually, it hardly seemed anything had changed, even in the world at large, although the War was over and there was comparative peace. Pope Benedict XV, so thoroughly disregarded by both sides during the War because of his condemnation of the war and his refusal to take sides, was still Pope in Rome. Only the future would reveal the wisdom of his position. Now the very year Mother Leonarda was transferred to St. Ann's, Benedict XV released to the world one of the most important documents of his pontificate, the great missionary encyclical *Maximum Illud,* called "the charter of the Catholic missionary movement of this century." It contained three fundamental principles: promotion of a native clergy; renunciation of all nationalistic attitudes; and respect for the civilization of the mission country."[1] Mother Leonarda would time and again re-iterate in her talks to the Sisters the importance of these very points for a missionary Sister.

In the United States, Wilson was still president, but the 1920 election would put Warren Harding in the presidency. The latter died in office three years later leaving a trail of scandals and corruption in politics and government. Vice-president Calvin Coolidge, a conservative, taciturn, and narrow-minded man took the oath of office as President and was re-elected the following year.

Economically, the period of the twenties had a beginning of prosperity, a period of slight depression, and then peaked to perhaps one of the best periods of prosperity the country had known. The "roaring twenties" it was called.[2]

But Mother Leonarda began her work at St. Ann's without even the slightest hint of any prosperity. There were more needs than money to take care of the needs.

Soon she was again helping where she could;

residents were coming to her with their problems and their needs; retreatants were coming in the hundreds, in fact, six hundred thirty-one retreatants came that first year forcing the Sisters again to seek sleeping quarters in the attic; summer visitors and guests increased; indeed, the Sisters knew that Mother Leonarda was once again the soul of the House. Since she was still a member of the Provincial Council, she continued to be the guiding spirit of the Province as well.

At the time when she had moved into the Provincial House four years ago, all the bookkeeping had gone along with her, and business matters for the Home and for the Convent and Academy were taken care of at Holy Ghost Convent. Now, however, a change was made. St. Ann's Home would now take care of its own business matters, and thus Sister Eucharista was appointed procurator at St. Ann's Home.

There were other changes and additions made at St. Ann's too. Ever since those first early years at St. Ann's when Mother Leonarda had to emphasize time and again that elderly people suffering from severe senility (senile dementia) could not be accepted at St. Ann's since the Home lacked the proper facilities for treating such people, she, nevertheless, continued to see the needs for making such facilities available. At last it was possible. A large section of the first floor was converted into living quarters for senile women—those mentally incapable of taking care of themselves. They had their private rooms and dining room in this section, and were cared for by a select number of Sisters. As with the rest of St. Ann's Home, this section, too, was always filled, and a much larger area could have been utilized. However, it was just four years after Mother Leonarda's death that the Holy Spirit Missionary Sisters were finally able to add an annex to St. Ann's. It was a cheerful looking building providing security, loving nursing care, and the conveniences and safeguards needed for these elderly women who, in addition to the burdens of age, were severely mentally handicapped with senility or severe nervous disorders. Mother Leonarda would have been happy to see this structure built. She had seen the ravages of mental affliction from her earliest years in this country, and her heart spilled over in love for those suffering from such a dreaded affliction.

For quite some time donations had been coming in to St. Ann's for the erection of a Lourdes Grotto on the grounds in gratitude for Mary's protection of the American soldiers during the war. Work on the Grotto began in October, was delayed somewhat during the winter months, but finally completed and dedicated in May, 1920. How many people over the years—Sisters, residents, retreatants, visitors—stopped a moment before Mary to pray and felt the peace of Lourdes in their hearts!

The feast of Corpus Christi that year fell on June 6, and five thousand people assembled in Techny to take part in the beautiful Eurcharistic procession. What a manifestation of pomp, elegance, devotion, reverence, and simple piety!

But behind the scenes the Sisters were busy as usual preparing dinner for the visitors. The Sisters in the seminary kitchen, of course, prepared dinner for the people who came there, but the overflow of three hundred twenty guests were given dinner and supper at St. Ann's. By 1920, the Corpus Christi procession and the meals and socializing had already become tradition. People looked forward to the day.

At the end of October, the Divine Word Fathers lost their Superior General. Reverend Nicholas Blum died on October 29. His successor was Father William Gier, elected in 1921. He was the brother of Sister Irenaea, who was the Assistant Provincial in Techny at the time.

At St. Ann's it seemed that for a while there were new surprises almost every day. One day as the Sisters were hurrying from their various places of duty to the chapel for the afternoon devotions, they were momentarily taken aback, and in the next instant, had big smiles as they saw standing on guard a short distance from the chapel a large imposing statue of St. Michael the Archangel with drawn sword and shining armor seeming to proclaim to everyone "Who Is Like God!"

Another gift came to the Sisters at St. Ann's around Easter. A huge box arrived and as it was opened it revealed parts of a large grandfather clock which chimed every quarter hour and showed the various phases of the moon. A nickel plate on the front of the clock bore the inscription "To the Good Sisters of St. Ann's Home in Memory of Mr. R. C. Gannon, 1921". Mr. Gannon had died unexpectedly some months before. Now he had the Sisters remembering him every quarter hour with a little prayer and surely a smile. He had been another of St. Ann's loyal friends.

Everything seemed to have settled down to a normal routine at St. Ann's when suddenly the sameness was shattered. During the night of May 20 to 21, thieves broke into St. Ann's kitchen through a window and disposed of a cake and a large amount of pastry, apples, and pears. It seemed that these thieves were just hungry for some sweets, but not so. They left the kitchen by way of the door and took with them on their way out the key which was fastened inside the door on an iron chain. Two days later, two harnesses disappeared from the barn. Then the thief or thieves went to the seminary across the street and took the best horse from the barn. An interval of a few days, and the thief was back at St. Ann's where he took a horse-drawn wagon.

For fourteen days the thief helped himself to quite a bit of movable property of the three Houses: Holy Ghost Convent, St. Ann's, and the SVD Mission House. From the convent he stole, in addition to other things, fifty chickens, killing them on the spot.

Night watches had been set up in all three places, but with little success. On the night of June 10-11, the farmers of the area made a cooperative effort to catch the thief, and they did. He was taken into custody, was tried in court, and sentenced to the State prison. It seems that burglarizing had been quite a habit with him.[3]

This was not the only time the Sisters were burglarized. At another time, some years later, the Sisters' car was stolen and was tracked down months later in Michigan—dirty, in need of repair, and perhaps in need of a new blessing for the Sisters were told the thief had used it in several robberies. The thief, however, as far as the Sisters knew, was never apprehended.[4]

But with the misfortune somewhere there would be a "silver lining", and so it was. One of the greatest joys that came to Mother Leonarda and to all the Sisters in the United States Province occurred in October 1921. Sister Clara, Sister Frances, Sister Matricia, and Sister Dolorosia received mission appointments for New Guinea. It was a day longed for by each Sister, and now the first American Sisters would be leaving for the island of New Guinea. Even the four happy missionaries could not have been happier than Mother Leonarda. All these years she had worked and struggled to keep the missionary aspect of the Congregation ever in the forefront. The missionary appointments and the reception of the mission cross, the coming mission departure were just the "shot in the arm" the Sisters needed to put them back again in the missionary spirit of their vocation.

The four Sisters left the United States in December, and as the future ordained, they never saw their country again, although they were to experience American kindness, generosity, and charity in a way they could never have imagined on that day in 1921 when they left their country.

During the Second World War on the South Pacific front when the Japanese invaded New Guinea, the American Sisters were put on a Japanese warship which was badly strafed by American air men. The ship carried no signs to inform "the enemy" that prisoners of war were on the ship. Sister Dolorosia lost her life; others were wounded, and all suffered physical and mental anguish.

When the Americans subdued the Japanese, the American marines rescued the Sisters who had been put ashore in some abandoned area. The joy was overwhelming on the part of the missionaries, and the military men were astounded at the heroism and quiet, prayerful acceptance of the almost total destruction of a mission that had taken more than forty years to build and the tragic loss of their friends and fellow Sisters.[5]

But this was in the future. All this Mother Leonarda could not have known now as she rejoiced with her Sisters in this first mission departure celebration.

Mother Theresia was finishing her twelfth year in office as the Mother General, and a time of change and elections was coming up. In December, the Sisters in the United States held a Provincial Chapter, electing delegates to the General Chapter in Steyl which was to take place in the spring of 1922. Mother Leonarda and Sister Irenea were elected to attend the Chapter in Steyl.

Before she left for the meeting, however, Mother Leonarda had a sad experience. On a cold February morning one of the elderly residents at St. Ann's took a brisk walk into the nearby woods. He found Lucy Gaesfeld lying in her small house next to a cold stove and only half conscious. Mother Leonarda immediately sent two Sisters to bring the 82 year old Lucy to the Home, but the sick woman was adamant about staying in her home, the very same home she had lived in for over fifty years. Mother Leonarda had asked Lucy repeatedly during the last years to come and live at St. Ann's where she could get the care she needed at her age. Lucy could not leave her little home and the plot of land she owned for so long and always refused Mother Leonarda's offer. The Sisters could do little more for her now except to try to make her warm and comfortable and give her something to eat. People in the neighborhood were asked for information regarding Lucy's relatives, and they told the Sisters that she had some distant relatives in Chicago. They were called immediately and came the next morning. A doctor was called, but he said he could do nothing for her anymore. A nearby neighbor, Mrs. Felderer, offered to take in Lucy Gaesfeld, but two days later Lucy died. She, who had befriended the Sisters when they came to Shermerville and had helped wherever she could, became a solitary hermit in her later years, seemingly abandoning even the faith she had embraced shortly after the Sisters came. However, she was given the Last Anointing of the Church and a burial from the Church. She had been that friend in need in 1901, and she would not be forgotten by the community of Sisters she had helped and befriended.[6]

On the first Sunday of April, 1922, a departure celebration was held at St. Ann's Home for the delegates going to Steyl. The girls of the Academy gave one of their plays—*St. Elizabeth of Hungary*.

The departure was almost a repeat of her leave-taking in 1909. Again, the Sisters feared their Mother would not return. Everyone knew that her health had been deteriorating and maybe the General Council would decide to keep her in Steyl. It was a sad occasion. The community of Sisters who assembled at the entrance at 8 A.M. on Wednesday, April 5, was not a happy one. Mother Leonarda went to each Sister again and shook her hand, and as always, the pressure of her hand was the same. If she loved one more than another, or was more grateful to one than to another, and, human as she was, this would not have been unusual or unfair,—she did not externalize that feeling. Each one felt love in the handshake, and that is what counted.

The General Chapter opened in Steyl on May 1, and on the third a cablegram went to the various missions around the world with the word: "Columba." The newly elected Mother General was Mother Columba, a kind mother, indeed.

During the time of the Chapter in Steyl, Mother Leonarda came to a milestone in her life as a missionary Sister. On June 13, she celebrated twenty-five years as a Holy Spirit Missionary Sister. Since she was the first Sister from the North American province to celebrate a Silver Jubilee, the community celebration in the Steyl Motherhouse was a bit more elaborate than usual.

At St. Ann's the Sisters celebrated Sister Borromaea's twenty-fifth Jubilee on the same day and regretted that Mother Leonarda was not with them. They would celebrate hers later.

The General Chapter closed on July 17, and a week later Sister Irenaea left with four new Sisters for the ocean voyage back to the United States. Mother Leonarda did not go along. As on the previous occasion when this happened, the Sisters were greatly distressed thinking that they surely lost her this time.

She was gone four months and returned August 7 with her re-appointment as Superior of St. Ann's Home for another three years.

One of her reasons for staying in Steyl so long was to discuss a number of problems with the Generalate; one of these was future building possibilities for St. Ann's. In a letter of October 1, 1921, she had written to Mother Theresia:

The house is completely filled.... There are not

enough homes for the present number of elderly people.

She had recognized this need to enlarge St. Ann's for some time and, possibly, her four months in the Motherhouse gave her an opportunity to lay the matter before the General Council first hand.

There was rejoicing among the Sisters and residents when the Sisters received the good news that they had permission to build a new wing accommodating a large chapel, a Sisters' department, and four dining rooms for the residents. The large steam-shovels arrived at the beginning of May, and workers began digging the foundation.

Mother Leonarda was always interested in the people in her care—her Sisters and the residents. She showed this same interest in people who came to visit and in the Sisters' relatives. To her St. Ann's was the people. And among the residents who came to St. Ann's there were some beautiful people.

For instance, there was Mrs. Jennie Rogers, who came to the Home in October, 1922. All her life she had belonged to the Episcopalian Church, but her brother, a convert to Catholicism for some years, had asked that she be taken in at St. Ann's. In time she asked to be instructed in the Faith and her date of Baptism was set for Easter. But severe illness intervened, and on February 25, death seemed imminent. She was, therefore, baptized, received the Last Anointing, and for the first time received Holy Communion. She was a very happy 82 year old. She rallied four more days, receiving Holy Communion each day, and was fully conscious up to the moment of her death.

There was another special person—a woman who was 103 years old when she came to St. Ann's in May,

1923. For her years, she still looked strong and healthy; she was in full possession of her faculties, had a clear memory for the present as well as for the past and for the very far back. She did not need glasses. She did, however, need her pipe. Every day at a definite time she had to smoke her pipe. She was a good-natured and courteous soul, full of good feeling towards everyone. She had said once that she could not remember ever having given a harsh word to anyone.

And then there was Mr. Collins. For thirteen years he had suffered from crippling arthritis until now there was not a single limb he could move. He was absolutely helpless and depended on the help of others for everything. His intellect was extremely clear, sharp, and penetrating. Everybody felt drawn to him. He never spoke of himself or his sufferings, and if someone began pitying him, he would cleverly turn the conversation to the Savior or the missions or the needs of the Church. No one heard a complaint from him. When penumonia finally overtook him and increased the pains that racked his poor body, he only whispered praises of God. Fully conscious to the end, he welcomed death with a smile. At his funeral Father Reichelt, who had the funeral Mass and services and who had been Mr. Collins' confessor for years, said: "I have known this man inside and out . . . . One should not mourn over the death of a Saint. May good Mr. Collins now in heaven pray for us."

St. Ann's had been blessed with these residents. A few such noble souls compensated for the troubles and problems the Sisters may have experienced elsewhere in their work. To have known just one person of such heroic spirituality as Mr. Collins was to have had the gift of a lifetime.

In June of 1923 Mother General Columba came to the United States to begin her visitation of the province. She was true to her name—the dove of peace—and wherever she went the Sisters loved her. In fact, on her first visit to St. Ann's she won the hearts of all, recognizing names immediately, and even remembering some family names. She was also a fond and capable musician, and upon Mother Leonarda's request, took over the directing of the choir on July 26, the Feast of St. Ann.

Mother Columba had as her companion Sister Sixta, but she also brought along four new Sisters for the United States mission. Sister Sixta was the sister of Sister Fabiola, who had come to the United States as a postulant. During her stay here, Sister Sixta gave instructions to the Sisters in choral work. She was well versed in music and was a writer. One of her later works was the life of Mother Theresia—*Gottes Kraft in Schwachen Haenden*.

The Mother General stayed in the United States until November, and because it was her wish that no departure ceremony be held, she left after the evening meal, shaking the Sisters' hands and waving goodbye. It was November 20. She would not leave the country immediately, though. First she would stop in Girard, Pennsylvania, and then in Hyattsville, Maryland, and leave from New York on December 8.

During the time of Mother Columba's visitation, work on the new wing for St. Ann's had been growing fast, but keeping pace with the builders was the ever rising financial debt. Mother Leonarda, as always, sought God's help and her friends' help. The residents and benefactors came up with various ideas for raising money. One resident gave her a diamond ring; another one gave a complete set of silverware; and another resident gave a surprise trunk with the directions that the contents of the trunk should be raffled off. Benefactors helped with raffle tickets. People were interested in St. Ann's and saw the need of the new wing. Their work was a definite financial help to the Sisters.

The new wing was finally completed in April, 1924. There were now two large dining rooms for men and women, a small dining room for the workingmen who took care of the maintenance; a smoking room for the men, and a recreation room for the women. Most of the first floor was now occupied by the Sisters—the cloister area; and on the second floor was a chapel, two stories high, with a sacristy.

It was this year, too, that St. Ann's came into possession of its very own car. One of the workmen, Albin Ostman, generously placed his car at the disposal of the Sisters, and then through sale, it became the property of St. Ann's Home. No more horse and wagon to get them to the Techny station! They now had a car! What a luxury!

With her usual energy and determination, Mother Leonarda had been going on as was her wont—helping here, helping there over and above her administration work and her work as the Superior of a large group of Sisters. She was now fifty years old, and the effort expended was greater. In the early months of the year, the Sisters noticed that their Superior was getting weaker and weaker. They became alarmed at how tired she looked and what a chore even walking was. Finally, she summoned whatever strength she had to travel to St. Joseph's Hospital in New Hampton to find medical help. She stayed at the hospital for ten days and received some relief and help to strengthen her. However, she probably gave more than she received. Writing about this occasion, a Sister at New Hampton at the time writes: "The Sisters considered her presence among them at that time as a special blessing of our Savior as they were going through some severe trials."[7]

She came back to St. Ann's feeling somewhat better. Yet, she was not better, and the following months she suffered quietly trying to do what she had to do and be what she had to be while suffering pain and extreme fatigue.

During the year Mother Columba wrote her to ease off a bit, for she, too, was worried about the Superior's failing health. Mother Leonarda's answer to this letter explains her state of health.

> *At present I am sitting in my room recuperating from tonsil surgery. I went in the hospital Monday, September 10, and the next day, I came home. The surgery is healing well. The doctor stitched it to stop the bleeding. The Sisters gave me very good care and today I can swallow pretty well except solid food. My tongue is swollen. The doctor said the tonsils were full of pus and that hindered my hearing. Lately I had a hard time hearing, and when the doctor checked my ears he found the eardrum swollen and infected. This is why I decided to go through the operation. Maybe the pus was also the reason for my not feeling well last February. I hope all will be well in the future.*

She goes on with the next paragraph showing that just as the situation was in 1901, so it was in 1924—and work grew almost spontaneously, so it seemed, but the number of Sisters grew only by one's and two's.

> *You say that I should take care of myself. Yes, that is easily said. If we do not have enough Sisters, it isn't possible. We got one Sister last year and 30-40 more people to care for. This is overlooked as well as the added work due to the addition, the cloister part. We have no one to do the work. Our Sisters have a lot to do and have no substitutes. Sister Hermana was also sick for two weeks and others had to do her work. You see, the situation is such that it does not allow for care of oneself. We have many more rooms occupied and this demands that another Sister be in the home . . .*[8]

It was true. Work was almost always overwhelming. And then when misfortune fell it was doubly so. Once again in May, fire destroyed a part of the Sisters' property. This time it was not in the Home, for which everyone was grateful, but still it was a loss. The petroleum stove in the chicken house exploded during the night and sent flames shooting out high in the air. Five men passing in their car saw the flames, immediately stopped, and offered their assistance to the Sisters and the workman from the Home who were already there. By means of a makeshift leather pipe, water was conducted from the house, and the fire was finally extinguished but with a total loss of the chicken house, 140 baby chicks, and the chickens on the roosts. Yet, there was gratitude, too, that the fire was contained and did not do further damage.

Although she was Superior of St. Ann's Home, Mother Leonarda was still the one who cared for the educational growth of the Sisters, the improvement in teaching, and the constant upward climb, intellectually, spiritually, psychologically of the teachers in the province. Hence for the summer of 1924, she organized an intensive six-week summer course for the Sisters to be given by a priest of the Society of Jesus. The Sisters coming in from the Southern stations, tired after a year of work, exhausted by the heat of a sub-tropical climate, wanted nothing else but a few weeks of rest, just a little vacation before they had to go back and start another year of teaching in conditions that certainly did not ease their work load. Their work was among the poor, for the poor, and they themselves lived in poverty conditions for the most part. It was not an easy life, and a couple weeks' vacation would not have been extravagance.

What the Sisters meant by vacation, however, must not be misunderstood. Vacation did not mean time to travel, go sight seeing, just sit and take it easy, etc. Not at all! It was several decades later that the Holy Spirit Missionary Sisters in Techny had a little more freedom in choosing a two weeks' vacation. It came about after Vatican Council II when certain changes were made in the Church at large and in Religious Orders. One of these changes was to recognize that Religious Sisters, too, like all people who work for their living, will greatly benefit from a relaxing vacation every year.

But while Mother Leonarda still lived, vacation simply meant no teaching. It usually meant a change in work—spending some weeks in the kitchen helping out; working in the garden; working with the housecleaning crew. So when the Sisters wanted a vacation what they meant was a rest from books and the demands of the classroom.

This summer, before they all had had a chance to

say hello to each other—the various stations arrived a few days apart—here was dear Mother Leonarda her smiling self introducing them to a Jesuit who was to give them a course, and before they knew it, they were so wrapped up in books, research work in the library, writing papers, that all thought of vacation was gone. Six weeks passed in a flash. It was over and they had grown in knowledge, and if that knowledge would be used to better themselves and others they were the wiser. Yet, they still must have wished for a vacation. It was very human.

Was Mother Leonarda unfeeling in her demands of the Sisters? On the surface it seems a bit hard. But actually there was little choice. To keep the community's schools academically sound institutions, approved by State and local authorities, she had to have qualified teachers. To have qualified teachers she had to insist that they continue taking courses, working toward degrees, and becoming accredited in their fields of teaching. Hence there was little that could be done except to keep them going on to universities during the summer and giving summer courses in Techny to accommodate a larger number of Sisters.

Also a good two-thirds of her Sisters in schools had come from Germany. For many the language, the customs, the country, the people were still new—really unknown to them. They needed every bit of education they could get to acquire the necessary knowledge of their subject and the people they taught. To have taken courses in Germany was not enough, for a person cannot translate knowledge in a classroom; she has to impart it and share it, and for that the person needed a definite feel for the language and history of the people. The Germans themselves had a word for it, "sprachgefuehl."

That is why Mother Leonarda never relaxed her position regarding the thorough education of her Sisters. That it was also a demanding life for the Sisters cannot be doubted. For the Sisters from Germany, it was their destiny to be pioneers, having to accept with everything else the necessary adjustments and sacrifices of pioneers. For the native American Sisters, it was also a matter of being a pioneer, adjusting to a community with a greater German cultural bent than American in its early years. Patience, forbearance, humility were needed on both sides, and Mother Leonarda was wise enough to know that a sound and well-rounded education would do as much for the Sisters in its way—leading to understanding—as a powerful Sunday sermon or an inspirational Chapter conference.

In these early years, too, there were very few Sisters who could be spared from community service in order to spend full time studying. Most of the Sisters earned their degrees by taking courses on Saturday and in the summer.

In the period after the First World War, there was nationwide an increase of women going in for higher education because there were now more women teachers than men teachers. Men were now going into fields affording them better pay to support their families. Although teachers' salaries rose somewhat after the War, the teacher's salary fell far below that of other fields requiring a similar amount of training. Because women now predominated the field, it was harder for the teaching profession to acquire the status of other fields. The reason? Historians and economists may give any number of reasons. However, basically it was, as it still is to some extent, a pure case of a narrow, unjust attitude toward women and their mental acumen. One aspect of a profession, however, did evolve—special graduate education.[9]

And Mother Leonarda was right up there in front sending her Sisters on to special graduate fields—in teaching, nursing, music, art, home economics—to fit into a new evolving American society in which women were beginning to make their mark.

The highlight of the summer of 1924 was another mission departure celebration. Sister Alvina and Sister Lima were departing for China; Sister Adalrica was going to New Guinea; and Sister Marian was missioned to the Philippines.

The departure celebration was held in the Divine Word Mission House for all the priests, Brothers, and Sisters who were leaving Techny for the Far East. It was September 18. Present for the celebration was His Eminence Cardinal Mundelein of Chicago, who later in the day paid a special visit to Holy Ghost Convent. He expressed his joy at the mission zeal shown by both Orders. His visit, his concern, and appreciation for what the Sisters did all helped to give the Sisters another booster shot of missionary enthusiasm.[10]

In the Fall of the year, the Sisters opened another mission in the South, Bay St. Louis on the southern tip of Mississippi. Sisters Matutina, Leonardine, Charitosa, Basilissa and Ellen were sent to the station and were received in a friendly way. They opened a parish school for elementary school children.

Ever since the First General Chapter, the Constitutions (Holy Rule) of the Holy Spirit Missionary

Sisters had been under close study by the Holy See in Rome. Good news regarding the Book of Rules finally emerged. The Holy See had given its approval to the Constitutions. The papal decree was issued on March 21, 1925, very appropriately the Feast of St. Benedict, founder of monastic life in the West, and Father of all religious Orders. The decree was signed on March 24, the Feast of St. Gabriel, the Archangel, and the day before the Feast of the Annunciation, or as the Founder Arnold Janssen called this special day, the Feast of the Immaculate Spouse of the Holy Spirit. Father Superior General William Gier sent his heartfelt congratulations from the Divine Word headquarters in Rome. With the Holy See's approval of the Holy Rule, the Congregation and the Holy Rule became all the more dear to each Sister. Rome's approval meant that the way of life outlined in the Constitutions was an approved and holy way of attaining personal sanctification.

During this period of her administration at St. Ann's, Mother Leonarda gave a lawn party for the benefit of the missions. It was the first in what became a yearly custom—a garden party to help raise money for the foreign missions.

The warm July sun was still high in the sky although it was already after four o'clock when the afternoon mail on July 24, 1925, brought Mother Leonarda the news of her appointment for the next three years as Provincial Superior of the North American Province. Sister Irenaea was appointed Superior of St. Ann's.

A letter written to Mother Theresia a couple weeks later gives an insight into what the appointment meant to Mother Leonarda. She writes:

The voting results arrived on July 24—just as I intended to start Chapter. I had a hard time bringing it to a close. Right afterwards, I went to Church. I placed my cross at the feet of the Sacred Heart and the Holy Spirit and expressed my readiness to do his will, to sanctify myself and others and to lead others to the Lord insomuch as it is within my strength. I thank you, dear Mother Theresia, for your hearty good wishes and your prayers. Your dear letter was a great consolation. It had eased my departure from St. Ann's.

Dear Mother Theresia, I do not deserve the confidence which you and the Sisters of the Generalate place in me. I will keep this before me and will try to live up to it. Another consolation for me is that the Sisters inspite of the critical years received me with confidence and joy—even those that opposed me. I have tried to forget everything and I will try to be to the Sisters what I should be, a mother and a leader ....[11]

For the next six years, Mother Leonarda again took up her duties as Head of the Province. During this period of her life up to about six months before her death, she kept an almost daily record in her diary. Heretofore, she had written in rather scattered periods of time. Now, however, she makes a daily entry, sometimes very brief but, nevertheless, a record of her work, sufferings, feelings, griefs, relationship with Sisters, visitations, community spirit—all on a day to day basis. In fact, there is such a fidelity in writing every day that when she misses a day, she still pens in the date and writes: "Forgot."

An ever-increasing heaviness of spirit pervades every page of her small diary notebooks. Even more so now than in those early difficult years, she is distressed in mind and body and labors under a prostrating anguish, and she is almost always in physical pain. So deep is her personal pain at times from some extremely difficult and hurtful situations that arose and from some of the treachery directed against her by people she trusted that from time to time it seems she is writing about two people—herself in anguish and her life outside her pure personal pain, in other words the external community life or the general state of affairs in the house.

From its very beginning the province was sadly burdened with sickness among its members and with the deaths of many Sisters. As the twenties headed into the thirties, this situation did not seem to change. In a letter to Mother Theresia in 1925, Mother Leonarda writes:

> *Last night at 9 o'clock Sister Praesentata died without a struggle, quietly and peacefully. . . . Sister Sophia is quite ill and coughs up much blood. I do not think she will live until spring. Sister Borromaea has lost a lot of weight. One also fears for her. God means it well with us. We are more sick than healthy Sisters. Sister Pauline is not in school anymore. She also suffers from tuberculosis and is taking treatments in New Hampton. It is questionable whether she will make it . . . .*[12]

Letter after letter mentions the sick of the Province and the deaths. Tuberculosis claimed a good number of Sisters. The Sisters had to be taken from their places of work and sent to a hospital or rest home for treatment and rest. For Mother Leonarda it means not only the pain of seeing another one of her Sisters suffering illness, but also the frustration of obtaining a replacement for the sick Sister from an already depleted community.[13]

The pages of her diary as well as letters to Mother Theresia and other members of the Generalate reveal that Mother Leonarda also had much trouble with some Sisters. They were put into teaching but showed no inclination in that line and in many cases had to be taken out for fear of creating bigger problems.[14] The trouble was that with most of these Sisters it was hard to find the right place for them. They found difficulty everywhere. Others were domineering and "bossy" and no one wanted to work with them.[15] In a letter to Mother Theresia, Mother Leonarda writes:

Since Sr. I. is also down South, there is peace and harmony among the teachers here.[16]

Again, she writes:

Sister M. is also a difficult character. Sister Euphrasia can hardly 'take it' when she is present.[17]

In her diary one reads such phrases as:

Much sorrow with Sister M.[18] *Heavy cross with Sister M.*[19]

A rather lengthy entry says:

Sister L. brought forth many complaints against me. I am so cold and have no sympathy, she said. She told me I was a northern German with no feeling for a southern German. Both Sister L. and Sister I. then spoke against me saying I did not care for the sick. The whole thing was a big condemnation of me. It hurt me very much . . . .[20]

There are many more passages in the diary which show that all the Sisters of the province were certainly not with her, and that she really had to take a lot from some. Once, incredible as it seems, she was slapped in the face by an angry nun, and another time was pushed down the stairs by a mentally disturbed Sister. At the end of her life, Mother Leonarda remarked that "gossip and slander brought me where I am."[21]

Why did someone who had given so much to God and others, so much to her Sisters, why did she have to also endure the pettiness and spite of some members of her community? How could these nuns who were supposed to be "striving for perfection" treat her in such a manner? One could give any number of spiritual reasons and give any number of excuses for these nuns. But there could have been very natural reasons. The whole Congregation was still very young but it had grown very rapidly. The North American Province had grown quickly in acquiring work and, therefore, in its need for Sisters. Perhaps in fulfilling these needs of the missions, the initial training was too fast and not thorough enough and Sisters were sent abroad too quickly and maybe with not enough discretion regarding ability, aptitude, psychological readiness to adjust to all the differences of living in a foreign culture. Once confronted with the newness of a country, a language, customs, climate, some were not able to adapt and adjust and showed their frustration in some negative behavior.

Today the missionary is much more thoroughly screened, prepared, and initiated into the new culture even before she ever sets foot in the mission land. Whatever Mother Leonarda may have suffered from some Sisters, her attitude toward all was the same. At one time Mother Theresia wrote in a letter to her that it is "natural" for Sister Leonarda to be a mother to the Sisters. Mother Leonarda commented on the statement in a return answer:

You write that it is natural for me to be a mother to the Sisters. I think that you are mistaken. It was always hard for me and required many a battle. Grace must do the main part. You may be convinced, dear Reverend Mother, that I try hard to be all that I should be. I trust the Holy Spirit will help me . . . .[22]

Having been a member of the Provincial Council for the past six years, Mother Leonarda was well apprised of what was going on in the Province regarding buildings, activities, etc. She went on making new contacts for the Congregation and opening new schools and making additions to existing buildings. St. Joseph's Hospital in Iowa was already too small and a new wing was added. The solemn blessing of the new wing took place on August 12, 1925.

As for the Provincial House itself, a new wing had been already added in 1922. Now there were additions and changes made on the grounds surrounding the building. She writes to Mother Theresia:

This autumn we planted over 100 fruit trees and in the spring some more trees will be added. We cleared a piece of land next to the vegetable garden for a park for the Sisters. The paths have been started and the shade trees, berry bushes, have been planted at the lower end. The park is for the Sisters' use. It will take a few years for the trees to get big. We had all the shade trees and only needed to transplant them. The Stations of the Cross, donated by some kind people for our garden, were set up by Brother Paul.[23]

In another letter she writes:

. . . This summer our grounds have been landscaped; roads were made, shrubs and flowers planted and here and there are small nooks where the Sisters can

pray and rest. Now they need no longer go to the garden at the South during retreat and pray the rosary. A kind benefactor donated a beautiful statue of St. Joseph for the park. Along the paths shade trees are planted. Behind the park we planted three hundred trees to serve as a windbreak and also as an area where the Sisters can take a walk. In spring we will plant a variety of berry bushes between the fruit trees. We hope in a few years we will have our own fruit . . . .[24]

She had, indeed, wisely planned for the future. Long after she was gone, the Sisters and their guests would be enjoying the raspberries, black and red currants, gooseberries that came off the bushes she had planted as well as the apples, pears, plums, and peaches from the orchard. She was the ever efficient Elise from Ahlen!

Another home for the elderly, Sacred Heart Home, was being built in Hyattsville, Maryland. At the beginning of 1926, only the framework of the building was up. It would be May before the Sisters and residents could move in. For the time being St. Ann's Home helped out both financially and with some equipment until there were enough residents at Sacred Heart Home for it to be self-supportive.

In the Fall of that year, a candidature was opened at Holy Ghost Convent, thus admitting girls of high school age who felt inclined to be missionary Sisters to the Academy. That year there were twenty-five novices, twenty postulants, and four candidates.

The schools in the South had grown in number since that day in 1906 when Father Heick had visited Mother Leonarda in Techny and pleaded for Sisters to come and staff his school. Unfortunately,

Father Heick was not there anymore, and some of the Pastors in the eight parishes where the Sisters worked had very little respect or use for the Sisters. How these Pastors had intended to carry on an elementary school and high school for several hundred students—and that with having paid the teaching Sisters not even $1.00 a day—*without* the Sisters now, is a question. The unpleasant situation, however, added up to more grief for the Foundress. In a letter to Mother Columba she writes:

> *Only a few Sisters were changed in the South. The greatest trouble is in Little Rock. The Pastor makes life difficult for the Sisters, especially for Sister Superior Otgera . . . . It would be better if Father had no S.Sp.S. Sisters. The Sisters have a nice house but of what good is it if Father makes life hard for them.*[25]

The next year Mother Leonarda wrote to Mother General Columba that some of the Pastors were angry that some Sisters were changed from their parishes, or they were dissatisfied with the Sisters they got. As she states it: "One hears all kinds of unpleasant things at such times."[26] This was not an easy problem for the Provincial Superior to solve satisfactorily always. For one thing, the Generalate in Steyl appointed the Superiors; and secondly there were many reasons for transfers, not the least important of which was teaching needs of a school and the qualifications of the teachers. Although a good rapport between Pastors and Sisters was considered important, it was extremely difficult for Mother Leonarda and her Council to position every Sister that would be of satisfaction to everyone and at the same time advantageous to the school where she would teach and to the community of Sisters with whom she would live.

It was after Mother Leonarda's time that a change came about in the schools in the South, and it helped solve some of these problems. As the Sisters got their degrees and were trained in administration and supervision, the Sisters became the Principals of the schools. The priests remained Pastor of the Parish and, of course, that included the Parish Church and the Parish school and all concerned with their up-keep. This separation of some of the administrative duties worked toward a better cooperative effort on the part of all.

It would be an error, though, to conclude that there was nothing but animosity and disagreements in the Southern Stations in those early years. Not at all! Personality clashes, yes, and perhaps a lack of understanding, but, for the most part, there was a harmonious working together which earned for all the schools of the SVD-SSpS in the South a fine reputation for learning and helped make the parish a community of zealous and Catholic-minded parish-ioners. They were already caring for many students as Mother Leonarda noted in one letter: "In Jackson our Sisters have 420 students, in Vicksburg and Greenville, 350, in Meridian, 250, in Little Rock 175 . . . ."[27]

Both the priests and Sisters together with their parishioners faced a lot of difficulties and problems those early years. They even braved catastrophes together.

On April 21, 1927, the whistle of the Greenville water works blew violently announcing to the people of the town that the levee had given way to the pressure of the swollen Mississippi River which was now gushing and rushing with great force over the Delta. In a detailed account, Father Jacobs, a Divine Word Father and Pastor in Greenville, gives a graphic description of the terror of the flood in that city. Thousands of people were homeless. For three months the city was under water, and when the water finally receded, Sacred Heart Mission, as Father Jacobs expresses it, "was a picture of the destruction of Jerusalem." Help began coming from the Red Cross, the Bishop, friends. The flood was also in a way a "blessing in disguise," Sister Gerasine wrote at the time. Such unstinted service and such admirable charity was shown by Father Jacobs and the Sisters at Sacred Heart Mission to the people of Greenville during the flood that the "prejudice against Catholics" so evident heretofore was given a death blow. Whereas before most people turned away when either Father Jacobs or the Sisters passed by, now the people called out, even from a distance, "Hi, Father! Hi, Sister!" The flood had destroyed the material possessions of thousands, and yet to these same people it brought an enormous wealth: the gifts of Faith and the joy of Hope. Many became converts to Catholicism.[28]

It was in this same year that Mother Leonarda received permission from the Generalate to take over a school in Milwaukee, Wisconsin—in the Whitefish Bay suburb. The Sisters were also working at St. Margaret's Guild in Milwaukee at the invitation of Bishop Messmer and Father Klopfer of the Vincent De Paul Society. The Guild was a home for young women, most of them in high school, who did not have a home. The building on 20th and Highland which housed the girls looked like an old Tudor mansion lifted out of the pages of English history. Although the Sisters did a tremendous amount of good for the girls, the Guild was another one of those pro and con situations. Mother Leonarda had accepted work at the Guild with the condition that the Sisters would be given a school in connection with the home, but this never materialized. The Provincial Council, therefore, was in favor of dropping the Guild. However, Father Klopfer again begged Mother Leonarda to let the Sisters stay on.

During their brief stay in Milwaukee, the Sisters experienced some positive attitudes toward them from the people of the city. Mother Leonarda wrote to the Assistant General and expressed these feelings:

> *. . .In Milwaukee an Auxiliary was formed which supports our Sisters in many ways, also financially. The Sisters reported that there has been a noticeable change among the children; they are more obedient and devoted to the Sisters. The Sisters are confident that they will be able to do much good . . . The Sisters love their apostolate in Milwaukee very much.*
>
> *A month ago we received an invitation to speak at a Catholic Women's meeting in Milwaukee. It was the wish of the Archbishop that we speak about modern dress. Sister Pauline, who accepted to give the talk, chose as the theme "A New Crusade" in which she spoke mainly about the influence of a mother upon her daughter and the relation between the two. Only indirectly did she speak of modern dress. It seems this talk put us in a good light with the clergy and the ladies. The priests congratulated Sister Pauline and asked for a copy of the talk to publish in their parish bulletins . . . .*[29]

It was only some years after the death of Mother Leonarda that the Guild was dropped as an apostolate, and this only because they could not get a school with the Guild; and to keep four Sisters in the House with such limited activity was more than the Order could afford in the matter of personnel. It is interesting to note, though, that several fine vocations came from among the girls who lived at the Guild.

Bishop Messmer from Milwaukee came again to call on Mother Leonarda in 1928 requesting Sisters for a school in Cudahy, Wisconsin. Thus for several years the Sisters worked in three places in Milwaukee and Cudahy. However, all three places were eventually dropped in the 1940's.

Mother Leonarda did not give up her desire to open a place in the West, preferably Colorado. Again in the 1920's she petitions the Generalate to allow her to open a convent in Colorado because of the ideal climate for some of the Sisters who were struggling with poor health. She also mentions the possibilities of opening a place in California. However, she did not get the required permission. As she writes to Mother Columba:

> *A house in Denver, Colorado, was not found advisable by the Generalate. Although it is far away, it would still be beneficial to have a house there since the climate is better . . .especially for Sisters with tuberculosis.*[30]

Her plans for the West were dropped for the moment, but she had so many other things to take care of right now. For years she had been looking for the right place in Chicago to build a hospital for Negroes. When a beautiful piece of property was for sale in an area in Chicago where many Blacks were moving in, Mother Leonarda began taking steps to acquire the property. However there were many meetings before getting anything done. The people in the area did not want a hospital; they thought their homes would depreciate in value. It took a long time to get the final approval from the people of the area. And still there were setbacks to keep the Sisters from getting the hospital "off the ground."

It was when Mother Leonarda went to see Bishop Hoban about the Negro Hospital that he told her that he and Cardinal Mundelein wanted her to find a suitable place in Lake County area and build a hospital there, since the people in that locality did not have a Catholic hospital.

Assuming this gigantic task of building a large up-to-date fully equipped hospital and seeing to its completion was perhaps the largest, most impressive, and most tiring and grief laden project of her life.

When the Bishop and later Cardinal Mundelein presented her with this request, it was during a time when financially her community in the United States was at a low ebb. She had just completed building Sacred Heart Home in Maryland which had drained her, and for which she was still in debt. Futhermore, she had also paid off the final sum of money to the Divine Word Fathers for St. Ann's Home. As she puts it in a letter to the Mother General:

> *The money matter with the SVD was settled on the 1st of October. We paid them $100,000.00 which we had to borrow and received the contract for St. Ann's. Thus everything is in order and we are on good terms with the Society.*[31]

Hence she was undertaking this new project with

much faith—or as some people saw it—rashness. Yet, she never took any work upon herself without placing her trust implicitly in the Holy Spirit. Because of this deep trust in the Holy Spirit, she could never have acted rashly. Just how important the Holy Spirit is in each one's life, she never seems to tire of telling the Sisters:

> *The Holy Spirit, then, enlightens the soul and moves the heart and thus precedes with His grace all our actions. It is He who arouses in the sinner thoughts of contrition, who spurs the lukewarm to greater zeal and makes the just desire the treasures of Heaven.*
>
> *It is more than conviction that induces Holy Mother Church to incessantly invoke the assistance of the Holy Spirit. She wants the faithful to call upon Him frequently in prayers like the VENI CREATOR SPIRITUS . . .God wants us to turn to the Holy Spirit for enlightenment and help whenever we are in need . . . .*[32]

And this she did!

As far as financial help the Sisters could rely on, there were only St. Ann's Home and the two small hospitals in Watertown and New Hampton. Friends advised the Sisters to start a fund-raising campaign.

For six months the Sisters were looking for a suitable place to build. They made a novena to St. Therese of the Child Jesus, in whose honor the hospital would be built. On the last day of the novena, the Sisters were told of fourteen acres that were for sale near the western boundary of Waukegan. The property was owned by a family named Grady. Mother Leonarda and her Council immediately went to look at the site and found it acceptable. The architect Herman Gaul was called to look over the land and draw up plans. Meanwhile the papers were signed by the proper parties, and the Congregation received the land for a sum of $46,000.00.

On October 24, 1927, the plans were complete and the ground breaking took place. Present were Mother Provincial Leonarda and her Councillors: Sister Maria, Sister Irenaea, and Sister Dafrosa, the provincial procurator. Also present were the architects, contractors, and citizens of Waukegan who were pleased that the hospital was being built. Mother Leonarda turned over the first spadeful of dirt; the other Sisters followed, and then all the other people.

St. Therese Hospital in Waukegan was in the making.

One day it would be a monument to her inexhaustible zeal for God's work and to that missionary love ever burning in her. It would be a place of healing for thousands and a place of life for countless newborns. But now in 1927 and as the following years unfolded, the hospital was for her the slowly devastating heartache of countless setbacks and disappointments. It was as if the burdens of a lifetime suddenly heaped themselves upon her all at one time.

It started with a harsh disappointment soon after that first spadeful of dirt was turned, Mother Leonarda wrote in her Diary:

Bishop Hoban called in the forenoon to tell me to give up the campaign (fund raising program) in Waukegan. The Cardinal didn't want the Drive. Deep sorrow over that!

Two days later she writes:

To St. Ann's Hospital. Many suggestions for our

hospital. Then to Monsignor Rempe. The place pleased him well; love it. Told him about Bishop Hoban regarding Waukegan campaign. He said we should have gone directly to the Cardinal not to Hoban. He said he wanted to talk to the Cardinal. The Little Flower had partly helped us.

October 8, she enters the following in her Diary:

To Bishop Hoban. He will talk to the priests in Waukegan in the morning. Everything hangs on that.

The next day the entry reads:

Today we will find out about the future of our hospital in Waukegan. Suspended for the time.

October 10:

Yesterday much trouble, anxiety. Today better. Outcome of Waukegan still doubtful.

October 14:

Tired. Bishop Hoban didn't permit the Drive. Now what? God knows.

October 17:

A little more hope. Monsignor Rempe whom I called up asked if I talked to the Cardinal as to why he did not want the Drive. All this almost crushed me.

In November Mother Leonarda wrote to Steyl, and she writes a paragraph on the development of matters in Waukegan:

. . .In regard to the new hospital in Waukegan, the situation seems to improve. We hope eventually to have success with our solicitation of funds. His Eminence Cardinal Mundelein wrote us a beautiful letter of recommendation which, I am sure, will promote our cause. We will personally contact the priests and leading persons and show them the Cardinal's let-

ter . . . .[33]

She was also negotiating the buying of the Carmelite Convent in St. Louis. It had been up for sale, and Mother Leonarda wanted to buy it in order to open Little Flower Retreat House; but the new Carmelite Convent was so slow in being built that Mother Leonarda was delayed a long time waiting for the Cloistered Carmelite nuns to move into their new convent.

Adding to the problems and sorrows she had as a Foundress, a Provincial Superior, and a religious Sister striving for perfection, she had also the problem of being an Aunt. One of her nephews had come to the United States with his wife, and he caused his aunt much grief and worry. One gathers from Mother Leonarda's numerous diary entries that this nephew was somewhat of a drifter, and as many times as his aunt tried to help him, or as often as she found a job for him, he would, through sheer negligence and a not-caring-attitude lose the job. Thus he drifted along, always coming back to Mother Leonarda when his funds were low and he needed help. She never let him go without help of some kind, but he also broke her heart.[34]

Although Mother Leonarda was still traveling around on her business and visitation trips as she had always done, there were times now when she could hardly walk. Her problem was diagnosed as varicose veins, and sometimes the inflammation of her legs was so painful, she could not stand on her feet. On May 31, 1928, the pain was so intense she could not stand. She was taken to St. Mary's Hospital in Watertown and was told to go to bed immediately and stay there. The doctor bandaged her legs, and after four hours she was at least able to stand. She went home the following day.

She had had her share of sorrows in life, but she was well aware of what she had chosen in becoming a religious missionary Sister. When Christ Himself called a person to His service, it was seldom to an easy life. She was contemplating this very thought one evening.

This was one of the most precious hours of the week—the hour just before evening prayer on Saturday. Every one of the one hundred sixty-eight hours every week was mapped out for each Sister in the Order of the Day. She knew exactly her hours for prayer, for work, for study, for meals, for recreation, for sleep and rest. Any deviation required permission. In an establishment housing so many people, where so much had to be done, and where all in some way depended on the other, adherence to the Order of the Day was a necessity.

For the religious who lived her life in a somewhat passive way, simply following the Order of the Day took care of a lot of decision-making problems. For the intense, actively striving religious, who relished her inner freedom and her ability to make decisions and was always cognizant of her power to choose, the Order of the Day was another discipline to keep one's self in check, seldom easy, but a means of strength, something like the stringent demands on time, diet, recreation made on the professional athlete who wants to reach a goal. For the religious it was simply the living of her vows: everything I do is part of my worship of God.

This one hour before evening prayer on Saturday was called "free time." During this hour each Sister could use her time as she wished: read, sew, work on a hobby, spend time in chapel, listen to music. Many of the Sisters would use the time to catch up on their personal sewing or writing; but perhaps, the majority took this free time to spend in prayer, spiritual reading, and meditation.

Perhaps one of the most erroneous ideas people outside the cloister have of religious Sisters is that they spend most of their time praying in chapel and walking down long corridors with grave faces and arms folded. Nothing could be farther from the truth. The active religious and the cloistered nuns work all day long, stopping only as the Order of the Day requires for meals, short recreation, and brief devotions during the day. Instead of arms folded, she probably has her sleeves rolled up and may be wiping the perspiration from her face. Or she may be at a desk preparing school work; or in an office working on accounts; in an operating room; or in the kitchen, etc., etc. Each one had an assigned place of work, but in addition all Sisters, even those engaged in school work, office work, nursing had their chores. Physical labor was part of each Sister's day.

So it was that many Sisters used the Saturday free hour to spend in prayer. Their life was a demanding one, one of almost constant giving: giving one's time, one's energies, one's talents, one's love, one's forgiveness, one's strength—giving it to whoever needed it that day, that moment, and being willing to accept thanks or no thanks or ridicule and hostility or misunderstanding in return. Its demands cannot be explained to be understood; they must be lived.

Such giving called for a constant replenishment, and so the Sister would try to get whatever time she could to commune with her One Love and from Him get strength and greater love to go on and forward. And yet, in this lay the very crux of her vocation: to go on day after day telling Someone, "I love You" and never hearing in human language the response: "I love you, too." Ah, that must, indeed, be a wholly unselfish love for the vows do not take away one's humanity nor one's desire for a human response.

Mother Leonarda seldom had this free hour for herself. There was always something that had to be done or someone to see her. Today, however, she had a moment of free time, and it came about in a rather amusing way.

Last Wednesday, Sister Lillian and Sister Ellen had supervision in the girls' dormitory. Since the girls had been sneaking in some midnight parties, the two nuns resolved that they would find the culprits tonight and put an end to the midnight dormitory parties. It wasn't twelve yet, but the two Sisters were making their rounds to check around a bit anyway. As they walked through the dormitories, they heard a terrible noise coming from somewhere below. The only thing they could think of was a burglar breaking in. Slowly they went down one flight of stairs after another. Following the sound, they found themselves in the sub basement, and here the noise was very loud. Slowly they went toward the butter making room, and the two terrified nuns found themselves face to face with Mother Leonarda, who did not look too graciously at them. She was scrubbing the basement floor, and the cleaning mop she was using to pick up the water swished and swooshed and the sound was eerie and frightening as it was echoed through the silent, empty halls. They had a good laugh, once Mother Leonarda found out what brought them to the basement. Sister Lillian and Sister Ellen begged her to let them clean the basement at least once so she could have some time. Mother Leonarda was reluctant to put any more work on the Sisters who all had their assigned jobs, but she gave in this time, but only once, she said.[35]

She thought about the Sisters now and wondered how they were enjoying the squeaky mop. She knew, too, that if she had said the word, any number of Sisters would have volunteered to clean the basement, but she had done it for so long, it seemed a natural thing. She also knew, though, that the ease and facility with which she had handled a mop and buckets and cleaned floors was no longer there. She was tired. Ah, but why waste this precious hour thinking of her tiredness.

Slowly, she prayed the Quarter Hour Prayer—"I believe in Thee, O My God . . . ."

She continued with her renewal of her Consecration to the Holy Spirit, a prayer she had composed many years ago.

"O Eternal Love, God Holy Ghost, I offer myself to You especially for Holy Church and its Head, my Superiors and all my Sisters, for missionaries, and for all my dear ones, for our benefactors, for the suffering and the dying, for all lovers of the Holy Spirit . . . Oh yes, dear Holy Spirit, for Thee I live, for Thee I die; I am Yours in life and in death."[36]

1. Thomas Bokenkotter, *A Concise History of the Catholic Church* (New York: Doubleday & Company, 1977), pp. 338-339.

2. David A. Shannon, *Twentieth Century America*, (Chicago: Rand McNally & Co., 1963), p. 206.

3. Chronicle of St. Ann's Home.

4. Chronicle of St. Ann's Home.
Mother Leonarda's letter to M. Theresia.

5. Accounts written by missionaries at the end of World War I.

6. Chronicle of St. Ann's Home.

7. Chronicle of St. Joseph's Hospital, account written by Sister Marilyn.

8. Letter of Mother Leonarda to M. Theresia (November 11, 1924).

9. Shannon, pp. 256 ff.

10. Chronicle of St. Ann's Home.

11. Letter of Mother Leonarda to M. Theresia (August 15, 1925).

12. Letter of Mother Leonarda to M. Theresia (October 28, 1925).

13. Letter of Mother Leonarda to M. Theresia (October 28, 1925).

14. Letter of Mother Leonarda to M. Salvatora (November 26, 1927).

15. Letter of Mother Leonarda to M. Salvatora (November 26, 1927).

16. Letter of Mother Leonarda to M. Theresia (January 1, 1926).

17. Letter of Mother Leonarda to M. Theresia (January 1, 1926).

18. Diary of Mother Leonarda (August 31, 1929).

19. Diary of Mother Leonarda (September 16, 1929).

20. Diary of Mother Leonarda (May 11, 1929).

21. An account of Sister Luciosa.

22. Letter of Mother Leonarda to M. Theresia (January 24, 1926).

23. Letter of Mother Leonarda to M. Theresia (January 24, 1926).

24. Letter of Mother Leonarda to M. Theresia (November 28, 1929).

25. Letter of Mother Leonarda to M. Columba (March 7, 1927).

26. Letter of Mother Leonarda to M. Columba (September 12, 1927).

27. Letter of Mother Leonarda to M. Theresia (November 26, 1927).

28. An account of Father Jacobs, S.V.D.
An account of Sister Gerasine, S.Sp.S.

29. Letter of Mother Leonarda to M. Theresia (November 26, 1927).

30. Letter of Mother Leonarda to M. Columba (March 7, 1927).

31. Letter of Mother Leonarda to M. Columba (March 25, 1926).

32. Chapter Conference (no date given).

33. Letter of Mother Leonarda to Rev. Mother Assistant General (November 26, 1927).

34. Diary of Mother Leonarda.

35. Diary and account of Sister Lillian.

36. Diary of Mother Leonarda—personal prayers.

Chapter Twelve

. . .The name, Servants of the Holy Spirit, is not merely a title; it is an obligation. By their lives of singular fidelity to the Spirit of God, by their profound adoration of Him, their love for Him, their untiring zeal to promote His veneration among others, the Sisters must prove that they are in very truth Servants of the Holy Spirit . . . .

—Diamond Jubilee Book of the S.Sp.S.

The period of the late 1920's was, at the time, the worst economic period in the country to date. The great depression that began in 1929 caused widespread suffering to people in just about all classes and all sections of the country. For the man who defeated Alfred E. Smith, the first Catholic nominee for President, in 1928, Herbert Hoover, who was also one of the first Presidents to enter the White House with an overwhelming popular approval—the depression leveled his name to a phrase of common sneering and slurs depicting human misery. Hoover, of course, was not the cause of the great depression, and, perhaps, his greatest fault or greatest lack in this time of turmoil was his total ineptness in politics. But, he was the President at the time, and the profound discontent among all people chose him as the one on whom to vent all their anger.[1]

The Church in the United States also felt the economic pressure, for there was hardly anyone in farm or city who was not touched by the depression. Yet life had to go on, and the Church kept going. In the aftermath of the lost election of 1928, some Catholics were discouraged that Al Smith did not get the Presidency, and still more discouraged that groups of fellow Americans persisted in suspicions and accusations that the Catholic faith was incompatible with democratic ideals, laws, and practices. One voice, however, set up a powerful slogan for the future. Father James Gillis, the Paulist Editor of the *Catholic World* in an editorial in December, 1928, proclaimed for everyone to hear: "We shall not wither up and blow away."[2]

His cry was taken up by many in the years to follow and in many ways.

A 34-year old professor at the Catholic University of America, Fulton J. Sheen, gave a talk at the National Catholic Educational Association and spoke of educating for a "Catholic Renaissance"; he subsequently became one of the most popular and eloquent radio speakers—later TV—and he aroused thinkers from all areas of life with his eloquence, religious philosophy, and deep faith.

In Chicago, William D. O'Brien, Auxiliary Bishop in that city, worked for many years for Catholics in poorer parts of the country through the Catholic

Extension Society.

Also in Chicago, Cardinal Mundelein, appointed Archbishop of Chicago in 1914, and almost killed at his installation banquet when an anarchist cook poisoned the soup, went on undaunted, using, if necessary political muscle, to work against bills in Springfield that misrepresented Catholic schools and orphanages and were adverse to the establishment and maintenance of such Catholic institutions. When the Cardinal died in 1939, he was known to be the Catholic bishop closest to Franklin D. Roosevelt.[3]

In 1929, however, Cardinal Mundelein was, perhaps, Mother Leonarda's greatest ally in the Church, encouraging her in her great efforts to finish the hospital she had begun before anyone had any hint of the great depression about to befall the country.

At the beginning of the year, although the hospital was not completed, Mother Leonarda sent three Sisters to St. Therese to work. The people had been begging to open the hospital at least "a little" at a time. Patients began coming even while the workmen were still in the building.

In a letter to Mother Columba she writes:

From the last letter, Reverend Mother, you could see that the hospital in Waukegan has brought us much trouble. I am sorry that we have caused you and the Generalate so much grief. We have had sorrows enough but now we hope that we shall receive a large donation. Rt. Rev. Bishop Hoban and Rev. Shea have caused us much trouble. Because of a strike, the plasterers were delayed eight weeks. For the last four weeks the Sisters have had patients on one floor because the people absolutely want to come. Every day there are more operations although only one operating room is ready.[4]

And then the day of dedication arrived. Dignitaries, priests, Sisters, and people from all the surrounding areas: Chicago, North Chicago, Mundelein, Evanston, Techny, and Waukegan had gathered for the solemn dedication of St. Therese Hospital in Waukegan, Illinois. The scholastics from the SVD Mission House in Techny were there to chant the Litany of all Saints. Rev. Bruno Hagspiel, SVD, was there to greet and welcome the Cardinal and the other Church dignitaries.

The day had begun with lovely spring-like weather, but as the people began to assemble, a hailstorm suddenly came up, and the the people sought shelter indoors. However, the storm did not last long. By the time the Cardinal came and the ceremony began, the sun was shining again.

It was an impressive ceremony. Cardinal Mundelein officiated and slowly went from room to room blessing each and every room in the building.

After the dedication, Cardinal Mundelein went to the Sisters' community room and addressed the Sisters. He congratulated them on the beautiful hospital they had built and commended them for the fine missionary work they carried on in this country. It was April 28, 1929.[5]

The architects, Herman Gaul and Sons designed the building in the Italian Renaissance style. It was pale yellow brick with a trim of limestone, and it rose six stories high surmounted by a tower which formed a solarium. The plan was T-shaped so as to allow for future additions.

In the June, 1929 edition of *Hospital Progress,* the official magazine of the Catholic Hospital Association, the following paragraph concludes a well written, detailed description of the new St. Therese Hospital:

All in all, the Sisters feel that they may well be proud of St. Therese Hospital. Ideal in location, efficient and pleasing in design, perfect in equipment, their hospital ranks as one of the best in the country, one which will in every way serve the needs of the community in which it is located for many years to come.

In the evening of the day of dedication, Mother Leonarda wrote in her diary that the people of the area were very pleased and happy about the hospital.

Even after the hospital was dedicated and opened, Mother Leonarda urged her Sisters time and time again to pray that the debts accrued from the building and upkeep of St. Therese Hospital could be satisfactorily met. The first years were extremely difficult and shaky.

Different from her concern with hospitals, schools, and homes, and yet in its own right, just as important, was the almost on-going worry Mother Leonarda had regarding farm hands. From the earliest years, the Sisters had tried to be as self-supporting as possible. They had their own farm and poultry yard, and their own vegetable garden. But finding suitable farm hands and maintenance workers for the buildings posed a problem. The Sisters were unfortunate in having hired over the years a number of workingmen for the farm who proved to be quite troublesome. Some had to be terminated because of poor work or poor morals or both.

In 1929, Mother Leonarda experienced a very stressful period of trouble on the farm. Simultaneous with the construction pains of St. Therese Hospital was an increasing turmoil on the farm. Beginning with March 24, Mother Leonarda begins writing of problems among the men on the farm.

March 24: *Heavy sorrow. Vincent will go away, also the shoemaker. Mr. Happ angry about it. Mr. Scherer sad over it. It is as if the devil looked at us.*

March 26: *Difficulty on the farm. Oh, it is almost too much!*

March 27: *Vincent left and also the shoemaker; Scherer is dissatisfied. Wants more money. Mr. Happ will have no tractor. Money need is great. Heavy cross!*

March 28: *Big trouble on the farm. Scherer is very agitated....*

And so she goes on, day after day, a new entry about a new problem, and a new sorrow. On one day she writes:

April 7: *The cross weighs heavy. Owe $750.00; I have only $200.00. 'Father, if it is possible, let this cross go away from me. Fiat voluntas tua.'*

Then she leaves to go to Watertown on business. Back home and then to Waukegan. Home again and to Chicago to register some Sisters at the Music Conservatory. Once again she goes to Watertown, and then to Milwaukee to St. Margaret's Guild and to a Music Convention. Finally on April 24, she is back with the problem again and writes: *"Mr. Scherer quits the farm."* Before he went, though, he had humiliated Mother Leonarda with the most slanderous remarks. And to top it all, he took Mother Leonarda to court, another humiliating experience.[6]

During these months practically every man who worked on the farm quit the job and Mother Leonarda was busy trying to find new help to work the farm. She did get some help, but she was still unsuccessful in getting good, solid help, such as the men who would come in later years and remain working for the Sisters for twenty-five to thirty years. Perhaps a lot of the problem lay in the fact that Mother Leonarda just had too soft a heart for some of her country-men who came to her with a hard luck story of being new in the country, unemployed, unfamiliar with the language and customs, and desperate. What they didn't tell her was that all they wanted was free room and board. They recognized her kindness and took advantage of it.[7]

On May 6, 1930, Sister Regis as a representative of the Generalate and her companion, Sister Maria, came to Techny to conduct a visitation of the province. Of all the Visitators who came to Techny, Sister Regis, was, perhaps, the most rigid and conservative. She believed in the letter of the law. An example of her law perfect mentality was clearly demonstrated on an exceptionally hot summer day in Techny. It was a hot, sticky, humid day, and in the chapel of the Convent, the humidity was always intensified when the chapel was filled with people. It was also a special feast for the Sisters, the Feast of the

Sacred Heart of Jesus, and hence the liturgy would be more elaborate and longer. According to regulations, the Sisters had to wear mantles (a heavy garment serving as a coat out doors in the winter but worn also for Church services on special feasts as part of the complete habit). Mother Leonarda knew how hot and extremely uncomfortable these mantles could be during a lengthy service in the chapel. She also knew that the mantle could even physically affect some of the Sisters who were not so well. Hence, for her it was a matter of common sense to dispense with the wearing of the mantle on this day. Upon coming to the chapel, Sister Regis was shocked to see not even one Sister wearing a mantle. She accepted no word of explanation. She simply told the Sisters to leave the chapel and get their mantles.[8]

Mother Leonarda was called before Sister Regis quite frequently to explain why this was done and that.[9] There were no serious infractions of the Rule nor was the spirit of the Founder and Foundresses suffering any diminution in the American province. It was simply that Mother Leonarda always saw the person; Sister Regis saw the word for word Rule.

If it were only for the Visitation in the United States, Sister Regis would appear as an unbending, almost unfeeling person; yet, some years later when she was the Mother General, she wrote beautiful, comforting letters to Mother Leonarda when the latter experienced a profound sorrow.

Once St. Therese Hospital was built, Mother Leonarda was not too involved with any new construction projects. A Sisters' Convent had been built in Girard. At St. Ann's Home the final wing was in the process of being built. Nothing yet had come of the

Negro Hospital that she had planned to build in Chicago.

Even without any new building project going on, the financial burden and obligations of the Province and the accounting and bookkeeping involved were a tremendous task. Mother Leonarda had a distinctive administrative ability and was, by no means, ignorant of finances and of keeping accounts, but some of her business dealings, as could be seen in her hiring of some farm help, were at times clouded by her implicit trust in human nature and her extraordinary kindness. She had good common sense and an innate ability to sense a future need. On the other hand the Provincial Treasurer or Procurator as she was then called, Sister Dafrosa, had a shrewd, adamant business mind. She had an almost obstinate, hard core manner of dealing with people, and her expressionless, unyielding way completely obliterated some of her more amicable personality traits. That the Foundress and the Procurator clashed at times on some issue was almost inevitable and understandable. Sister Dafrosa, however, used the "silent treatment" sometimes and went her own way as Mother Leonarda notes in her Diary for June 11, 1931:

Sister Dafrosa again angry with me . . . . A heavy cross. Yesterday she did not talk to me, but without telling me she changed banks. Fiat voluntas tua!

Then on June 15, Mother Leonarda writes another entry in her Diary:

Today Sister Dafrosa talked with me again.

Those piqued egos that can cause so much heartache!

Although she was always burdened with the weight of numerous problems, Mother Leonarda had the joy also of seeing some of the goals she had worked for in the province attained. One of these was the accrediting of Holy Ghost Academy by the North Central Association. She had paid much in mental anguish and determination in achieving this approval. In fact, this accreditation is what she wanted for all the schools. This is what she fought for in sending her Sisters to schools for degrees. Now it came—a precious piece of paper—on April 19, 1931.[10]

The end of her term as Provincial Superior was fast approaching but not before she was able to see the request she had made to the Generalate years ago come to fruition. Her great love for the Holy Spirit would now be the distinctive mark of the entire province. The Generalate gave permission for the North American Province to be called "Paraclete Province" having for its Titular the Holy Spirit Himself.[11]

The community prepared for the solemn celebration consecrating this to the Holy Spirit by three days of special prayers and adoration before the Blessed Sacrament. Mother Leonarda wrote a short discourse for the occasion, and every line is saturated with meaning. It is as if all that went before, difficult as it may have been, has been forgotten in the joy that the Holy Spirit has been officially designated the Comforter, the Paraclete of the Province.[12] She tells the Sisters:

> *The Holy Spirit, whom our Lord promised to His disciples had comforted and filled them in times of trial and tribulation. When He had sent out the seventy-two disciples, and they returned to Him full of joy and elated because of their success, He must have looked out over the years to come and must have seen the great harvest fields of the world and the*

thousands of mission undertakings of all centuries, and what a joy and comfort this must have been to Him. But from whom does He receive this comfort? Holy Scripture tells us in another place: 'The Savior rejoiced in the Holy Spirit . . . .'

. . .Soon we will start again our activities in the various houses and stations. It is immaterial where we work, we all are engaged as Servants of the Holy Spirit, in one big task which He has assigned to us. We should often recall the words of Holy Scripture: 'I will ask the Father that He may abide with you forever, the Spirit of Truth; He shall abide with you and be in you. The Paraclete, the Holy Spirit, whom the Father will send in my name, will teach you all things and bring all things to your mind whatsoever I shall have said to you.'

. . .If this feast has promoted in any way love and devotion to the Holy Spirit within our souls; if we have rendered Him a little gratitude and love; if we have tried to make reparation for all we have done to grieve Him; and if, through our prayers and sacrifices the love of the Holy Spirit has struck a chord in the souls of others, then we may look back with joy and confidence upon the days of this Triduum. The blessing of these days will follow us through life until the day comes when we have finished the task assigned to us.[13]

A large beautiful painting of the Holy Spirit, the Dove, hovering over the deep was placed on the wall opposite the entrance to the chapel commemorating this most happy occasion, August 17, 1931.

Late in August the new appointments came for the Paraclete Province. Mother Leonarda was appointed Superior of St. Ann's Home, and Sister Irenaea was appointed the new Provincial Superior. Before she left the Provincial House, Mother Leonarda went to each workroom in the house and to work areas outside and spoke to each Sister at her work. This had been her custom during all her years as Superior at St. Ann's or as Provincial Superior at Holy Ghost Convent. If possible, weekly, she visited each work place. Now she said her "Auf wiedersehen!"[14]

In the evening of August 28, Mother Leonarda returned to St. Ann's Home and was received with much love and good cheer.

Three days later she wrote in her Diary:

Nothing of importance. Must first settle down.

On September 1, she helped in the laundry all day, and on September 2, she canned peaches. She wrote:

Very tired. Fiat.

On September 5 she made the entry:

Tired. I'm not really so right at home.

She tried to carry on, helping out all over as she had done in the past, but she couldn't follow the pace. Each day she helped where she could, but each day her Diary entry reads:

Tired, very hot. Very tired. Tired in my feet.

The heat also seems to be bothering her more than ever before for she enters time and again:

Very hot and humid. Heat too much...

in her little notebooks.

In October she had a surprise for the Sisters. When they entered the community room in the evening of October 24, for an hour of recreation, they saw before them a huge painting of the Holy Spirit, with the inscription: "In Memoriam Dedicationis Provinciae Nostrae in Honorem Spiritus Sancti Paracliti. August 17, 1931." It was a painting similar to the one at the Convent. Mother Leonarda wanted her Sisters to be ever mindful of their unique calling—Servants of the Holy Spirit—and of the Presence of the Divine Paraclete in the world. It was from Him she wanted her Sisters to know, that they would obtain light and strength. They must not forget this.

In November there was another happy day when Mr. and Mrs. Happ celebrated their Golden Wedding anniversary. They had been the Sisters' dear friends and generous benefactors for so many years, and they still lived in their little home near the Sisters' Convent. For the special occasion, the Happs and their guests had breakfast with the Sisters in the cloister.[15]

On the Wednesday in Easter week, 1932, Mother Leonarda had to go to bed so severe was her pain. For days before Easter she had been running around helping with the work wherever she could, and she was almost always on her feet. Her blood pressure went up to 220, and her leg became so inflamed she could no longer step on it. The Doctor ordered complete bed rest, and there she stayed for ten days.[16]

Her intense physical pain was but the prelude to one of the most severe heartaches of her administration. She herself writes:

> *October 4, 1932: The heaviest and darkest day of my life. Mr. Glaeser (the convent attorney) declared bankruptcy and we lost $11,000 to $12,000.*

She writes the sad news to Mother Columba:

> *. . .With a sad and heavy heart I write to you to give you the following report. . . . On October 3, Mr. Glaeser turned himself in at court and confessed that*

over the period of the last ten years he has defrauded his clients and stolen from them the sum of $500,000.00 . . . .Mr.Glaeser became acquainted with the Home through his mother-in-law who died at the Home. From the beginning he has been a friend of the Home; he handled many legal and business matters for us, always to our satisfaction and free of charge . . . .

Mother Leonarda then details exactly what Mr. Glaeser did. He took an estate of $7,000.00 which a deceased resident, Mr. Folz, had willed to the Sisters and invested it in bonds. He did the same thing for a woman in the Home who just sold some property for $3,000.00. But the bonds never materialized, and after months of dissembling and courteous dishonesty, he had to admit he had appropriated the money for himself.

No one, not even his family and friends knew or suspected anything of this fraud. The revelation was a great shock to his family and clients. Everyone had trusted him and this made it possible to get so much money until the fraud came to a standstill.

Mother Leonarda, of course, blamed herself. She should never have signed any papers or notices without getting advice from her higher superiors. She tells Mother Columba:

I wonder whether the high blood pressure of 220 which I suffered at the time impaired my ability of concentration. I do not know; I have no explanation. This is not meant as an excuse. I submit to any penance you may wish to impose on me . . . .

All in all, the Sisters' loss was $7,000.00, $3,000.00, and $4,000.00. The whole matter was a heavy burden for her.[17]

The incident devastated her. Again, she had been betrayed by someone she trusted, but what made this especially heart-rending for her was the fact that she, too, felt as if she had betrayed her community. It was after all their money—community money—that had been entrusted to her, and she had acted unwisely and imprudently. At first Sister Irenaea, shocked also at the great loss, made Mother Leonarda feel the full brunt of her action, and the Foundress was overcome with grief.[18] In the ensuing weeks her body reacted to the mental anguish she was undergoing. Her blood pressure rose alarmingly, and she was in severe bodily pain almost always. Her Superiors, both here and in Steyl, having had time to appraise the unfortunate incident more calmly, now became alarmed by her continuous grief and her rapid decline in an already failing health. Sister Provincial Irenaea wrote her:

> *. . .Please do not grieve and worry any more; it is poison for your condition. Your health and presence is for us* ***worth more*** *than all the money in question. I feel very sorry, if I, either on Saturday or yesterday, did say anything, that could have increased or caused more grief and worry. It was not my intention. Of course, I must confess, it took me all last week, to get over it, but now I think quite differently about the whole matter. . . .There was not one bit of ill will in the transaction on your part. . . . Regarding Mr. Glaeser, . . .I too, had no thought of mistrust. Moreover, I am fully convinced of being liable to make far greater blunders. I do believe the whole thing was providential, and that much good and blessing will come out of it.*
>
> *I cannot bear the thought that you suffer mentally*

and physically under the strain of worry and grief. God is very good. Our property is His property, and He has more than that . . . .I pray that the dear Holy Spirit may strengthen and comfort you in this hour of trial . . . .[19]

It was a beautiful letter and was a soothing balm for Mother Leonarda, but deep inside she still hurt. Mother Theresia was on Visitation in China, but she wrote at least a few lines to Mother Leonarda to calm her and to reassure her.

. . .You have only material loss to bewail which our dear Lord can take or repay. Of course this tribulation is hard for the province and especially for you. Our dear Lord allowed it in order to make you very small and humble and detached from everything in order to draw you ever more to Himself. There is a reason why Thomas a Kempis calls suffering "The Royal Way of the Cross." Therefore, do not lose courage but follow courageously in the footsteps of our cross-bearing Savior. From suffering grace and blessings will flow . . . .[20]

Toward the last weeks of the year things began looking a little better. The many prayers had pierced the clouds and a few rays of sun shone upon Mother Leonarda and her Sisters. They received a sum of money from new residents who had been admitted, and the Sisters benefited from an inheritance settlement.

Mother Leonarda had answered the letter she received from Mother Theresia expressing her acceptance of the cross.

. . .Your kind letter of October 10th was comforting and I thank you for your kindness and understanding. Although I feel the burden of the cross heavily, I

still give my 'fiat' and leave all to the will of my heavenly Father who has everything in His hands and can send help when He wishes. Whatever is demanded of me in reparation I am willing to accept as I wrote to you earlier.

Good people are working hard to help us. If the times weren't so bad, the loss could be restored quicker. I pray and hope that the dear God will give me time until the loss is made up . . . .[21]

However, even with things looking up, Mother Leonarda began the New Year with an extremely high fever—103° to 104°—and was forced to bed. Her blood pressure soared again to 210. Yet by January 28, she was back helping in the laundry and going on as usual.

Her Diary shows, though, that life had become a daily struggle. Illness, pain never leave her. She is going on sheer will power and, as she would surely have said, the strength of the Holy Spirit from day to day.

On March 4, 1933, she records in her little diary notebook that the nation was celebrating the Inauguration of Franklin Delano Roosevelt. She thought it proper for the Sisters to join in the celebration, and she gave her permission for the Sisters to converse at the noon meal and evening meal instead of the usual silence and reading.

In his Inaugural Address, Roosevelt has a sentence which sounds so much like something Mother Leonarda would have said, not so much for the country (Roosevelt's reference) but for her Order and her Province.

Roosevelt's words: "This great Nation will endure as it has endured, will revive and will prosper.

So first of all let me assert my firm belief that the only thing we have to fear is fear itself." Mother Leonarda would have encouraged her Sisters in a similar way. How many times had she told her Sisters that the work of the Holy Spirit would endure.

So long as her community needed her, and so long as she was yet able to get around and had a sound mind, she went on doing what she could to further the development of the Paraclete Province.

In 1934, a General Chapter was to be held in Steyl, Holland. Mother Leonarda was again chosen a delegate to this Chapter. Although she was not at all well, she made the necessary preparations and finally was on her way once again across the Atlantic. One of the women at St. Ann's had a Mass said for Mother Leonarda for a safe journey and another Mass when she got on the steamer in New York.

This time when the Chapter was over, Mother Leonarda did not delay her stay in Steyl. Immediately after the Chapter she was on her way home and was welcomed most heartily at St. Ann's—so heartily, in fact, they forgot to light the elaborate Welcome sign they had made and put up for her.

She began her second three-year term as Superior of St. Ann's Home. The Sisters could expect her anywhere, helping here, helping there, and always ready and available for anyone who wished to see her. The Sisters began to notice now that during her conferences, she would sometimes lose her trend of thought or she was struggling to remember her next point. Her memory was sometimes a blank. Not only did she have the burdens of infirmity, but also the embarrassment of a poor memory and forgetfulness.

When Mother's Day came in May, the Sisters

surprised her by decorating her place in the dining room with garlands of flowers and two large bouquets. One of the Sisters read a poem; another read a letter of gratitude. Then came the reading of a brief biography of Mother Leonarda, and finally Sister Rudolpha, as a letter carrier, brought in an armful of packages and letters for Mother Leonarda from all over the world. It was a delightful little program, and Mother Leonarda again laughed heartily till the tears came. In her Diary she expresses how much happiness the Sisters gave her.

On her feastday, too, November 26th, the Sisters tried to show her their love and appreciation by a tastefully decorated room, by poems, songs, and skits.

She ws always grateful for the least little favor done for her, and now these beautiful manifestations of the Sisters' love for their Foundress touched her deeply.[22]

As the Superior of St. Ann's she did not have to travel back and forth to the various stations on Visitation as she did when she was the Provincial Superior. Yet, as a Provincial Councilor, she was called on frequently for her knowledge and expertise in the matters of the province.

She was not surprised when the Sisters had to leave the school in Whitefish Bay. Father Dietz, the Pastor, had ideas of his own as to who should teach in the schools.

On June 29, 1935, Mother Leonarda had the happiness of welcoming Reverend Mother Columba once more to the Paraclete Province. She arrived in Chicago promptly at 12:30 P.M., and Mother Leonarda and Sister Irenaea met her at the station.

Later that summer Mother Leonarda was forced to bed again with a badly inflamed leg and a fever of 102°. As soon as the inflammation went down a little and her temperature was almost normal, she was back again at work. There was extra work in the house but no extra Sisters so every Sister used whatever time she could spare, and Mother Leonarda lent her hand to canning eighty bushels of peaches, fourteen bushels of plums, as many bushels of pears, and many bushels of apples, which one of the workmen had brought in from Michigan.

Canning occupied quite a big portion of the summer. These preserves of fruit would be used the rest of the year for the residents and Sisters as a nutritional dessert for lunch or dinner. It was a lot of work, but the fruit could be bought at a cheaper price directly from the orchards in Michigan, and transportation and delivery charges were saved by having the men get the fruit in the truck.

When the fruit was canned, it was time to begin canning vegetables. The Sisters spent all their recreation periods now in cutting and preparing carrots, beans, beets, etc. for preserving. There were no freezers yet; at least the Sisters had none.

Two more times that summer, in August and September, Mother Leonarda was forced to bed with an inflamed leg and fever. She was not alone in suffering. Perhaps she did not know that across the Atlantic in Rome, Italy, in the Vatican, Pope Pius XI was also suffering from an acute painful leg ailment. His right leg was paralyzed, and his heart could hardly take the pain. Yet, characteristically, Pius XI said: "The Pope cannot be ill. The Pope is in the hands of God who will call him from his labors in His own good time. We shall continue to work until called." Only to the few at his bed did he acknowledge: "The pains are atrocious; yes, most atrocious."[23]

Mother Leonarda, too, continued to work as long as she could. She was not one to hide behind invalidism or her continuous pain as an excuse from work, although it would have been a most legitimate excuse.

At times during the course of the next months, she sometimes had to go with Mother Columba on business trips to Chicago or some nearby houses. It was Mother Leonarda who still had the pulse of the Province under her sensitive fingers, and who, though she did not carry on the immediate business of the Province, was still totally cognizant of what was going on and how it was going on even to such seemingly insignificant matters as to write in her little notebook on Christmas Day, 1935, after she had just written a detailed description of the beautiful Church service—this almost humorous sentence:

> *The plums at dinner were not good. Didn't give them enough attention in canning them.*

This was Mother Leonarda! She may have been in the middle of building problems, worrisome financial problems, community troubles—matters that would have made others oblivious to the smaller details of life; yet she mentions the preserves not tasting up to par; little pigs born that morning; the Filke Mass that the Sisters sang this morning for the liturgy was sung so well—or poorly. Everything had some importance for her because they all added up to community living.

The new year, 1936, began as all the new years

began with some Sisters on retreat at the Provincial House, and some of that group preparing to make first Vows. Mother Leonarda, of course, never missed these most beautiful Clothing and Profession days. She was at the Provincial House that January 6, to witness the clothing ceremony of the new novices and the profession of some Sisters. It was always a happy moment for her because the great love she had for her vocation and the depth of meaning her title Missionary Sister Servant of the Holy Spirit had for her overflowed in happiness for the young women who now became special to the Holy Spirit.

At the beginning of Lent that year she wrote in her notebook a list that she called

> *Some practical points regarding mortification as free chosen penance:*
>
> 1. *Do not complain about the weather, heat or cold, nor about persons or things without good reason.*
> 2. *Be content with everything—occupation, work, food, clothing.*
> 3. *When oppressed do not show your feelings; try to be cheerful, kind, and affable; do not let others suffer from your ill temper or melancholy.*
> 4. *Always, everywhere observe good manners in carriage, in conversation.*
> 5. *Ever be obliging, never refuse assistance when it can be rendered without neglecting your own duty.*
> 6. *At prayer, also at table, manifest always a reverential attitude that portrays respect for the presence of God . . . .*

Lent began with Ash Wednesday on February 26, and the very next day, Mother Leonarda fell, and although she did not break anything, she bruised herself badly and was in pain for weeks. The pain also kept her awake at night.

On March 8, she was sixty-two years old.

Mother Columba had come to St. Ann's several times for lunch and to talk to Mother Leonarda. On May 6, the Visitator left the United States.

The heat of summer bothered Mother Leonarda more and more, and so the summer of 1936 was hard on her. Other than that the rest of the year passed uneventfully.

In January, she makes just a few notations in her Diary, some of them rather confusing, but that is the last of the Diary entries.

One of the great sorrows she had to endure in these last months was to be unable to sing. She could no longer hold a tone or a melody, and this for her was a terrible cross. She had once said that when she can no longer sing, then her end will be near.

Regarding this cross, Mother Columba wrote to the Foundress:

> *From experience I know how hard it must be for you, that you cannot sing anymore. But it has to come that way, dear Sister Leonarda. If we take the striving for perfection seriously, then our dear Lord detaches us from everything, even from the most innocent pleasures. Happy those who understand God's intentions and who submit with a willing heart. Perhaps or rather certainly your condition will demand that you must let others do things which you would rather do yourself. That is the best preparation for union with our Lord, as we shall realize when we are seriously striving.*[24]

Spring came early to Techny that year. It was only April 2, and the grass was already a beautiful emerald green. The buds on the trees were still quite small, but some of the braver forsythia bushes had sprigs of sunshine yellow flowers cheerfully announcing the arrival of spring.

At Holy Ghost Convent the Provincial Councilors had just concluded a council meeting and were going back to their places of work. Mother Leonarda stopped and said a few words to Sister Irenaea, and then she said, "I think I'll just walk around the grounds a little while. I told the driver to pick me up about 3:30, and it is still quite early."

She went down the front stairs, very wide palatial-looking stairs that started at sidewalk level and sloped up to the first floor. She also told Sister Anthony, the Portress, that she would walk outside and wait for the car.

Once outside, she turned around and looked at the front of the building. In her mind she saw the rest of the building as it would look when all the wings would be added and the convent would then be architecturally complete. Some years ago she had written to Mother Theresia explaining the building plans for the completed convent. At the time she knew nothing could be done just then, so she writes:

> *. . . I think it is of no use to think only of the present and do patch-up-work. In reflecting on the future need, insofar as it can be reasonably foreseen, a plan can turn out quite differently. It must not be narrow-minded but broad-minded . . . . If the Holy Spirit continues to bless our work during the next twenty-five years as he did during the first twenty-five years, we can certainly hope for more vocations . . . . The plan must be practical and the building presentable from the street. I thought out the enclosed plan and naturally present only a sketch.*

...What is now building 'A' would become a side wing when everything has been completed. The new main building would be located in the back in the center. ...We could later on add a side wing 'F' parallel to what is now building 'A' and building 'B'. ...We could also make 'B' up to the newly planned chapel. Since the garden below the chapel is located much lower, the lower section would lend itself to beautiful dining rooms without any excavation. Later on 'E' could be used as a novitiate ....[24]

She had written that in 1926, more than ten years ago. She looked up again at the Convent-Academy building. In itself the Convent was not really an imposing structure. Built of yellow brick, it was a rather plain rectangular shaped building, but there was a quaintness in a row of dormer windows on the north and south sides, and it had an artistic look in a set of seven exquisite stained glass windows, rich in symbolism, that stretched across the length of the chapel and in height from the second through the third floor.

If the building was plain, the grounds surrounding the Convent, though, were landscaped beautifully. A sunken rock garden with every kind of spring, summer, and fall flower covered one area of the north side of the building. The other three-fourths was covered with grass and trees, a linden—reminiscent of one of the first convents in Steyl, the Convent of the Three Linden,—a large shady weeping willow and borders of forsythia, bridal wreath, and honeysuckle along Willow Road and Waukegan Road. In the middle of the lovely trees and the green grass stood a picturesque white gazebo.

On the north side of Willow Road was a large

playground with swings and slides, teeter totters and merry-go-round, a tennis court, a large pond for boating, and a bowling alley—all for the recreational enjoyment of the students of the Academy.

Going around to the south end and close to the building was a rather large summer house, screened against insects. The girls of the Academy dubbed it "Tramps' Hotel." Up until the Second World War, there were many beggars who came regularly to the convent door for something to eat. In the summer, they took their bread and butter sandwich, cup of coffee, and apple to the little summer house to eat. Hence the girls gave the summer house a name.

Two blossoming hawthorn trees stood near the summer house on the south and straight from them was a narrow path that led to a small rustic bridge—water flowing beneath—; a rose arbor decorated each end of the bridge, and the path continued to an area of trees. It was called the circle of pines. Once inside the circle, one stood on soft green grass. There was a stone bird bath in the center, and pine trees formed a circle of sentinels on guard. This was the perfect place for moments of solitude and contemplation.

As one faced south to the left of the circle was a quaint airy castle made of stones, like a miniature "schloss" lifted from old world Germany. Later the aspirants mounted a small statue of our Lady in the castle and called it the castle of our Lady of Royalty. Close to the castle was a unique horse chestnut tree with its large digitate leaves and its sticky buds.

Walking west along the path one came to a large stone statue of the Sacred Heart, arms extended to all; then a large Lourdes Grotto, and the Stations of the Cross circling the whole path.

The paths that went farther west went into the cloister gardens, that part of the grounds reserved for Sisters only. These gardens were just as exquisitely landscaped. Here and there were statues always beautifully laid out with decorative flowers. There was a statue of St. Joseph and one of the Founder, Arnold Janssen, and a large Crucifixion group—Jesus on the Cross, Mary and John standing beneath. A white trellised grape arbor took up one whole length of the path. In this part of the garden, too, large Stations of the Cross circled an inner area, and in the middle was a picture-book water-lily pond with gold fish. The cloister gardens were rich in flowers of every kind beginning with the courageous early spring flowers, crocuses, wild violets, lilies of the valley, tulips—down to the hardy zinnias, marigolds and yellow and rust pompons of fall. There were bushes of every kind: lilac, bridal wreath, honeysuckle, barberry, snow-ball bushes (guelder-rose), and the ever lovely blossoming quince. One had to be absolutely blind to beauty not to revel in the glories of Nature as laid out here in the gardens surrounding the American Motherhouse of the Holy Spirit Missionary Sisters.

Mother Leonarda finished her long walk around the grounds and felt as if she had planted every flower, laid down every stone, so dear to her was this place in which God had placed her. She thought again of the Convent and how beautiful it would be when completed. But she knew very well that she would never see it. She smiled: "Well, today it is my dream; tomorrow it is another's accomplishment."

Then she had another thought. Smilingly she looked upward with a kind of mischievous look on her face and said softly, "A Bauernfrau, Papa? Is that what you wanted me to be in Ahlen—someone who could manage a big farm? Look, Papa, how good God has been to me—a beautiful land, a large farm, and so many dear, dear Sisters who have been my responsibility as if they were my own children. God has given me all and more!"

She was standing now on the sidewalk near the windows on the first floor that opened onto the music rooms. She heard a music student playing a Bach exercise and Sister Marysia counting exactly and emphatically like a metronome. Pupils took a lot from Sister Marysia; she was one tough "drill sargeant" in the music room; but, oh, did those students learn and how they could play eventually! Some even went on becoming concert pianists. Sister Marysia was a good soul, kind and helpful, but her temperament could make her demanding in more than music, and she could try a person's patience by her insistence on what she thought should be done or not be done. For Mother Leonarda she was at once a source of joy and admiration especially in her talent, and she was at times a source of exasperation and frazzled nerves.[26] She would long outlive the Superior who was now listening to her music lesson, and that notwithstanding the fact that all through her Religious life, Sister Marysia would be almost always on the sick list.

There was another melody coming from another music room. Mother Leonarda listened. No, this was not a piano lesson; it was a full orchestra, a record surely. What was the composition? She knew she had heard it. What a nostalgic, serene melody—like the fields of Ahlen when she listened to the larks—

like green pastures and wooded hills—like a brook, rippling smoothly over stones—like the Breath of God, the Holy Spirit, in the soul! What was the composition? And then it came to her. She had heard it in November when the Candidates gave a play commemorating the one-hundredth birthday of Arnold Janssen and the music for the play was taken from Edvard Grieg's **Peer Gynt Suite.**[27] Yes, that was it. This was the lovely "Morning Mood" from *Peer Gynt*. Evidently Sister Fabiola is working on an assignment for one of her classes at the Conservatory. Like Sister Marysia, Sister Fabiola, too, had musical talent, but in character she was a much more quiet and peaceful soul. She gave indescribable joy to the Sisters of the Province for many years by her superb mastery of the organ. Every year at Christmas, it was her gift to the Sisters, to spend an hour or so in the late afternoon on Christmas Day playing all the lovely Christmas melodies on the Chapel pipe organ. One heard the flutes, the bells, the chimes. "The shepherds are serenading the Infant Jesus in the crib," she would always say.

Mother Leonarda knew that if she were to walk a little farther listening in at the music room windows, somewhere she just might find someone practicing Gregorian chant for next Sunday's liturgy. She loved the chant. It had the purity and simplicity of the Divine. She thought if anyone would be praticing chant, it would most probably be Sister Othmara. Ah, another talented Sister, another personality—aggressive, active, very intelligent, a leader, and quite independent. Yes, the Province of Sisters that she directed for so many years had just about all the movements of a symphony.

Much work and sacrifice and prayer had gone into the building of the Province and its charitable works, she mused, but who could know the work, the prayer, and the sacrifice involved in helping so many women of so many diverse personalities, such different backgrounds—cultural, language, social differences—of so many levels of intelligence—the ordinary to the sharp penetrating intellectuals—the timid, quiet personality always needing encouragement to the aggressive, dominating personality needing wise guidance.

How many times did she slip into chapel for a moment to utter a quick prayer for the Sister she knew was having a personal problem or was suffering severe depression; and then again, how many times did she settle a problem with a Sister or Sisters only to hasten to her room to jot quickly in her diary a few quick words showing that the incident tried her patience to the limit and she was angry. She had to get it out of her system; in her diary it did no harm, and she did not hurt anyone. But if she did hurt someone, she never failed to apologize. Friend of the Holy Spirit that she was, she could not do otherwise.

Ah, yes, it was the task of forming the Sisters into a unified whole, a Province of Missionary Sisters Servants of the Holy Spirit—not German or American or whatever nationality, but Servants of the Holy Spirit—Missionary Sisters—whose vision recognized the greatness of each nationality but encompassed the world. This was the task. This was what cost! The buildings she saw; the unified spirit?—She hoped the greater part was there. After she was gone, she would continue to pray for it.

She thought she would walk slowly to the front to

see if the car was there to take her back to St. Ann's She was extremely tired. Just then she saw Sister Casparina come from the workingmen's dining room, and she had to smile. Besides teaching sewing, Sister Casparina took care of the dining room for the workingmen and their laundry. Mother Leonarda recalled what Sister Casparina said one day, and she laughed. One Monday evening when the Sisters sat for recreation, in walked Sister Casparina with an armful of men's socks. She began matching pairs and then proceeded to darn the torn ones mumbling all the time, "For this I entered the convent to darn men's socks and iron their shirts? That is what I wanted to get rid of. I choose celibacy, and in return I get twenty men to look after!" Of course, she was grinning all the while she was talking, and the Sisters knew it was all said in fun. They all laughed and each one picked up a pair of socks. Mother Leonarda smiled at the memory. A missionary Sister has to be ready for every kind of work! And, yes, Sister Casparina was another type of person in the community. She made the costumes for the plays the girls gave, and each costume was a work of art.

Mother Leonarda was just about at the front of the convent now. She turned slowly around, trying to capture it all in her memory. She knew she wasn't well, and her memory was so poor nowadays, although she rememberd things from long ago better than more recent happenings. She was embarrassed at how she forgot the most simple things now. Her term of office was almost over, and she knew she would not be able to accept another position of authority. Others must now carry on without her.

The car was waiting for her and she got in. As she

drove down the one mile to St. Ann's, she looked at the stretch of land along the way. It was so different now from what it had been when she came in 1901. To think that it all started on the great financial asset of forty-seven cents. She thought of the Parable of the Talents in the New Testament. Indeed, she had invested that forty-seven cents in the love of the Holy Spirit and He had increased it a hundred fold.

A few days later, On April 7, Mother Leonarda called Sister Irenaea and told her she was not feeling well and would like to go to St. Joseph's Hospital in New Hampton and find out just what the problem was. Sister Provincial Irenaea accompanied her to the hospital.

It was thought that she needed a long rest, and that is what the Sisters were told. Nothing was said about her condition of health.

Then on May 9, Mother Leonarda suffered a very severe heart attack and was anointed by the chaplain. After a few days, however, she seemed to rally a bit, and the Sisters thought she would be getting better. They were happy.

In Steyl, the Superiors were saddened by the reports that had come to them concerning Mother Leonarda. Mother General Regis wrote:

I would like so much to come to your sick bed in order to say a few loving words to you. . . .Through Sister Provincial I heard that . . .you received Extreme Unction. Extreme Unction is a powerful means of restoring bodily well being. . . .I hope that you will feel better when these lines are read . . . .We hope that by and by your health will improve, but should the Holy and loving God ordain otherwise because he wants you with Himself in eternal joy, then unite your great last sacrifice most ardently with the sufferings and death of your beloved Savior so that your death will be precious in His eyes. . . .[28]

Mother Theresia who had gone through so much herself and could sympathize with Mother Leonarda sent her a message of concern and love.

. . .I heard that your health is poor again. The reception of the Holy Sacrament of Extreme Unction is a God-given remedy for soul and body . . . . I would be so happy to know that your health has improved, but I am convinced that you are satisfied should God ordain otherwise. Should you, dear Sister Superior Leonarda, go home before I do, I wish to thank you for all the work, labor, and sacrifices that you made for our Congregation. Also for all the joys and all the consolation that you have given me. Our Blessed Savior will repay His spouse most richly. He knows your ceaseless labor. We will pray very much for one another till we see each other in the beautiful heaven. Should you really die before I do, I beg you to remember me in heaven.[29]

When the feast of St. Aloysius, June 21, came along, Mother Leonarda asked the doctor for permission to get out of bed and sit up in a chair. He, however, was reluctant to let her do this, but on June 24, he said she could sit in a chair for thirty minutes each day. She was so happy, and the very first thing she requested was that one of the Sisters should take her to the chapel in a wheelchair. Her visit to her Lord in the Tabernacle was a great joy to her. The next day she got up again and also the next day, Saturday.

But Saturday morning as she sat in the chair, she

seemed to get extremely tired and weak. She asked Sister Antoinette who was with her in the room to call Sister Domitilla, her nurse, so that the latter could help her get into bed.

Sister Domitilla who had been working in a room across the hall came immediately and was shocked to find Mother Leonarda lying on the floor. Other Sisters came to the room, and they helped to put Mother Leonarda into bed. Her face was blue, and her pulse was weak. The priest and the doctor were called, but there was nothing the doctor could do for her any more. While the chaplain and another priest visiting the area were saying the prayers for the dying, Mother Leonarda quietly slipped into eternity—surely to her eternal reward—just as she had years ago slipped away early in the morning from the Provincial House to St. Ann's.

Since it was summer and the time of retreat, there were many Sisters in the Provincial House from the various houses of the Province. In fact just about every house was represented. It was as if Mother Leonarda wanted to have all her Sisters together for this last meeting.

She was laid out in state for one day in the Provincial House and one day in St. Ann's. In both places she was laid out in a parlor so that other people, too, might come to see and pray for her. She lay in the coffin peacefully beautiful. Her lips closed naturally into that ever present pleasant expression; it was not really a smile but a look expressing interest, care, understanding, and the peace of a person on good terms with God, her fellow human beings, and herself. The many people who came to see her and bid her farewell saw that peaceful look and paid little attention to the fact that there was little camouflaging of death. Her face—cheeks and lips—were colorless and had truly the hue of death. Her worn out fingers with the rosary twined around them were also emaciated, white, almost transparent. It was not customary for the Sisters to be made up with any cosmetics even in death. Her head was decorated with a wreath of natural myrtle with red roses. On one side of the coffin were beautiful palms, a large crucifix, and two huge burning candles; on the other side of the coffin were the Sisters crying and praying, coming and going. In spite of all the peace surrounding the deceased, death was a rigorous preacher.

Monday, about five o'clock in the afternoon, the casket was placed in the hearse for its journey to St. Ann's. The Sisters stood in the various windows watching the hearse. It began to rain gently, and then when the car was on the road, the rain came in torrents completely hiding the hearse from view. Yet, when the car approached St. Ann's, pleasant sunshine greeted Mother Leonarda once again.

At St. Ann's too, the stream of people coming and going to see the deceased was tremendous.

The funeral was on Wednesday, and the day turned out to be a pleasantly cool day, the kind Mother Leonarda liked. The Sisters formed a procession walking from St. Ann's across the road to the cemetery. The graveside prayers were said, and then the Sisters and friends slowly returned home. In the cemetery Mother Leonarda was laid in a row with the graves of the other Sisters who had died. As in life, she would always be a Mother in the midst of her Sisters—in work, in recreation, in prayer, in their joys and sorrows, and in their hearts.

Letters of condolence poured into the Provincial House and into St. Ann's. One can only marvel that this woman, an unknown nun and stranger in this country when she came in 1901, left with having made a veritable chain of friends from all walks of life and spanning this country and across the ocean to Europe and mission lands.

It is also interesting to note that in so many letters a reference is made to Mother Leonarda's great love for the Holy Spirit. She truly spread her own love for this Divine Spirit among hundreds, and in her way she helped to fill the hearts of others with the fire of His love.

1. Link, S. & William B. Cotton, *American Epoch, A History of the United States Since the 1890's* (New York: Alfred A. Knopf), pp, 361 ff.

2. James Hennesey, S.J., *American Catholics, a History of the Roman Catholic Community in the United States* (Oxford University Press, 1981), p. 253.

3. Hennessey, p. 242.

4. Letter of Mother Leonarda to M. Columba (March 26, 1929).

5. Chronicle of St. Therese Hospital.

6. Diary of Mother Leonarda.

7. An account of a Sister (no name given).

8. Diary of Mother Leonarda.

9. Diary of Mother Leonarda.

10. Diary of Mother Leonarda.

11. Diary of Mother Leonarda.
Chronicle of St. Ann's Home.

12. Diary of Mother Leonarda.

13. Chapter Conference.

14. Diary of Mother Leonarda.

15. Diary of Mother Leonarda
Chronicle of St. Ann's Home.

16. Diary of Mother Leonarda.
Chronicle of St. Ann's Home.

17. Letter of Mother Leonarda to M. Columba (October 9, 1932).

18. Diary of Mother Leonarda.

19. Letter of Sister Irenaea to Mother Leonarda (October 10, 1932).

20. Letter of M. Theresia to Mother Leonarda (October 10, 1932).

21. Letter of Mother Leonarda to M. Theresia (November 15, 1932).

22. Diary of Mother Leonarda.

23. Francis Sugrue, *Popes in the Modern World* (New York: Thomas Y. Crowell Co., 1934), p. 184.

24. Letter of M. Columba to Mother Leonarda (October 28, 1936).

25. Letter of Mother Leonarda to M. Theresia (January 24, 1926).

26. Diary of Mother Leonarda.

27. Personal remembrances.

28. Letter of M. Regis to Mother Leonarda (June 2, 1937).

29. Letter of M. Theresia to Mother Leonarda (June 5, 1937).

Epilogue

The classroom was buzzing with excitement. High school seniors in their caps and gowns were pinning on corsages and boutonnieres. It was a big night—high school graduation for St. Mary's seniors in Vicksburg. Three boys, actually three young men, handsomely dressed, with ear to ear smiles approached the nun at the front of the classroom, their homeroom teacher and principal, and shook her hand repeating, "Thank you, Sister, Thank you!" One of the boys was especially happy. For the first time in St. Mary's history, this young man would be receiving tonight before a proud audience of parents, relatives, and friends, and faculty a $4,000.00 medical scholarship to St. Louis University. Three other scholarships would also be given out.

As the nun lifted her eyes to the back of the room, in her memory she could envision Mother Leonarda standing there in that classroom, smiling in her benign way, as she had stood so many years ago, smiling at the young people, encouraging them, whispering an answer to a timid youngster. It seemed she was saying, "For this we came here in those poor early years to give these people a chance for bigger and nobler things in life."

But times have changed, and with the advent of the intensive Civil Rights movement in the country, the Blacks went into the mainstream of life, finding educational opportunities on all levels now in integrated schools of their choice. The mission schools for the Blacks, having fulfilled a great need during the interim of a hundred years or so, silently closed their doors.

*****

St. Therese Hospital in Waukegan had grown rapidly. Already it had graduated many young women from its school of nursing. Now, however, the patient intake was so great that every available part of the hospital had to be utilized for the patients and patient care. The Mother Leonarda Memorial, St. Therese School of Nursing and School of Medical Technology, was built next to the hospital in answer to the increasing patient admissions every year.

The beautiful Memorial building was dedicated August 21, 1955. There was also the solemn unveiling of a large portrait of Mother Leonarda which would hang in the front lobby. So she is there now, demure and kind, with soft, interested eyes, looking at everyone who enters the building and almost seeming to say as she did so often in life: "Hello. I am Sister Leonarda. What can I do for you?"

Again the changing times, advances in medicine, technology, requirements in educational background, and all the cooperative ventures in medical care and patient care have changed things at St. Therese's also. There are special needs now again for the hospital, and the Sisters count on their good

Mother Leonarda.

* * * * *

The doorbell rang, and the Portress at the Convent of the Holy Spirit in Techny opened the door to a man and woman. The man said, "We have passed your convent several times, and each time we are just intrigued by the beautiful stained glass windows. Could we see your chapel?"

The request was not an isolated one. Ever since the new Convent of the Holy Spirit was built, visitors to see the chapel came in large numbers.

Mother Leonarda would have been delighted with the new convent. It was quite similar to what she had wanted years ago. Yes, her dream had been accomplished.

But, above all, she would have been especially thrilled to see the large exquisite mosaic of the Holy Spirit, the art work of one of the Sisters, Sister Agnes Paul, high on the wall behind the marble altar. She herself would have wanted Him there hovering over the whole community and the world because one can almost hear her saying again as she did one Pentecost:

> *. . .The Church has come to look upon the Holy Spirit as another Redeemer,—a Savior. What the Messiah was to the people of old—that the Holy Spirit is to the world of the present day. As such, then He has to be looked upon. God wants us to turn to Him for enlightenment . . . .*
>
> —Pentecost Chapter

* * * * *

Bibliography

Primary Sources

Chronicles of some of the Houses of the Province containing detailed information about events, activities, and development of that particular House:

Chronicle of St. Ann's Home, Techny, Illinois,
Chronicle of St. Therese Hospital, Waukegan, Illinois,
Chronicle of the Paraclete Province, Techny, Illinois.

Diary of Mother Leonarda.

Documents, reports, reminiscences concerning Mother Leonarda's life work, and activities and character submitted by her brothers and sisters, relatives, friends, teachers, priests, Holy Spirit Missionary Sisters, and Sisters of various Orders:

Private documents in the archives of Sacred Heart Motherhouse in Steyl, Holland.
Private documents in the archives of Holy Spirit Convent in Techny, Illinois.

Letters (all unpublished):
Letters of Mother Leonarda,
Letters of Bl. Arnold Janssen,
Letters of Mother Theresia,
Letters of Mother Columba,
Letters of Mother Regis,
Letters of other Sisters in the Generalate,
Letters of relatives, friends,
Letters of Fr. T. Grabe.

Private spiritual writings and admonitions of Mother Leonarda.

Secondary Sources

Anderson, Robin. *Between Two Wars: The Story of Pope Pius XI.* Chicago: Franciscan Herald Press, 1977.

Angle, Paul M. *The American Reader*. New York: Rand McNally & Co., 1958.

Bode, Carl. *Midcentury America.* Southern Illinois University Press, 1972.

Bokenkotter, Thomas. *A Concise History of the Catholic Church.* Garden City: Doubleday & Co., 1977.

Claudel, Paul. Trans. Helen Weaver. *I Believe in God—A Meditation on the Apostles' Creed.* Agnes du Sarment, ed. New York: Holt Rhinehart & Winston, 1961.

Dulles, Foster. *The United States Since 1965.* Ann Arbor: The University of Michigan Press, 1969.

Ellis, John Tracy. *American Catholicism.* Chicago: The University of Chicago Press, 1955.

Ellis, John Tracy. *Documents of American Catholic History.* Milwaukee: Bruce Publishing Co., 1955.

Forbes, F. A. *Life of Pius X.* London: Burns, Oates, & Washbourne Ltd., 1918.

Guerry, Archbishop Emile. *The Pope and World Government.* Baltimore: Helicon Press, 1964.

Hennesey, S.J., James. *American Catholics, A History of Roman Catholic Community in the United States.* Oxford: Oxford University Press, 1981.

Hobe, Hans. *The Wounded Land.* Trans. Ewon Butler. New York: Coward-McCann, Inc., 1964.

Hoskins, Lotte, ed. *I Have a Dream.* New York: Grosset & Dunlap, 1968.

Jones, Howard Mumford. *Strange New World.* New York: The Viking Press, 1952.

Lerner, Max. *America as a Civilization.* New York: Simon and Schuster, 1957.

Link, S. & William B. Cotton. *American Epoch, A History of the United States Since the 1890's*. New York: Alfred A. Knopf, 1955.

Morris, Richard B., ed. *Encyclopedia of American History*. New York: Harper and Row, Publishers, 1953.

Murphy, Francis, C.SS. R. *The Papacy Today*. New York: Macmillan Publishing Co., 1981.

Noel, Gerard. *The Anatomy of the Catholic Church—Roman Catholicism in an Age of Revolution*. New York: Doubleday & Co., 1980.

Perrett, Geoffrey. *America in the Twenties*. New York: Simon & Schuster, 1980.

Planner, Mabel G. & William L. Neff. *Freedom Under the Law*. Milwaukee: Bruce Publishing Co., 1962.

Schlesinger, Arthur Meier. *Political & Social Growth in the United States: 1852-1933*. New York: Macmillan Company, 1933.

Seven Great Encyclicals. Glen Rock: Paulist Press, 1939.

Shannon, David A. *Twentieth Century America*. Chicago: Rand McNally & Co., 1963.

Sheen, Rev. Fulton J. *Way to Inner Peace*. New York: Garden City Books, 1955.

Stockton, Lewis J. *A Topical Survey of American History*. New York: Barnes & Noble, Inc., 1937.

Sugrue, Francis. *Popes in the Modern World*. New York: Thomas Y. Crowell, 1961.

Zinn, Howard. *A People's History of the United States*. New York: Harper Colophon Books, 1980.

Reference Works

"Ahlen," *Encylopedia Brittanica*, I, 152.

"Fernando Po," *Encylopedia Brittanica*, IV.

"Germany," *History of Nations*, XVIII, 440-441.

"Westphalia," *Catholic Encylopedia*, XV, 602.

History of the Congregation Background Information

Fisher, Hermann, S.V.D. *Life of Arnold Janssen*. Trans. Rev. F.M. Lynk, S.V.D. Techny: Mission Press, 1925.

Mutter Maria Michaele Mitgruenderin und erste Generaloberin der Steyler Anbetungschwestern. Steyl: Mission Press, 1938.

Sister Assumpta, S.Sp.S. *Life of Mother Maria Stollenwerk and Mother Josepha Stenmanns*. Trans. a Servant of the Holy Spirit. Techny: Unpublished, 1931.

Sister Sixta, S.Sp.S. *Gottes Kraft in Schwachen Haenden, Lebensbild und Lebenswerk von Mutter Theresia, Margareta Messner, S.Sp.S.* Steyl: Mission Press, 1951.

Spiritual Book References

The Jerusalem Bible.

DeChardin Teilhard. *Le Milieu Divin*. London: Fontana Books, 1957.

Lepp, Ignace. *The Challenges of Life*. New York: Doubleday & Co., 1969.

Merton, Thomas. *The True Solitude*. Kansas City: Hallmark Editions, 1969.

Van Kamm, Adrian. *Books on Spirituality, Studies in Formative Spirituality*, Volume 1.

Josephine Allendorf Lentrup, M. Leonarda's mother

Heinrich Lentrup, M. Leonarda's father

Allendorf, Germany - Birthplace of M. Leonarda

Elizabeth Lentrup, now Mother Leonarda Lentrup

One room school attended by M. Leonarda

M. Leonarda's Final Vows, Sept. 8, 1904

Rear: Sr. Maria, Pauline Heinemann, 1st postulant and novice
Sr. Josepha, Mary Delort, 1st postulant and novice
Front: M. Leonarda, Elizabeth Lentrup, Foundress of the U.S. Province
Sr. Borromaea, Anna Maria Schneider

M. Leonarda